Vital Memory and Affect

Vital Memory and Affect takes as its subject the autobiographical memories of 'vulnerable' groups, including survivors of child sexual abuse, adopted children and their families, forensic mental health service users, and elderly persons in care-home settings. In particular, the focus is on a specific class of memory within this group: recollected episodes that are difficult and painful, sometimes contested, but always with enormous significance for a current and past sense of self. These 'vital memories', integral and irreversible, can come to appear as a defining feature of a person's life.

In *Vital Memory and Affect*, authors Steven D. Brown and Paula Reavey explore the highly productive ways in which individuals make sense of a difficult past, situated as they are within a highly specific cultural and social landscape. Via an exploration of their vital memories, the book combines insights from social and cognitive psychology to open up the possibility of a new approach to memory, one that pays full attention to the contextual conditions of all acts of remembering.

This path-breaking study brings together a unique set of empirical material and maps out an agenda for research into memory and affect that will be important reading for students and scholars of social psychology, memory studies, cultural studies, philosophy, and other related fields.

Steven D. Brown is Professor of Organisational and Social Psychology, University of Leicester, UK.

Paula Reavey is Professor of Psychology, London South Bank University, UK.

Vital Memory and Affect

Living with a difficult past

Steven D. Brown and
Paula Reavey

LONDON AND NEW YORK

First published 2015
by Routledge
Church Road, Hove, East Sussex BN3 2FA

and by Routledge
Third Avenue, New York, NY

Routledge is an imprint of the Taylor & Francis Group, an informa business

© 2015 Steven D. Brown and Paula Reavey

The right of Steven D. Brown and Paula Reavey to be identified as the authors of this work has been asserted by them in accordance with sections 77 and 78 of the Copyright, Designs and Patents Act 1988.

All rights reserved. No part of this book may be reprinted or reproduced or utilised in any form or by any electronic, mechanical, or other means, now known or hereafter invented, including photocopying and recording, or in any information storage or retrieval system, without permission in writing from the publishers.

Trademark notice: Product or corporate names may be trademarks or registered trademarks, and are used only for identification and explanation without intent to infringe.

British Library Cataloguing in Publication Data
A catalogue record for this book is available from the British Library

Library of Congress Cataloging in Publication Data
Brown, Steven D. (Psychologist)
  Vital memory and affect: living with a difficult past/
  Steven Brown, Paula Reavey. – 1 Edition.
    pages cm
  1. Memory. 2. Social psychology. I. Reavey, Paula. II. Title.
  BF371.B767 2015
  153.1'3 – dc23
  2014049466

ISBN: 978-0-415-68399-9 (hbk)
ISBN: 978-0-415-68401-9 (pbk)
ISBN: 978-1-315-71393-9 (ebk)

Typeset in Bembo and Calibri
by Florence Production Ltd, Stoodleigh, Devon, UK

Printed and bound in the United States of America by Publishers Graphics, LLC on sustainably sourced paper.

To my dear dad, Victor Reavey. A generous and
warm-hearted soul, with a vital memory or
two of his own. Paula x

In memory of Edna Dexter (1909–98). Steve x

Contents

Acknowledgements	ix
Preface	xii

1	The seven virtues of vital memory	1
2	The expanded view of memory	22
3	Memory and life-space: affect, forgetting and ethics	48
4	Feeling an ambivalent past: survivors of child sexual abuse	86
5	Managing the memories of others: adoptive parents and their children	107
6	Remembering with, through and for others: surviving the 2005 London bombings	133
7	Forgetting who you were: the forensic psychiatric unit	155
8	Recollection in later life: the reminiscence museum	178

9	Ordinary people living with a difficult past	210

References	226
Index	239

Acknowledgements

This book is based on theoretical and empirical work we have carried out together over the past decade. Our participants are the first people we wish to thank. We hope we have done justice to the immensely brave and articulate manner in which they have shared their experiences with us. We have learned so much by carefully observing the nuanced and creative ways these people have approached the difficult task of remembering.

We have met many other wonderful individuals on the way, who, in their different ways, also try to conceptualise memory as bound to experience, contexts and settings. One particularly critical moment was attending the workshop 'Memory in Context', in Bielefeld, Germany, in 2012. Our ideas on autobiographical memory, in particular, emerged anew, largely through our contact with some great scholars, including Charlie Stone, Lucas Bietti, William Hirst, Andy Hoskins, along with others.

It is always difficult to remember everyone who has contributed to the ideas that have made up this book. There are a few that we do recollect distinctly, and with affection, including David Middleton, Andy Hoskins, Jacqui Dillon, Janice Haaken, Matt Allen and, in particular, Sue Campbell, who sadly will not see this work published. To Sue, we owe a great debt, as she pushed feminist and philosophical thoughts on memory to a whole new level. Without her work, who knows where we might be.

We would also like to thank the wonderful colleagues whose participant experiences we have shared and worked on together: Matt Allen, from the London bombings studies, Elena Bendien, on the reminiscence museum study, and Helen Brookfield, on the adoption study. Your contribution is alive throughout the book, and we thank you for your permission to use various materials. The same, of course, is true of the participants themselves.

We would like to acknowledge the following support provided to fund the research we discuss in this book. The work in Chapter 4 was supported by Sheffield Hallam University in the form of a university PhD scholarship for Paula. The work in Chapter 6 was supported by the Arts and Humanities Research Council through the grant 'Conflicts of Memory: Commemorating and mediating the 2005 London Bombings' (AH/E002579/1). The work in Chapter 8 was supported by Humanitas and the Universiteit voor Humanistiek, Utrecht, in the form of a PhD scholarship for Elena Bendien. We would also like to thank Libby Volke and Michael Strang at Routledge, for their unfailing support and guidance during the difficult days of writing and editing.

Finally, thank you to our family, friends and colleagues who have joined in our discussions over time, within a variety of settings, including the pub, conferences and workshops: Alex John, Elanor Cowland, Lilliana Del Busso, Nicola Carter, Victor Reavey, Paul Stenner, John Cromby, Darren Ellis, Lewis Goodings, Ian Tucker, Dave Harper, Rob Cluley, Malcolm Ashmore and Laura McGrath – thank you for your friendship and the laughs.

Personal notes

Thank you as ever to Alex, Oskar and Viktor for ongoing love and support. Well-being and writing go hand in hand, and your contribution to the latter, in particular, is always so very much appreciated. Paula.

To A+K, with love always. Steve.

Publishing acknowledgements

In writing the book, we have drawn upon some previously published work, which we have duly revisited, revised and adapted. We would like to acknow-ledge the use of elements of previous publications from the following:

Chapter 1

Brown, S.D. and P. Reavey (2014). Vital memories: Movements in and between affect, ethics and self. In L. Bietti and C. Stone (eds) Special issue, *Memory Studies: Remembering in context* 7: 328–38.

Chapter 2

Brown, S.D. and P. Reavey (2013). Experience and memory. In E. Keightley and M. Pickering (eds) *Research Methods for Memory Studies*. Edinburgh, UK: Edinburgh University Press, pp. 45–59.

Chapter 3

Brown, S.D., P. Reavey and H. Brookfield (2012). Spectral objects: material links to difficult pasts for adoptive families. In P. Harvey *et al.* (ESRC Centre for Research on Socio-Cultural Change) (eds) *Objects and Materials: A Routledge companion*. London: Routledge, pp. 173–82.

Chapter 4

Brown, S.D., M.A. Allen and P. Reavey (2015). Remembering 7/7: The collective shaping of survivors' personal memories of the 2005 London Bombing. In T. Hagen and A. Tota (eds) *Routledge International Handbook of Memory Studies*. London: Routledge.

Chapter 5

Bendien, L., S.D. Brown and P. Reavey (2010). Social remembering as an art of living: Analysis of a 'reminiscence'. In M. Schillmeier and M. Domenech (eds) *New Technologies and Emerging Spaces of Care*. London: Ashgate, pp. 149–67.

Preface

To remember is to experience a sense of continuity of a life that we feel is uniquely ours. However, we feel at times that our memories slip away from us and become ambiguous, perhaps overly defined by others, such that we hardly recognise them at all. We may also feel ambivalent about what we can and cannot recall. At times, we question whether a recollection is accurate, though it may feel real; at other times, we feel absolutely certain that our version of events is superior and unremittingly accurate. Memory can feel at times hazy, like smoke, and at other times, well defined and wonderfully clear. Whom we remember with and for is, of course, crucial to understanding our relationship to matters of accuracy and ambiguity.

Relationships are central to memorial activities. We do not exist as atomised units of memory; we recall with others, through others and for others. We remember in the context of relationships with others, as collectives, and we actively forget via these same modes. Relational models of memory are hardly new. Frederick Bartlett, Maurice Halbwachs, Henri Bergson, Kurt Lewin and, later, David Middleton, Katherine Nelson and Robyn Fivush have all argued for a sociocultural understanding of memory, examining how the process of remembering emerges through our scaffolded relations and interactions with others.

Our purpose in writing this book has been to speak to the various ways in which memory emerges through relations, including the affective relations we have with others, as well as the settings in which those relations operate, within the ongoing flow of experience (or duration, as Bergson would describe it). We want to situate our readings in a very particular type of memory, which we refer to throughout as vital memories. By vital memories, we mean memories that are in some way fundamental to a sense of who we are as persons. These are memories that are difficult, irreversible, that create deep marks in the ongoing flow of our experience. Vital memories are not easily displaced (whether we recognise this or not) or discounted.

Like many contemporary psychological studies of how the present self shapes and is shaped by the past, we have set out to explore here the variety of ways in which the past flows into the present and is shaped by manifold relations that include both human and non-human elements. People, places and objects intertwine together to mark memorial processes in specific ways. It is these sets of relations that constitute a person's life-space that we will explore in relation to each of the groups of people we have had the privilege of working with over the past few years. Blurring the boundaries between the collective and the individual, the individual and the setting, the emotional and the rational is a guiding concern for us.

The issues we write about in the book are, in turn, partially grounded in our own experiences. Our memories of the London bombings have become tragically entangled with memories of the death of Paula's mother. Paula clearly remembers how travelling into work, seeing the helicopters flying overhead and hearing the blurred screech of sirens became heavily filtered through her recollection of the last time she spoke to her mother on the telephone. It was just three days after the bombings when Paula received a phone call about her mother's unexpected and rapid decline. Such experiences are obviously overwhelming, truly terrible and shape everything that comes after. They also impact on our way of thinking about memory. In certain ways, the London bombings will never truly be separated from the personal tragedy described, for either of us. This event revealed to us something important about the ways we need to think about the relationship between the collective and the individual. They are complex, interweaving movements that cannot be separated in any meaningful sense. The accounts from survivors of the bombing we describe in Chapter 6 are testament to this. Acknowledging our personal stakes and involvement in events does not taint scholarship through some kind of subjective bias, but rather reflects an effort to expand our relationship to enquiry by connecting our experiences to those of participants.

Our working together on this project represents a coming together of a series of shared and individual concerns with how memory 'works' in everyday life, across legal, care, therapeutic and clinical settings. We both work in psychology, though in somewhat different ways. Steve has, for many years, explored the ways in which persons move and act within institutions and organisations, and Paula has focused on experiences of mental distress, violence and abuse. Our recent projects on memory have brought these approaches together. We have experimented with a range of methods, including visual techniques and memory work, that reflect our mutual concern with how psychological enquiry might accommodate elements of interaction and continuity in people's accounts of their lives, while in turn situating those accounts in the settings and spaces through which they emerge.

Quite unexpectedly, our concern with continuity, interaction and setting has led to a re-engagement with elements of cognitive and experimental psychology. The work of Martin Conway, John Sutton, Katherine Nelson, Robyn Fivush and others, who predominantly use experimental techniques to examine the relationship between memory, culture and the broader environment, has shaped the way we now think about how people experience their lives across time. We now consider a dialogue as possible between what have often been seen as approaches opposed to one another. Though we work outside the laboratory, our aim has been to make our work and ideas accessible to those working both inside and outside the mainstream of psychology. We hope that, in turn, service users, practitioners and those involved in policy and strategy might benefit from hearing about the vast entanglements and culturally saturated values and meanings that come into play through situated acts of remembering. It is this *expanded* concept of memory that we believe will lead to an enhanced understanding of memory as a context-bound, fluid, ethical and affective practice.

Transcription conventions

Throughout this book, we have used a basic transcription system in the presentation of extracts. In this system, (.) or . . . represent audible pauses, underlining marks an emphasis placed on particular words, and interruptions or overlapping speech are indicated by the insertion of another speaker's words within the same turn: for example, F: And as I was saying (M: yes, yes) she often thought. In Chapter 8, the translation from Dutch to English was done by Elena Bendien, and we offer her our thanks for her permission to reproduce the translation here.

Chapter 1

The seven virtues of vital memory

You can't unring a bell

From the court records, it seems that Salomon R. Sandez had been very unlucky. Sat in his Chevrolet convertible outside the New Main motel in Los Angeles, on a spring evening in 1955, Sandez had probably not noticed the undercover police officers parked in front. Perhaps they in turn would not have noticed him, had it not been for the Mexican licence plate and his odd, anxious demeanour. He twice left the car, paced backwards and forwards, looked around and – as the officers later put it – 'sort of wrung his hands'. In any case, this was enough to arrest him. At 8 p.m., a federal agent posing as 'Benny Bean' completed a sting operation in one of the motel rooms, arresting Vince Perno after a brief shoot out. 'Benny' fired a further shot outside the room to alert the waiting officers, who promptly pounced on Sandez. His bad luck put him in the dock along with Perno and four other defendants, all charged with importing narcotics into the USA.

The case against Sandez was not exactly watertight. When arrested, he was carrying a business card from a doctor in Tijuana. Written on the reverse side was the cryptic message 'Vince, ? PL-97818'. The prosecution argued that, if the numerals were reversed, they matched the phone number of a local apartment from where Perno had made one of his many calls to 'Benny Bean'. Other defendants had spoken of a mysterious middleman called Tutu. When asked by the arresting officers whether he was, in fact, 'Tutu', Sandez had agreed. Or at least, it appeared that he had agreed, because, as became clear during the trial, Sandez's command of English was so limited that one witness was led to claim, 'The man can't speak English. He understands maybe a word or two'. Nevertheless, the jury felt they had enough to find him guilty.

2 The seven virtues of vital memory

Sandez appealed. His lawyers argued that his conviction had been influenced by a letter shown to the jury written by a defendant who had not been involved in the trial. Although it made reference to Tutu, the letter had not been thought sufficiently incriminating to bring its author to trial (not least because of some peculiar attempts to redact details in red ink). In fact, toward the end of the case, the prosecution had asked the jury to disregard this particular piece of evidence in relation to all the defendants, except Perno. However, could the jury members actually forget what they had read and heard described in open court? Or, as the appeal judges put it, was it possible to 'unring the bell' at such a late stage? For once, Sandez's luck turned, and some, but not all, of his convictions were quashed.

The case of *Sandez v. United States of America* (1956) uses a neat piece of legal-speak to restate what we all find out at some point in our lives – *you can't unring a bell.* You cannot simply forget, either when instructed or through sheer force of will, some piece of prior knowledge or an aspect of one's past experience. To know something, to have seen or felt something, is to live with it, however inconvenient or difficult that may be. Chief Justice McBride, in a much earlier case (*State vs Rader*, 62 Oregon, 1912) commented on similar legal dilemmas with the observation that, 'It is not an easy task to unring a bell, nor to remove from the mind an impression once firmly imprinted there'. The phrases 'impression' and 'imprinting' here are striking. They describe the act of making a mark in a surface through pressure. The empiricist philosopher David Hume made the notion of impressions on the mind central to his account of knowledge and understanding.[1] Much later, the ethologist Konrad Lorenz would use the term 'imprinting' for the rapid, automatic learning by newly hatched birds of the characteristics of key stimuli, which then become behavioural models.[2] Stephanie Meyer most likely had this in mind when writing the *Twilight* books, giving werewolves the ability to 'imprint' or 'fall in love at first sight' with significant others, to whom they are then unconditionally bound, as though by some gravitational force.[3] However, it may be that McBride had in mind the still relatively new technology of still photography, where images of the world were literally imprinted on light-sensitive plates and then transferred to photographic paper. One rapid exposure gives rise to a permanent mark. What we see in all these cases is the effects of a process that is immediate, irreversible and, to some degree, intractable. *You can't unring a bell . . .*

This book explores the consequences of the irreversibility of particular kinds of experience for memory. We are concerned with experiences that are difficult, distressing, sometimes painful to recall and troublesome to accommodate in one's current sense of self and ongoing personal relationships. These are experiences that 'leave a mark', that cannot be simply ignored or made irrelevant. Difficult experiences can become central to how a personal past is narrated. They become embedded in patterns of recollection that extend into other kinds of memory, lending them shape and emotional tones that they would not otherwise possess. Memories of troubling events can take on the status of defining experiences, becoming central to the life of the person who lays claim to them. It is in this sense that we use the term 'vital memories': memories that become pivotal to trying to make sense of a life.

The intractability of memory is not a new theme in psychology. One of Freud's most significant insights is, of course, the idea that we never really forget anything that happens to us.[4] For Freud, knowledge of past events is permanently etched in our unconscious, much like the marks on the waxy surface of a child's 'magical writing pad'. Yet it is very difficult to read any individual mark, as each tends to disappear into the messy confusion of previous and subsequent marks.[5] Contemporary psychologists would refer to these kinds of memory as 'available' but not 'accessible'.[6] They are there waiting for us, but there seems to be no sure or immediate route by which we can reach them (save that of dreams, free associations or slippages in consciousness for Freud).

The particular memorial qualities of difficult experiences have led to the widespread use of the notion of 'trauma'.[7] Based around an explicit analogy with a physical wound, 'traumatic memories' are considered to be thoroughly disruptive, as corrosive of personal identity. There have been suggestions that traumatic memory constitutes a completely different means of accessing the past, compared with other forms of memory.[8] However, although it is undoubtedly the case that memories of events such as physical or sexual violence can be entirely overwhelming, they become interwoven with other kinds of memory. It is the patterns that result from the efforts to incorporate difficult aspects of one's past into an accounting for oneself that concerns us in this book.

Mixtures and flows

Metaphors are indispensable tools for thinking about memory.[9] We have already encountered the ideas of impressions and imprinting and the analogies with wax tablets and physical wounds. None of these seems to us to capture the patterned, blended and composite nature of how one reflects on past experience. We invite you to think instead of memories of past events as mixtures formed by a huge series of individual elements blended together. It is possible to discern recognisable patterns or the outlines of particular episodes, but, over time, these fall rapidly back into the tangled whole. In Balzac's short story *The Unknown Masterpiece*, the celebrated artist Frenhofer has spent many years working on his masterpiece, a painting called *La belle noiseuse*.[10] When he finally unveils it, no one can make out what it is meant to be. If closely studied, in one portion of the canvas there appears to be something resembling a foot emerging from a swirl of colours. The problem is that the painting is destined to never be finished – Frenhofer has continuously added more and more layers of paint and would undoubtedly carry on doing so if he had the chance. The outcomes of any given individual painting session are still there and could perhaps be partially discerned under particular conditions, but it is the perpetually unfinished whole that takes centre stage.[11]

Remembering is sometimes thought of using other metaphors, such as being like looking at a set of old photographs or searching through folders and libraries of stored information on a computer. However, it comes closer to our everyday experience to compare it to finding the outline of the foot in *La belle noiseuse*. Memories are part of a whole constituted by our ongoing, unfolding experiences. They become more or less visible and change in nature as that whole changes. William James tried to convince his peers in the late nineteenth century that any theorising of the psychological had to start from the idea that we are all works in progress, unfinished and changing as our lives progress.[12] He promoted the phrase 'stream of thought' to describe personal experience as in motion, flowing, seeking out the as yet unknown. The image of a flowing stream suggests some powerful ideas about how we think and remember. A stream appears to flow in one direction, but in fact there are all kinds of patterns of turbulence and counter-flows. As the flow pushes forward, what happens downstream affects the patterns of flow upstream. If we try to trace the origins of the stream, we find ourselves lost in a mass of tributaries that come together in a confluence. As physicists have now come to see, apparently simple phenomena such as streams behave in very complex ways that are often not linear and involve changes in properties of the whole.[13] If we treat memory as a flow, it makes sense to say that, although we can never physically change the events we have experienced, their properties and qualities can be and are dramatically changed at any given moment by the overall movement of the 'stream of thought'.

The French philosopher Henri Bergson, whose ideas were engaged with William James's, used a related word, 'duration', to talk about the flow of experience.[14] Bergson, like James, argued that the psychological had to be treated from the perspective of movement and change. The fundamental fact of our existence is that we are never quite the same as we were, or will become. Bergson was well aware that this way of thinking about our lives could appear counter-intuitive. It is difficult, he claimed, to think about movement without starting from the idea of a clearly defined progression between points.[15] Surely our lives cannot be without order or predictability? Bergson addressed this with the example of waking up to the sound of a bell tolling.[16] When we first hear, we are taken with the sound itself. As it repeats, we start perhaps to count the tolls. In doing so, we are breaking our experience into parts, punctuating it into one chime following another. However, if we stop counting, we slip back into the sounds of the bells ringing, where each chime appears to partly merge with the last, as the pattern unfolds. This would be like listening to music, where the various lines of melody and rhythm combine such that what we have just heard already points forward to what is to come, without any apparent breaks: we are carried along with the flow. Bergson argues that 'duration', this form of experience without division, but with continuous qualitative transformation, is fundamental. We can, of course, attempt to break up our experience into distinct temporal or spatial units – and this is what the entire social machinery of modern bureaucratic and administrative techniques seeks to do – but this is a secondary process. Our lives flow, only subsequently do we add in the breaks and punctuations.

Approaching memory from notions of the 'stream of thought' or 'duration' presents certain challenges. If our lives flow, then the past is never really over as such, as it remains intimately connected to our ongoing experience, in a relation of the upstream and the downstream. However, we cannot simply access past experiences in a straightforward way – a process that psychologists sometimes refer to as 'mental time travel'.[17] If we could swim backwards to reach the 'upstream' of the flow of past experiences, we would find it to be different to how we recalled it, as the flow is, by definition, in perpetual movement. Moreover, our point of departure always begins from where we are right now and is shaped by our current concerns, needs and self-definitions. If one feels in despair, that one has arrived at a dead end in life, then it is considerably more likely that one will interpret past events in a way that is congruent with this feeling, such that present distress seems to be the breaking wave of a tidal pattern that originated long ago.[18] The past can never really be experienced as it was at the time. It is reconstructed, felt again on the basis of the current directions our lives appear to be taking.

The key idea that the past is reconstructed rather than simply re-presented in memory is now so widely shared across the various disciplines that together make up contemporary 'memory studies' that it is entirely uncontroversial.[19] The question is, rather, how this reconstruction happens and what its significance is for the way we understand the ongoing flow of our lives. In one of the remaining fragments of the writings of the pre-Socratic philosopher Heraclitus, the pithy phrase appears that is translated as 'On those stepping into rivers staying the same other and other waters flow'.[20] This is a strange juxtaposition of opposites – a river is both 'the same' and 'other'. Sometimes, this phrase is taken to be a claim that everything is in flux, that change is everything, but this would be to ignore the reference to sameness. The phrase is better grasped as an invitation to think how something may be said to endure or persist while becoming different to what it was. In the case of vital memories – these recollections of difficult events that are irreversible parts of our personal history – we remain 'the same' over time, in the sense that we have an ongoing felt engagement with this bell that cannot be unrung. However, we are also 'other', in that the flow of experiences in which the sound of the bell is prolonged is perpetually changing its arrangement and qualities.

Psychologists have found it difficult to think sameness and otherness together, because they have been drawn towards models from the natural sciences that emphasise stability and consistency.[21] One of the oldest of these models is that of *homeostasis*. A homeostatic process involves attempts to maintain a continuous state across an internal environment to which it returns after disturbance. Good examples of this are the maintenance of core body temperature or blood pressure. It is tempting to extend the model from the biological to the psychological and treat diverse matters such as emotions, subjectivity and the maintenance of personal and family relationships as homeostatic efforts at preserving steady states.[22] However, this provides a highly insufficient description of psychological life. Our emotions, for example, wax and wane, flow one into the other without appearing to settle in any particular state or other. A better model would that of *homeorhesis*, where a process oscillates around a moving trajectory rather than a given point. We could then see emotions as weaving their way around our unfolding experiences, such that they emphasise and intensify our sense of the directions our lives take.

Homeorhesis deals with pathways, or chreods, that are picked out through a series of possibilities.[23] A chreod is a dominant tendency, like a pathway that

The seven virtues of vital memory   7

gradually emerges across a stretch of grass as more walkers take the same route.[24] In the geography of rivers, this is known as the thalweg, the lowest points of a downward flow that come to define its course. Over time, this tendency attracts more activity to itself, in such a way that it can appear the only possibility. Vital memories operate in this way. They are but one portion of the life experience of the person who recollects them, but they seem to cut out or define what that life amounts to. One does not simply choose when and where to recall vital memories – they are always and everywhere perpetually significant. Yet, a chreod emerges as one among many possibilities. It has a could-be-otherwise character, no matter how well established it becomes.[25] And a trajectory for a homeorhetic process is not fixed and given, but rather continuously remade through a flow. In this way, we might see vital memories, not as determining ongoing life experiences, but rather as semi-stable patterns in movement.

Perhaps it is easier to think about these patterns if we move away from visual metaphors. The psychology of memory has used a range of striking images – the stylus marks the wax, the file is placed in a folder, the flashbulb light has illuminated everything in its glare for an instant. Visual metaphors suggest causal relations – encoding memories is a kind of writing, mental or neural storage that has a clear structure, striking events make concurrent trivial details highly memorable. However, this causality may well be an artefact of metaphorisation, something akin to what Alfred North Whitehead once called 'the fallacy of misplaced concreteness'.[26]

In the case of memory, there is something to be gained by using auditory, rather than visual, metaphors. In a piece of music, for example, the notes and sounds are contiguous with one another and have clear and definite relationships. However, we are not tempted to say that hearing one note determines the next, in the way that we are with visual metaphors, such as with so-called flashbulb memories. Sounds are events that have an intrinsically temporal character, a 'one-offness'. This makes it more difficult to impute a core structure or to reduce the sound to basic information to be retained, such that numerous events can be readily subsumed under one category. Hearing is, by its very nature, composite, lacking in initial selectivity. When one walks into a crowded room, for example, it takes some time to adjust to or focus on a particular conversation. Even when one does so, the remaining background noise remains part of the experience; it is never entirely irrelevant. By contrast, visual metaphors lead us to think that we can process parts as distinct from wholes. We are always being exposed to sound, even when asleep or half-awake, unlike with our visual faculty. Sound is omnipresent; we never encounter absolute silence. The performance of John Cage's '4'33"', a score that requires performers to not play their instruments for just over four minutes, is not silent. The audience instead hears the ambient noises of the auditorium for that duration. If memory is more analogous to hearing rather than seeing, it suggests that our control over what to encode in memory and over our memories themselves is far more diffuse than that suggested by visual metaphors.

Indeed, take a moment to try and recollect the voice of a person who, for whatever reason, has not been present in your life for a few years. Does it return instantly? Or does it instead take a few attempts to 'get it'? Can you think of their voice in the abstract, or do you need to think of the contexts wherein it was heard? Maybe how they spoke when they were excited, or that time when they were most angry with you. Perhaps it is not the words, but rather the sound of their voice that starts to emerge – their laugh, the way they whispered when you were close. Does that start to work? Or do you begin to feel that you cannot quite catch hold of it, that there is something not quite right or missing? Do you become increasingly aware of the absence rather than the presence, and of the irreversible gap between then and now?

Ordinary people managing difficult pasts

The research that we have been involved with over a number of years has been concerned with particular kinds of difficult personal memory among so-called 'vulnerable' groups. These include survivors of child sexual abuse (CSA), adopted children and their families, people close to the 2005 London bombings, forensic mental health service users, and elderly persons in care-home settings. Each of these groups is very different. Some are managing circumstances that they have chosen; others are dealing with events that were entirely unwanted and outside their control. The contexts in which these pasts are recollected vary. Some groups are engaged with social and welfare services, others with legal or political processes. Institutions or organised care settings are a feature of some groups' lives, either directly or through the experiences of others, but not all. What we have been particularly struck with across all these groups is both the irreversible nature of the experiences they recollect and the range of capacities and strategies that individuals across these groups have for 'taming' their personal pasts. These are ordinary people managing difficult experiences and, on the whole, doing this well. We would contrast this with what might be termed the 'extremity' and 'deficit' models that are commonly adopted in psychology.

The *extremity model* typically appears in discussions of CSA or mental health. It refers to events that are held to be on the very edges of culturally normative life experiences. These are seen to create discontinuities in experience that require significant intervention. Persons who have undergone these kinds of experience are typically seen to have a range of 'memory problems' – such as problems with recollection, difficulties in integrating memories and/or persistent, intrusive concern with aspects of the unwanted experience. The way their memory works is 'other' to what would be considered normal functioning, with the result that they have difficulties sustaining a coherent sense of self. In this model, extreme experience disrupts memory and fragments identity.

The *deficit model* also features in discussions of mental health, along with consideration of persons at the two end points of the life-course, namely children and the elderly. Here, memory is treated as following a specific developmental course. Persons diagnosed with an underlying psychiatric disorder, such as schizophrenia, are taken to have developed unreliable memories as a consequence of their long-term condition. Children and the elderly are meanwhile similarly unreliable in their memories, because their memorial capacities are either not yet fully formed or in a process of natural disrepair. This calls into question whether persons viewed through the deficit model can be considered as adequate witnesses to their own experiences. Here, poor memory is a defining feature of certain normative and supra-normative conditions.

What we find problematic in these two models is their focus on what persons are supposed to *not* be able to do, rather than on their actual accomplishments. For example, elderly visitors to the reminiscence museum that we will discuss in Chapter 8 are able to produce very rich recollections about their past at certain moments, although at other moments appearing uninterested and disengaged. One of the reasons for this is that the space of the museum itself appears to have a role in facilitating and shaping certain kinds of memory. The central role of context – whether that is the part played by others, or by the features of the space where recollection happens, or the affordances of objects – is ignored in both the extremity and deficit models.

Equally problematic is the view that experiences that depart from cultural norms will always create significant memory problems. The women who had experienced CSA from whom we hear in Chapter 4, for instance, reflect on the place of their experiences in subtle and complex ways. They are also clear that their lives are far broader and richer than the past difficulties that they manage in the present. We are not denying that unwanted, distressing experiences offer significant challenges for personal identity and a sense of agency. However, rather than see such challenges as exceeding cultural norms, we would locate them within a diversity of 'problems with the past' that are a shared across a great many lives.

Out of all of the issues that arise from uses of extremity and deficit models, the one we find most troubling is the conflation of different kinds of questions. Psychologists have often treated memories of difficult events strictly in terms of their literal accuracy – is this particular memory true or false?[27] However, in Chapter 5, we will meet adoptive parents who wrestle with the dilemma of how to preserve the personal history of their adopted children without forcing them to engage with all the details immediately. These parents use a mixture of fact, opinion, abstraction, revision and even invention in order to leave the space for their children to tell their own stories about their pasts at some point in the future. This is an ethical rather than a narrowly psychological problem. It concerns the ways that we jointly make use of the past with others to make the present liveable and the future desirable.

In a similar vein, the forensic mental health service users who feature in Chapter 7 are engaged in complex work around the past. However, in their case, they are principally concerned with events for which they are legally accountable and that have resulted in their being detained under a section of the Mental Health Act in a secure forensic psychiatric unit. Their current well-being and future prospects strongly depend on their willingness to publicly reconstruct those events as caused by their 'illness', such that they can demonstrate engagement with the programme that will ultimately lead to their rehabilitation. However, this comes at the cost of discounting other aspects of their past life, such as personal relationships or sexuality, which are deemed irrelevant to their current condition. The question is not how an individual patient's memory is affected by their mental health status, as the deficit model would have it, but rather the ways in which legal and psychiatric practices 'take hold' of personal memory and shape it along specific lines.

In Chapter 6, these issues acquire a definite political character as we describe how survivors of the 2005 London bombings found that their own personal experiences had become public property. They tell of the difficulties of finding that one is now an object of overwhelming media interest, at a point where one's life has suddenly and irrevocably changed. They also describe what it is like to be recruited into a political project of building collective memory, and of the dilemmas and ambiguities that this creates. Clearly these are people who have undergone extreme and distressing experiences, but the central issue is not the kinds of memory problem that are the focus of the extremity model. It is instead around how personal experience can become interdependent with broader collective commemorative, media and political processes, and what this means for the persons concerned.

Seven themes

Throughout the book we will work around a series of themes. These themes could be applied to any class of memory – they do not define memories of difficult pasts as such. However, when taken as a set of lenses through which to view vital memories, they draw out their particular contours, as distinct from other kinds of memory. In no particular order the themes are as follows:

Autobiography

Psychologists have traditionally made distinctions between different kinds of learning and memory, such as remembering how to perform various actions (*implicit* or *procedural* memory); remembering meanings and factual information (*semantic* memory); and remembering context-bound, specific events (*episodic* memory).[28] This last form of memory has been of particular concern to contemporary psychology. Martin Conway has led the way in demonstrating that memory of events that have personal relevance – or *autobiographical* memory – is a subset of episodic memory. Conway's work has shown a range of interesting effects around this kind of memory.[29] It appears that what we can recall from our past experience is driven to a large extent by how we currently view ourselves. Memories that are congruent with the present image of self are more readily accessible. If, right now, you think of yourself as someone who is too quick to trust others and, as a consequence, unlucky in love, it is likely that you will be able to find a whole host of autobiographical memories that seem to confirm this. Conversely, shifts in self-definition surface different kinds of similarly oriented autobiographical memory.

Conway's work has increasingly come to resonate with another tradition within psychology, the study of self-narratives. Research here has explored how telling stories about oneself is a critical life skill.[30] Historically, it appears to be the case that, in Western Europe, from at least the seventeenth century onwards, personhood was linked to memory – what we are is the product of how we relate to our own past.[31] The ability to tell a self-narrative is, then, critical to constituting oneself as a person, socially, morally, legally and politically. From this, it follows that the inability to construct coherent self-narratives invites suspicion at the very least, and at worst can lead to a disqualification of individual rights (such as the right to give legal evidence or to manage one's own affairs). We see vital memories as a particular class of autobiographical memory that typically take the form of self-narratives. Like all self-narratives, they do the work of accounting for who and what we are. Unlike many other self-narratives, however, because they deal with distressing experiences, vital memories come with challenges to a present view of self. They cut out chreods, life trajectories that point in directions that the person may wish to contest or resist. If we must tell our pasts, or risk being held to account for not doing so, then vital memories require considerable skill in the telling.

Agency

Discussions of agency in relation to memory tend to treat agency as something that we either fully possess or have in some way lost. The extremity model, for instance, posits that agency is unravelled by memories of traumatic experiences and only restored once those experiences are contained through practice such as the neo-Freudian idea of 'working through' trauma. In his study of Veterans Administration patients being treated for post-traumatic stress disorder (PTSD) on a psychiatric ward, Allan Young shows that linking current agency to a working through of trauma creates a different and complex relationship to personal history that he calls 'traumatic time'.[32] The experience of this time is characterised by a continuous deferral of a perpetually just-out-of-reach agency. The problem, as we see it, comes from treating agency as something we have or don't have. It would perhaps be better to think of the relationship between agency and memory using Bartlett's notion of 'turning on one's schema'.[33] Bartlett coined this enigmatic phrase to describe how we may reflect upon the organisation of our past experiences and, in so doing, interrupt or create pauses in how memory informs our current activities. For example, persons who have strong connections to the 2005 London bombings typically spend considerable time reflecting on both what they remember and the ways in which they and others ought to remember this event in the future. In this way, agency expands or dilates according to our capacity for such 'turning around'.

To reflect on the past does not mean that the past is put in some clear order, nor is it necessarily expressed as a kind of autonomy or freedom in relation to our personal history. For example, survivors of CSA may routinely reflect on episodes of abuse and may derive complex and contradictory feelings about their abuser and their own involvement in what happened.[34] This may include struggles to determine whether there was some element of 'choice' on their part, along with attributions about the motivations of the abuser. In some therapeutic practices (such as those studied by Young), this kind of ambivalence would be seen as an obstacle to achieving some kind of settlement with the past – to 'moving on'. However, ambivalence may also be seen, in certain circumstances, as a powerful resource.[35] Through the refusal to fix clear intentions and definitions of what happened, a space is opened up between past and present that can be productive, because it allows difficult questions about one's moral character and personal capacities to be reformulated. At the heart of agency, therefore, has to be an understanding of the deep ambivalence individuals can feel about the actions performed in the past.

Forgetting

There are a number of detailed historical analyses of the changing ways in which memory has been conceived in Western culture and of the shifts in corresponding memory practices.[36] However, forgetting also has a history. As Harald Weinrich shows in his literary–philosophical treatment, there are a great many classical sources, from Cicero to Kant, that promote the practice of 'active forgetting' as providing salvation from a fixation on the past.[37] Nietzsche, for instance, argued that, although historical reflection provides a source of belonging and noteworthy examples, it can also suffocate and paralyse the vitality of the present by chaining it to the weight of the past, and thus what is required is a 'critical' attitude to history that takes the form of 'active forgetting'.[38] This has led some commentators, such as Paul Connerton, to characterise modernity as dominated by the self-conscious erasure of the past in the name of the 'new'.[39] We live in modern cultures of organised and systematic forgetting, Connerton claims. But, as Weinrich shows, this is a very partial reading of the history of forgetting. For many writers – including Nietzsche – the problem is not that of disposing or having done with the past entirely, but rather of acknowledging the dilemma of balancing 'too much' with 'too little' historical sensibility.

Active forgetting should be seen instead as the effort to defer or displace the relevance of the past in the present, such that alternative futures are opened

14 The seven virtues of vital memory

up. For example, adopted children who are aware of some difficult aspects of their early family life pre-adoption, such as violence or criminality, may project this forward to imagine that they are predestined to repeat similar acts in the future. These early experiences, which in some cases are reconstructions or 'vicarious memories' based on partial stories told by siblings or relatives, establish powerful chreods, as the child attempts to make sense of where their life is taking them. Adoptive parents typically try to support their children in resisting these chreods by a selective reframing of the past that minimises or occludes problematic aspects. However, parents cannot risk erasing these details entirely, as they may be held accountable for doing so by the child in the future (for example, the child may wish, on becoming an adult, to contact a biological parent). Active forgetting here takes the form of what we might call, to modify the psychological definition slightly, the 'managed accessibility' of memories. It helps here to recognise that both remembering and forgetting are distributed activities that involve a range of material artefacts (i.e. diaries, records, photographs) and other people (through both direct and mediated interaction, such as social media). The managed accessibility of vital memories is, to a great degree, a collective rather than an individual project.

Ethics

The collective nature of projects of remembering and forgetting immediately raises questions of ethics and morality. Two of the most significant recent contributions to this debate are by the philosophers Avishai Margalit (in *The Ethics of Memory*) and Jeffrey Blustein (in *The Moral Demands of Memory*).[40] Despite the cogent and persuasive arguments presented in both texts, there are some difficulties with the approaches taken by both Margalit and Blustein. Contemporary philosophy encourages a distinction between ethics and morality. This is particularly acute in the work of Margalit, who sees ethical questions, such as duties of care, as only relevant to the 'thick relations' constituted by families or communities, whereas moral obligations around what is right and wrong are abstractions that apply to the 'thin relations' of nationhood or common humanity. This makes it difficult to apply evaluative criteria within a community of memory, as, by Margalit's definition, the presence of caring in thick relations means that they cannot be immoral (as caring is an unalloyed good). Both philosophers also offer normative treatments of ethics. For example, Blustein formulates the conditions under which remembering a dead family member can become a moral imperative.[41] But how does this imperative apply to a survivor of CSA remembering an abusive parent? Are they relieved of this imperative? If not, then at what cost to themselves do they choose to uphold it, and, more importantly, what, for them, is the cost, both personally and socially, of *not* upholding the imperative?

The problem is with the imposition of unambiguous external moral standards and ethical goods on remembering rather than attempting to derive an ethics from the way that memory functions as part of the self-constitution of persons and collectives. Extending the previous example, we might say that, at certain moments, the survivor might choose to actively forget his or her abusive parent to assert their autonomy. On other occasions, however, they might want to remember, but not honour, their parent, because this affirms their place in broader family relationships. And on still further occasions, they may wish to both remember and partially honour the parent, because they were, in the past, the source of love and care, as well as abuse and harm. What criterion could we possibly apply to judge the ethical merits of the different decisions? It would be the extent to which the choice to remember or not remember enhances personal powers to act and expands the capacity to relate to and affectively engage with the others on each particular occasion. This criterion is developed from Spinoza's treatment of ethics, which has been developed recently by political philosophers such as Gilles Deleuze and Antonio Negri and feminist philosophers such as Moira Gatens and Rosi Braidotti.[42] For a Spinozist ethics, there is no universal good or bad, only what is contingently good or bad for given persons engaged in a specific encounter with one other. If this were to be applied to vital memories, we would argue that ethical judgements of what we ought and ought not to remember must be radically specific to particular occasions and practices and be concerned with the question of what increases the vibrancy, capacities and modalities through which persons relate to each other as they jointly remember.

Affect

At the centre of Spinoza's ethics is *affect*. Over the past 10 years, there has been a huge renewed interest in emotion in the social sciences.[43] The term affect is sometimes used as distinct from the patterned forms of felt evaluations that we call emotions, to indicate a prior, relational and to some extent non-conscious engagement with the world.[44] In Spinoza's philosophy, affect is the intensive, qualitative dimension of the encounter between bodies. For example, on entering a space such as a secure forensic mental health ward, one is immediately struck with a particular feeling that emerges from the ordering of bodies within that environment. This feeling is not immediately resolvable into a specific emotion, such as anxiety, but nevertheless has a definite, phenomenological reality. Referring to affect as an 'intensive' rather than 'extensive' property (e.g. as akin to temperature or pressure rather than distance or height) indicates that affect changes when it is divided through evaluation.[45] When we try to appraise what we are feeling, the outcome is an emotion that is qualitatively different from the affective relational form out of which it emerges. Affect might be best thought of as an 'atmosphere' and, crucially, as involving time (here, the convenient double meaning in French of *le temps* as both 'the weather' and 'time' is helpful).[46] Perhaps we can speak of there being 'affective climates' along with 'sites of memory', or even of the impossibility of thinking social memory apart from affect.

Thinking affect as an arrangement of relations, rather than purely an individual response, presents some challenges. For example, in previous work we have discussed how a CSA survivor recalls an incident from her childhood where her brother abused her.[47] A key element in the memory is of the brother locking the door to the room where the abuse subsequently occurred. We would argue that affect emerges here as a relational, intensive property of the arrangement of the brother, the setting, the locked door. It is the arrangement of all these things together that gives the memory its affective charge. Each time the incident is recalled, the survivor is reconnected to that affective atmosphere, despite the physical and temporal distance. Despite its power, this affect is relatively undifferentiated; it does not initially deliver a clear meaning. However, when the survivor focuses on the moment the door was locked, everything changes. The locking of the door is a moment of qualification and subjectification of the affect. Focusing on that moment resolves the atmosphere into a discrete emotional experience (in this case, anger). Yet this need not necessarily be the case. Affect is non-deterministic. The survivor has had a wide range of emotional experiences around this recollection. This suggests that rationalising one's emotional responses is unlikely to be sufficient to manage this memory — what needs to be done is to explore means of feeling a way through the atmosphere differently — to discovering new possibilities in what that atmosphere can offer.

Space

The idea that we are still connected to past affective atmospheres is difficult to entertain because of the way we think about space. Bergson famously argued that our conceptual difficulties in approaching memory come from the transposing of a spatial framework to a process that is, by definition, temporal.[48] We cannot think of memories as stored in a given site – irrespective of whether that is the brain, the archive or the group – because they are not entities with spatial properties. Nevertheless, remembering reconstructs events that can be clearly indexed to particular times and places, such as with recollections of the 2005 London bombings. And place often appears to 'hold' our memories in a way that defines who we are, such that, as the folklorist Kent Ryden puts it, 'we sense we are reaching the edge of our world when we run out of stories to tell about the places we see'.[49] The challenge is to break with our usual perception of space as a container of experience and action. We must instead move towards a relational conception of space.

One means of doing this is through topological description. Topology is a branch of mathematics that is concerned with the effects of continuous transformation on relations between points. To do this, it conceives of space in terms of regions, edges and boundaries distributed across n-dimensional surfaces known as 'manifolds'.[50] The questions asked of this space are not, primarily, to do with calculating the distance between points, but are instead around the properties of the relations that are preserved as the space is deformed (thus, very different spatial forms are considered as equivalent – homomorphic – if relations between points remain intact). The social psychologist Kurt Lewin argued that experience (or 'life-space') ought to be understood as a manifold.[51] In doing so, he was rejecting the idea of clear separation between the psychological subject and her or his external environment. Experience is constituted by the totality of actual and possible relations (for Lewin, these are both physical and mental) that define us as part of the world. For example, we might be tempted to treat the experiences of forensic mental health patients on secure wards as bounded by the physical locked doors and walls of the institution. However, patients are embedded in relationships that cross these apparent barriers through mediated means such as telephones, letters, photographs and music. The topological boundaries of the life-space of the forensic mental health patient do not map on to the metric space of the ward – they are considerably broader, spatially complex and porous. In this way, we can begin to think that remembering must also follow these topological planes of connections that diverge considerably from our usual understanding of (Euclidean) space and (chronological) time.

Institutional practices

In her classic *How Institutions Think*, Mary Douglas demonstrated how the psychological (i.e. thinking, feeling, acting) was profoundly shaped by organisational and institutional contexts.[52] Organisations such as large corporations have their own logic and practices for preserving authorised versions of the past, in which staff then become inculcated, even when that version of the past seems at odds with their own experiences. This raises the question of how institutions recruit or take hold of individual and collective modes of remembering. In pursuing this, it is worth noting the basic constraint identified by Luhmann in his systems theoretical approach.[53] A given social system, such as the law, can only communicate through its own particular practices for synthesising information and extracting meaning. Were it to attempt to do otherwise, it would lose its identity as a system. When it comes to remembering, therefore, we would expect the legal system to demand that individual and collective memory delivers on matters such as evidence, accuracy, lack of ambiguity etc. However, institutions that are embedded in different social systems, such as medicine or art, will require very different things from memory. Therapy, for instance, asks for emotional significance, symbolic value, evidence of current patterns of thought and so on. We cannot then expect the law to communicate in anything other than a 'legal' manner, and therapy to communicate in anything other than a 'therapeutic' manner. But, if this is so, what happens when the law and therapy converge on a given memory problem – such as when a person who recollects CSA seeks both legal and therapeutic redress?

Conway characterises the quality of autobiographical memory in the following way:

> Memories can be wrong – sometimes very wrong. Memories can also be 'forgotten' for long periods of time and later remembered with surprise. These are the facts of memory, they are not hypotheses or speculative beliefs . . . But autobiographical memory (AM) also has other (redeeming) properties, two of which are that the representations of the past which the system creates are often basically accurate and the rememberer has some, limited, ability to assess memory accuracy. Volatility of access, errors,

incompleteness, and even wholly false memories in the context of basic accuracy are the hallmarks of AM.[54]

If we leave aside differences over whether autobiographical remembering is best considered as a purely personal or a distributed activity, there is little here that diverges from what feminist theoreticians Janice Haaken and Sue Campbell would say about remembering CSA.[55] However, these 'facts of memory' will show up in very different ways to the law and therapy, which have very different thresholds of tolerance for the sorts of metaphor, symbolisation and narrative structure in which CSA memories are typically framed. This will inevitably create continuities and discontinuities in how remembering is treated, which all too often will be left to the survivor herself or himself to manage. We argue that, when vital memories become the joint object of concern for several different institutional practices, we need to acknowledge that the kinds of recollection that are produced in the different institutional contexts may appear to be contradictory and may not be readily synthesised. For example, in ongoing work, we are finding that the way that police officers engage with witness statements from mental health service users differs considerably from how the same recollections would be handled in a therapeutic setting.[56] We propose that what is needed in such cases is a formal recognition of the fact that what we can do with our memory and the forms our remembering takes are interdependent with institutional contexts; that the resulting contradictions across recollections ought not to be taken as undermining the credibility of the person concerned; and that this recognition should be backed up with procedures for allowing institutional practices to jointly manage the divergences in remembered accounts that they themselves act to create through their own functioning.

In the coming chapters, we return to the seven themes and expand upon their utility in considering vital memory in specific contexts. In turn, we also elaborate on what it means to treat memory as duration or as flow, by exploring the expanded view of autobiographical memory in the works of cognitive, sociocultural developmental psychologists, as well as the perspectives of those working within discursive psychology, in the following chapter. Our specific aim here is to examine these perspectives more closely in order to examine relations between people, things and settings and to establish a dialogue between these seemingly opposed perspectives. Here, we argue that much of the current work taking place within psychology is already extending memory beyond the confines of the skull, reaching successfully into broader contexts, or what we call, in Chapter 3, the 'life-world' of individuals. Here, relations between people, things and setting become necessarily morphed, moving together to produce 'experience', through which memory flows.

Notes

1 Hume, 1739/1985.
2 Lorenz, 2002.
3 Meyer, 2009.
4 Freud, 2001.
5 See Derrida, 1978.
6 Singer and Conway, 2008.
7 Trauma 'theory' became a major approach to memory in literature studies, with the widespread influence of the work of Cathy Caruth (1995, 1996). However, following the critical re-evaluation of Leys (2013), the approach has lost ground in recent years. For a thoroughgoing critique of trauma theory in memory studies, see Pickering and Keightley (2009).
8 Notably in the work of Bessel van der Kolk (2014). For a critique of this position, see Leys (2013).
9 See Draaisma (2000) and Danziger (2008).
10 Balzac, 2002.
11 Michel Serres (1995a) makes a reading of *The Unknown Masterpiece* central to his theorising of multiplicity and complexity.
12 James, 1890/1950.
13 See Mitchell (2011) and Waldrop (1992). Isabelle Stengers' (2010, 2011a) is probably the best place to start for establishing the relevance of this kind of thought for the social sciences.
14 Bergson, 1908/1991.
15 See his influential lecture on 'The Perception of Change' given at Oxford in 1911, which appears in Bergson (1933/1992).
16 See Bergson, 1913/2001.
17 Tulving, 1985b.
18 This is a central point made by Conway in relation to selectivity in autobiographical memory (see Conway, 1990; Conway and Pleydell-Pearce, 2000).
19 See, for example, recent surveys of the field in Erll (2011), Olick *et al.* (2011), and Hagen and Tota (2015).
20 See Kahn, 1981.
21 See Brown and Stenner, 2009.
22 This is done routinely in psychological approaches to 'stress' that emphasise the recovery of balance through coping mechanisms, such as with the influential model of Lazarus and Folkman (1984).
23 Serres's work, although rather forbidding for the uninitiated, is fascinating for its ability to demonstrate how natural science concepts may be thought of in relation to the human and social sciences. See, in particular, Serres (1982, 2007) and, for overviews, Brown (2002) and Abbas (2005).
24 Sometimes also referred to as a 'cow path'. In IT, the problem of whether or not emergent pathways ought to be formalised gives rise to the cautionary injunction, 'Don't pave the cow path'.
25 This concept is developed extensively in developmental systems theory – see Oyama (2000).
26 Whitehead (1925/1967: 51).

27 This is notably the case in debates around 'recovered' and 'false' memory. For various perspectives on this, see Loftus and Ketcham (1996), Conway (1997) and Campbell (2003).
28 See Schachter (1996, 2003) for readable discussions of these distinctions.
29 Conway *et al.*, 2004, 2005; Conway, 2005.
30 See Polkinghorner, 1988; Riessman, 2008; Andrews *et al.*, 2013.
31 Nelson, 2003.
32 Young, 1995.
33 Bartlett, 1932.
34 See the contributions to Reavey and Warner (2003) for further discussion.
35 Reavey and Brown, 2006.
36 For example, Yates, 1966; Matsuda, 1996; Ricoeur 2004; Carruthers, 2008.
37 Weinrich, 2004.
38 Nietzsche, 1997.
39 Connerton, 2008, 2009, 2011.
40 Margalit, 2002; Blustein, 2008.
41 Blustein, 2008.
42 Spinoza, 1677/1996. See Deleuze, 1988, 1992; Negri, 1991, 2013; Gatens, 1996; Braidotti, 2006.
43 See Gregg and Seigworth, 2010; Blackman, 2012; Wetherell, 2012.
44 This position is associated with what Thrift (2008) calls the 'Deleuzian ethological approach'.
45 See DeLanda, 2002.
46 See Serres, 1995b.
47 Reavey and Brown, 2009.
48 Bergson, 1908/1991, 1933/1992.
49 Ryden, 1993: 68.
50 Jänich, 1995. For applications of topological thinking to social science, see DeLanda (2002), Blum and Secor (2011), Brown (2012a) and Phillips (2013).
51 Lewin, 1936.
52 Douglas, 1987.
53 Luhman, 1996, 2008.
54 Conway, 1997: 150.
55 See Haaken, 1998; Campbell, 2003.
56 Reavey *et al.*, forthcoming.

Chapter 2

The expanded view of memory

Out from the laboratory

There was something unusual about the child, her parents thought. After she had been tucked in for the night, following story time, the 2-year-old would continue talking to herself. What was she saying? What did it mean? The parents did something equally unusual – they placed a tape recorder by the child's bed and made audio tapes of her bedtime monologues. These tapes were eventually passed on to a family friend, the psychologist Katherine Nelson, who in turn shared them with colleagues. Together, they analysed the child's recorded speech and published their findings as a series of essays, *Narratives from the Crib.*[1]

Contrast this story with the typical way in which data are collected within the experimental psychology of memory. A student who requires course credits waits outside a small, windowless room. They are eventually shown in by a postgraduate researcher and sat at a small desk with a computer. The researcher, following a script, will talk the student through what they will be required to do for the next 30 or 40 minutes. The door closes, the student clicks the mouse, and a program starts up, guiding them through a series of repetitive tasks. Somewhere nearby, the data from the experimental trial are captured by another machine, overseen by the researcher, who sits back dreaming of the day when they will be in charge of the experiments. Or perhaps just of the next coffee and cigarette.

Experimentation remains central to the vast majority of psychological studies of memory. Its current form can be traced back to the very origins of psychology. Hermann Ebbinghaus developed the first experimental approach to remembering in the late nineteenth century.[2] In these studies, participants would be required to learn and then subsequently recall 'nonsense syllables'. In common with the practice of the time, Ebbinghaus served as his own 'test subject' most of the time.[3] To the modern observer this may appear impossibly amateurish, but it is important to understand the revolutionary nature of what Ebbinghaus attempted. In order to legitimately claim that what was being studied was 'memory', Ebbinghaus needed to be able to purify the phenomenon under controlled conditions, such that it became visible and recordable. This meant constructing a task apparently free from confounding variables – nonsense syllables were used to eliminate the possibility that semantic association rather than pure recall was being tested – and using what was then the latest development in time-recording technology (e.g. the kymograph). It was vital that the accuracy of his recall of the previously learned nonsense syllables be established, because this allowed a supposedly objective mathematical relationship to be posited between factors such as number of repetitions and length of recall. This enabled Ebbinghaus to claim a kind of statistical reality for an otherwise intangible phenomenon: mental processes could be made manifest empirically when imputed through patterns formed by numerical records of carefully observed behaviour.

This approach came to full fruition in the cognitive experimental work around memory that gathered pace from the 1970s onwards. Cognitive science provided the conceptual resources to model mental processes in increasingly sophisticated ways (such as in terms of 'executive' and 'slave' systems[4]) or as spread across 'levels of processing'.[5] Experimental paradigms, while retaining the basic set-up of participants learning target stimuli (either explicitly or implicitly), were refined to explore a vast range of possible contributing variables. However, the cognitive approach tended to further reify the status of memory processes from having a 'mathematical being' to an independent existence. Memories were treated as informational bits within an ordered system for storage and retrieval, thereby acquiring an entitative (or 'thing-like') status. Moreover, despite the early call made by Frederick Bartlett to redirect focus upon the uses we make of our memory, accuracy remained the most important criterion that was studied.[6]

However, something changed in the early 1980s. One of the most eminent cognitive psychologists of the time, Ulrich Neisser, called for psychologists to step outside the comfort zone of the laboratory and to study memory in 'natural contexts'.[7] By way of example, he offered his own study of testimony given by White House aide John Dean to the Senate inquiry following the infamous Watergate political scandal. Dean had been advisor to President Richard Nixon, and both had been caught discussing unfolding events around the Watergate incident on audio recordings made at the White House. During the subsequent hearings, Dean was asked to recall events from the time of the recordings. Neisser had noticed that this meant, in effect, that there was a baseline measure – the original recordings – against which to evaluate Dean's ability to recall at the hearings. This could be treated as a 'natural experiment'. In his analysis, Neisser noted that, although Dean made a good many errors in his recollection, his overall sense of what was happening in the events he recollected was more or less faithful.[8] This would have been overlooked in a laboratory study, where literal accuracy rather than general faithfulness to the past is the primary concern.

At around the same time, Jerome Bruner, who, like Neisser, was considered one of the major influences on the 'cognitive revolution' in psychology, offered a different way forward for psychological research.[9] Bruner argued that psychologists had failed to adequately grasp one of the key insights from the arts and humanities, namely that human thought operates in at least two different modes. The first is the mode sought by Ebbinghaus and those who followed in his tradition – the presentation of bits of information in causal relation to one another. This mode, or *paradigmatic thinking* for Bruner, is shared across logic and mathematics. It is concerned with premises, deductions, consistency in the identity of terms and non-contradictions. The second – and equally important – mode is *narrative thinking*. Here, knowledge is organised in terms of plots, characters and meaningful actions with consequences. If paradigmatic thinking has its own particular logical conventions, then narrative thinking is no less deeply structured by specific cultural conventions. Bruner argued that a plausible description of the psychological needed to recognise the co-presence of both modes of thinking in human thought and action. The student who clicks away in the experiment for course credit is, at the very same time, constructing a narrative about why exactly they are doing this right now and how to tell a funny story about it to their friends later on.

Since the 1980s, the psychology of memory has engaged with the arguments about method and thinking offered by Neisser and Bruner. Some, such as Martin Conway, have expanded their research to include a range of data sources (e.g. diaries, questionnaires, interviews, neurological data) and have built models of remembering that explicitly engage with non-paradigmatic thinking and cultural influences. Others, such as Katherine Nelson, begin with the idea of narrative and then look to recruit empirical material – such as that collected by puzzled parents – that will help to bring this mode of remembering into focus. We will call this approach the 'expanded view' of memory. It uses multiple forms of evidence and is sensitive to the idea that there is not a single modality through which memories are enacted in the present. By contrast, the 'restricted view' of memory insists that a single empirical practice (usually experimentation) meets the demands of scientificity, and that the accuracy, or otherwise, of recollection is the primary matter to be explained. The work of Elizabeth Loftus is a good illustration of this latter view. Despite her interest in 'real-world' issues such as eyewitness testimony and recollections of CSA, Loftus is notorious for her rigid insistence on paradigmatic thinking and experimentation as the only respectable sources of data.[10]

In this chapter, we will discuss how an expanded view of autobiographical memory informs our treatment of vital memories. However, as we will show, the study of autobiographical memory needs to be enhanced with a greater concern for the interactional processes within which stories about our personal pasts are mobilised. Here, we will draw on work from discursive psychology, in particular the social remembering approach developed by David Middleton. This will lead us to consider some of the contexts and spaces in which these interactions occur in greater detail.

Autobiographical memory: the expanded view

The study of autobiographical memory in psychology began with Endel Tulving's distinction between procedural, semantic and episodic memory.[11] Procedural memory is the retained knowledge of how to do things, whether that be using a spoon properly or retrieving a voicemail message. Semantic memory is the general range of information about the world held by the person in the form of symbolic representations, from knowing one's own name to the chemical symbol for mercury. Episodic memories are of events that are bounded in time and space and have been personally experienced, such as moving house or witnessing a road accident. Tulving treated these forms of memory as distinct systems, nested Russian-doll-like inside one another.[12] He argued that episodic memory was a psychological capacity that grew out of these more fundamental forms of memory, which served as its conditions. For example, it is difficult to conceive how a person could remember an event as belonging in the past without having some symbolic means of distinguishing what is currently absent from the immediate present.

This distinction between different kinds of memory has considerable face value – it seems to capture something of how remembering 'feels' to us. Typing a PIN into a cash machine usually requires little conscious effort (except when we make an error), but recalling the last time and place we laughed heartily with a close friend may require considerably more. Phenomenal awareness appears to vary with each form of memory. In particular, whereas procedural memory has a 'timeless' feel, episodic memory involves a self-awareness of one's place in a personal temporal flow. Tulving called this self-awareness 'autonoetic consciousness'.[13] One of its principal characteristics, as he saw it, was the ability consciously to place oneself into remembered past events or anticipate future events, which he gnomically referred to as 'mental time travel'.[14]

One of the interesting questions that Tulving poses about this ability is why it should arise in the first place. Speaking in a loosely evolutionary sense, we can see that knowing how to recognise potential food from poison, or being able to symbolically represent water as both life and danger, has some adaptive purpose. But what use is memory of things past to us in the present? Tulving's answer is that, 'by enhancing the perceived orderliness of an organism's universe, episodic memory and autonoetic consciousness lead to more decisive action in the present and more effective planning in the future'.[15]

This functional approach to episodic memory is carried forward in Conway's approach to autobiographical memory. Conway proposes a 'self-memory system' built around a 'working self', a 'long-term self' and an 'episodic memory system'.[16] The working self is a cognitive process that is constituted around a dynamic hierarchy of goals and a set of abstract knowledges (i.e. semantic knowledge) about how to accomplish these goals. Conway sees this process as dynamic as the ordering of goals is perpetually shifting, as circumstances change. However, shifting goals comes at some cost. This can be comparatively minor, such as deciding against a planned trip to the shops because it is raining, to hugely disruptive, as in deciding that one is in the wrong job or personal relationship. Therefore, Conway reasons, the working self needs to be as well informed as possible to avoid such shifts in goal orientation and, consequently, draws upon episodic memory to increase the 'perceived orderliness' of the world in which the person acts.[17] From this, it follows that episodic memories that are relevant to current goals will be of the greatest value and, hence, are more likely to be drawn upon. What is called autobiographical memory is this reshuffling of past experiences to create an orderly present and coherent life trajectory – or 'long-term self' – where what we are doing now appears entirely congruent with what we have done before.

In subsequent work, Conway has modified the model, introducing greater reference to the cultural backdrop against which autobiographical memories are reconstructed.[18] The 'long-term self' is now formally divided into two further elements. The 'autobiographical knowledge base' is a set of knowledge structures based on culturally meaningful 'general events', 'lifetime periods' and normative 'life story schemas'. These represent ways of bundling together experiences into recognisable units, divisions and patterns, such as 'first-time experiences' (e.g. our first kiss), 'transitions' (e.g. leaving home) and 'types of lives' (e.g. with another person, or by ourselves). The second element, the 'conceptual self', is a set of 'socially-constructed schemas and categories that help to define the self, other people, and typical interactions with others and the social world'.[19] In other words, these are patterns of symbolic relations that render our world and us meaningful. For example, when asked to recall significant autobiographical memories, many adults recollect disproportionately more memories from when they were between 10 and 30 years old. This 'reminiscence bump' is thought to occur for a variety of reasons: it may be because it contains a significant number of 'first-time' experiences, or events that became thought of as 'self-defining', or perhaps simply because this period from pre-adolescence to early adulthood is especially culturally valorised.[20] Whatever the answer, these additions to Conway's theory aim to demonstrate that the mental models through which autobiographical memories are reconstructed are derived from the particular sociocultural milieus in which we dwell.

Despite such addition, Katherine Nelson and Robyn Fivush claim that theories such as Conway's place too great an emphasis on the 'internal' features of cognitive models and underlying neurological patterns, at the cost of understanding how a sense of self emerges developmentally in a social context:

> Rather than viewing the self in this construction as an autonomous construction of the mind or the brain, we view it as a product of innumerable social experiences in cultural space that provide for the developmental differentiation of the sense of a unique self from that of undifferentiated personal experience.[21]

The difference between the approaches is grounded in part in the type of material each works with. Whereas Conway's work places great emphasis on data drawn from neurological patients with various forms of amnesia, Nelson and Fivush's work draws primarily on studies of remembering in younger children. There is evidence that suggests children possess the ability to recall past events from as early as 9 months old.[22] As soon as children begin to speak, at around 16 months, they start to refer to recent past experiences spontaneously.[23] These recollections are typically 'scaffolded' (i.e. supported, encouraged and guided)[24] by adults, who ask sequences of questions about the recent past: 'For example, the mother will ask, "Did we have fun at the park today? What did we do? Did we go on the swings?" and wait for some confirmation by the child before continuing, "Yes, and didn't we swing high? Wasn't that fun?"'[25] Much turns on how one treats these linguistically mediated forms of interaction. Do parents simply assist the child to better express publicly the cognitive event of recollection, or do they provide a framework that shapes and structures the child's ability to place themselves in relation to the past?

Nelson and Fivush's *sociocultural developmental model of autobiographical memory* elaborates the second of these two possibilities.[26] They argue that interactions with parents and carers provide a narrative framework that enables the child to arrange episodic memories into meaningful sequences of experience that have personal relevance. In this sense, autobiographical memory emerges from, and is different in kind to, general episodic memory. The ability to produce autobiographical memories – which they peg at around 4-and-a-half years old – is a 'critical developmental skill' that supervenes upon a range of earlier cognitive capacities.[27] To put this in Bruner's terms, autobiographical memory is a form of learned narrative thinking that has a transformative effect on existing paradigmatic thinking. One of the key transformations is the development of autonoetic consciousness (which, unlike Tulving, Nelson and Fivush do not see as a given part of episodic memory), such that the child is not merely able to recollect some past event, but is also able to situate herself or himself as both having experienced that event in the past and as recalling the event in the present. The child comes to distinguish the 'self-that-experienced' the event and the 'self-as-rememberer' as both 'the same' and 'different'.[28]

This kind of approach has its roots in the sociocultural psychology inspired by Lev Vygotsky.[29] One of Vygotksy's key propositions is that thinking is restructured by external mediation and the use of cultural tools, such as language.[30] Development is not the unfolding of a set of capacities solely within the child, but rather a dynamic relationship, where the child is both shaped by the world and acts to shape the world around them, a cycle of 'mutual constitution'.[31] Of crucial importance in this relationship is the 'reminiscence style' adopted by parents and carers in their scaffolding of children's recollections. Fivush argues that 'elaborative' reminiscence styles – where adults ask more questions and do more interactional work in weaving together the recollections they elicit from children into coherent narratives – are the major factor, producing richer and more detailed autobiographical recall in children.[32] Moreover, gendered styles of telling stories about oneself appear by the age of 4, and explicit cultural differences appear in autobiographical narratives by age 6.[33] Taken together, these differences suggest that the form autobiographical memory takes is informed by, and hence varies across, cultural and historical context.

How do 'vital memories' fit into this expanded view of autobiographical memory? The sorts of memory we will be describing in the following chapters have some similarities to what Conway calls 'self-defining memories' – specific types of autobiographical memory that have significant affective intensity and vividness and refer to matters of long-term concern.[34] However, whereas Conway sees these memories as crystallised through abstract mental models, we think these memories are better treated as footholds on personal pasts that are embedded in social, affective, spatial and material contexts – they are not simply 'in the head'. Furthermore, Conway treats self-defining memories as threats to accurate recollection. Making difficult, painful events central to how we view major life transitions can create a coherence in the 'long-term self', Conway claims, but it runs the risk of becoming the script to which we turn whenever we need to make sense of changing goals, hence distorting our ability accurately to encode new memories.[35] Again, we think this is a narrowly 'internalist' conception of how we make sense of the past. It may be that, as Janice Haaken has claimed in relation to memories of CSA, certain compelling stories or 'master narratives' have a particular power to create meaning out of distress (e.g. seeing all experiences of CSA as necessarily setting in motion a catalogue of disastrous life choices and mental distress), but these narratives, which arise from cultural sources, are usually shared, negotiated and contested with others, where they may be subject to just the kind of 'reality testing' that Conway claims as absent.[36]

Given the concern for the sociocultural derivation of narratives, vital memories appear to fit better into Nelson and Fivush's model. We certainly share their view that, if vital memories are a subset of autobiographical memory, they are distinct from, and irreducible to, the mass of general episodic memories. However, the focus on narrative thinking suggests an orderliness that vital memories can lack. Recollections of difficult pasts do not always have clear plot line and protagonists or stable evaluative attributions. They are messy, shifting and changeable across the occasions when they are enacted. Sometimes there is a clear plot; on other occasions, the same events will be told 'out of order'. Visual or emotional elements may come to the fore, rather than characters and their actions. Moral judgements may not be stable; they may be continuously contested or even rejected altogether. It is not that vital memories lack culturally derived narrative frames altogether, rather that they are consciously recollected as sitting at the centre of multiple narratives that intersect, resonate and disrupt one another in variable ways. Vital memories are messy, ambiguous and unsettled.

This leads us back to the question about autobiographical memories that has recurred since Tulving first posed it: what purpose do they serve? The answer typically given is that they are functional in some sense. They make us better planners, better communicators, perhaps even worthier social beings, as Nelson and Fivush imply. If we apply this criterion to vital memories, we seem to be led back towards the extremity and deficit models we described in the last chapter. Perhaps vital memories are a last defence against complete self-disintegration following extreme circumstances. Or instead, they might be the 'dysfunctional' exception that proves the general rule, the 'bad' auto-biographical memories that create a perfectly coherent life of unremitting misery.

Of course, neither of these alternatives comes anywhere close to adequately describing the ordinary people doing their best with difficult lives who feature throughout this book. The problem with a unitary functional explanation is that it is insensitive to the wide variety of pragmatic accomplishments that are enacted in the performance of the phenomenon in question. Vital memories are recollected, shared and contested for very different reasons in different settings. If they appear to be caught between competing narrative frames, then that is because contradictions between these frames are embedded in the milieus in which vital memories are meaningful (e.g. families, institutions, social welfare, health services, juridical practices). From this, it follows that we need to attend to the 'natural contexts' that Neisser recommended as the proper sites for the study of memory. In this way, we can better explore the interweaving of different lives and the different situations and settings through which memory flows.

Collective remembering and discursive psychology

The starting point for the interactional approach to memory is the volume on *Collective Remembering*, edited by David Middleton and Derek Edwards in 1990, that represented a firm break with the experimental tradition. Like Nelson and Fivush's, Middleton and Edwards' background was in developmental psychology. David Middleton had been part of the research group at the University of Nottingham that had conducted some of the experimental demonstrations of 'scaffolding'.[37] Along with fellow member John Shotter, Middleton's concerns had turned towards an explication of the social contexts that shaped the development of psychological capacities. Derek Edwards' early work had dealt with language development in both family and classroom settings.[38] Using tape-recorded 'naturalistic data', where the researcher observes and tape-records an activity occurring in its usual context, Edwards had argued that lexical development was not the gradual accumulation of conceptual understanding, but could be shown instead to be part of the everyday pragmatics of adult–child interaction.[39] Children use language functionally to 'do things' (e.g. direct a parent to a toy that they need, or to request a drink) within interactional contexts before they can be said to understand the referential meaning of the words they acquire.

From this perspective on social development, they took issue with what they saw as the limited and limiting concern with the individual that dominated the psychology of memory as a whole. Key to their argument was the idea that psychological processes have social foundations – personal memories are located in a broader collective framework. Maurice Halbwachs famously developed the notion of 'collective frameworks' to describe the formative role of context in shaping individual memory,[40] but what was dramatically different about the work brought together by Middleton and Edwards was the systematic way in which they showed how persons participate in social mnemonic practices through skilful displays of 'public mentation'. They argued that the psychological is not some private realm that is shaped by social context and then expressed through individual behaviour. What we typically call 'memory' is instead the social-communicative act of remembering and forgetting with others in the course of some activity. The contrast with experimental psychology is, then, as follows:

> In experimental designs, meaning and context are defined as variables, factors whose effects on the accuracy of recall are manipulable. In the study of discursive remembering, significance and context are intrinsic to the activity, constitutive of it and constituted by it, rather than causally influential upon some other thing called 'memory'.[41]

Psychological experiments are designed to explore the causal effects of varying *independent variables* (i.e. those controlled by the experimenter, such as the information provided to participants, or aspects of the environment in which it is presented) upon *dependent variables* (i.e. a measurable response made by the participant, such as the accuracy of their subsequent recollections). The logic of experimentation forces a conceptual separation between these variables, such that 'memory' is treated as independent of, yet influenced by, the contexts in which remembering happens. Middleton and Edwards here argue against that separation, claiming that what it means to remember something on a given occasion is utterly intrinsic to the nature of the act itself. Memory is never independent of the context where it is enacted; rather, those contexts form an indivisible part of the phenomenon that psychologists study. Remembering is a social accomplishment performed as a joint activity with others, on particular occasions, in specific contexts.

One of the first empirical demonstrations of this approach was a quasi-experimental study where student participants were asked to jointly recall the feature film *E. T.*[42] The resulting data showed how participants constructed a shared understanding of what they were collectively recalling, which was systematically built up within the interaction, and involved the use of a range of conversational pragmatics. Edwards and Middleton proposed that verbal statements made during the task, such as 'I remember' or 'Don't you recall', were not verifiable expressions related to an underlying cognitive event, but were rather interactional strategies for legitimating or agreeing with or hedging jointly accomplished accounts of past events.[43] This is not to say that there are no cognitive mechanics underpinning public claims to recollection, just that the postulation of such processes is not needed to explain the empirical findings. Mind could be 'bracketed out' from the explanandum.[44]

In subsequent work, Edwards and Middleton turned towards using naturalistic data, but maintained the key scene of 'instruction', this time involving conversations between adults and children around family photographs.[45] The following example comes from their study of conversations around family photographs. Here, a young boy, Paul, and his mother are looking through photographs of family holidays:

Example 1 (from Edwards and Middleton, 1988)

> *Mother:* oh look (.) there's when we went to the riding
> [stables wasn't it?
> *Paul:* [yeh (.) er er
> *Mother:* you was trying to reach up and stroke that horse.

Paul:	where? (laughs)
Mother:	would you like to do that again?
Paul:	yeh
Mother:	you don't look very happy though
Paul:	because I thought I was going to fall off
Mother:	you thought you was going to fall off did you? (.) right misery (.) daddy was holding on to you so that you didn't (.) did it FEEL very bumpy?
Paul:	yeh.
Mother:	did it make your legs ache? [Paul laughs] Rebecca enjoyed it.
Paul:	yeh
Mother:	she's a bit older wasn't she? (.) you were a little boy there.

In this extract, we see how remembering operates as a shared activity. Paul and his mother are working together, assisted by the use of the photographs, to establish an account of a past event (in this case, a particular family day out). The mother offers a series of turns where she makes claims about the past event in relation to some aspect of the photograph ('there's when we went to the riding stables', 'you was trying to reach up and stroke that horse'). These are framed as interrogative inferences that appoint Paul as the next speaker to respond. In this way, Paul is being gradually committed to the account of the past that is being progressively built. As the extract progresses, Paul's mother shifts to offering candidate experiential claims – 'you don't look very happy though', 'you thought you was going to fall off did you?' – that invite completion by Paul, albeit in fairly minimal terms ('yeh'). The details and significance of 'what happened' are jointly accomplished in the unfolding interaction between parent and child.

The data here bear strong resemblance to the kind of adult–child interactions discussed by Fivush and Nelson. The manner in which Paul's mother steers her son through the activity of remembering could certainly be glossed as 'scaffolding'. However, what is at stake is not merely producing an account of the past event, but also establishing its contemporary relevance. For example, the question 'would you like to do that again?' sets up a contrast between Paul's interests and desires at the time and in the present, as does the concluding statement, 'you were a little boy then'. Similarly, the statement 'daddy was holding on to you' does not just respond to parental accountability at the time, but also serves as a restatement of an ongoing relationship of care. Paul is being actively tutored, not simply in telling a story about the past, but also in how to use that story to demonstrate family togetherness. From this perspective, we can treat the various cognitive ascriptions of intentions, feelings and emotions as rhetorically organised formulations that are designed to establish a continuity between family membership and belonging in the recollected past and the present activity of shared recollection. This is not to say that matters of accuracy – what 'really happened', what was 'really felt' at the time – are entirely irrelevant, merely that they are subservient to the conversational pragmatics of family remembering.

Middleton and Edward's approach to qualitative data was informed by an emerging turn towards discourse analysis (DA) in psychology, in the UK. Initially, this developed from work in the sociology of scientific knowledge, most notably Gilbert and Mulkay's study of scientific discourse around the nature of research.[46] Gilbert and Mulkay had shown that what appeared to be contradictions in scientists' expressed attitudes and beliefs were explicable when analysed in the argumentative context in which the utterances were made – scientists describe the nature of scientific work differently when they are explaining successful and unsuccessful research. Jonathan Potter (who had studied with Mulkay) and Margaret Wetherell took this analytic point further to propose that the social-psychological study of attitudes and attributions could be revolutionised through DA as the study of interactionally occasioned and rhetorically organised claims about self and others. Their jointly authored *Discourse and Social Psychology* had an enormous methodological impact on the discipline, as it finally offered a viable empirical strategy in which the conceptual and philosophical alternative to experimental psychology could be pushed forward.[47]

Potter and Wetherell's work on attitudes and Middleton and Edward's work on memory were brought together under the umbrella discursive psychology.[48] This revised approach was also highly influenced by conversation analysis.[49] As a consequence, there was an explicit rejection of formal theorisation in favour of close readings of transcripts of audio recordings. These readings were guided by knowledge of the patterns and regularities found in ordinary conversation identified by Harvey Sacks and his followers (e.g. Gail Jefferson, Emmanuel Schegloff), such as turn-taking, repair and action formulation. Following this approach, Edwards and Potter argued that, if a cognitive process such as memory is studied in the 'real-world' settings within which it is occasioned, the central focus needs to be on the conversational pragmatics through which the psychological act is accomplished.[50]

The discursive psychological approach to memory follows Neisser in calling for the study of remembering in context. However, it has a very different understanding of what 'context' does to memory. Neisser's study of John Dean claimed that the original tapes acted as a benchmark record of 'what happened' in the past, but, in a re-analysis of the study, Edwards and Potter argue that working out 'what happened' is precisely what the participants in the Watergate hearings were trying to establish.[51] Dean's claims as to what he can and cannot remember are not to be taken as neutral statements that can be checked for their accuracy; they are situated and occasioned utterances that are designed to manage Dean's accountability in the present. Dean is in a tricky situation. He has to show that he is co-operating with the inquiry, while avoiding incriminating himself for what might be treated as past wrong-doing. Sitting before the senators, he must appear to be an 'honest broker', but, if he speaks ill of Richard Nixon, to whom he was a trusted advisor, without apparent good cause, this will cast doubt on his honesty and reliability. So, Dean has to weave a careful and nuanced story about the past, one that is likely to have strategic narrative turns and gaps in order to meet these competing demands. These he explains away by making various 'meta-cognitive claims' about his ability to remember. The point is that context is not some form of external constraint on cognitive capacities, but is rather an active feature of ongoing social interaction that the participants orient towards in the way they talk about the past.

Edwards and Potter offer a counter example from the UK involving contested accounts of what was said in a private, off-the-record press briefing given by the then Chancellor of the Exchequer, Nigel Lawson, in 1988.[52] Lawson's account of, not just what he said, but the correct interpretation of those words, was at odds with those of the journalists present, resulting in a major public dispute. Edwards and Potter show, through careful analysis of media reports, how the various claims were established and warranted through the use of discursive devices. For example, the following extract comes from an exchange in the Houses of Parliament:

Example 2 (from Edwards and Potter, 1992b)

> *Mr Lawson*: . . . the statements that appeared in the press on Sunday bore no relation whatever to what I in fact said. What I have said to them is that, while we were absolutely, totally committed to maintaining-

Ms Clare Short (Birmingham, Ladywood): They will have their shorthand notes.

Mr Lawson: Oh yes, they will have their shorthand notes and they will know it, and they will know they went behind afterwards and they thought there was not a good enough story and so they produced that (Hansard, 7 November)

Edwards and Potter note that each side here (Lawson, the journalists) uses a variety of strategies to discount the version of events given by the other. Some media articles had blamed Lawson's efforts at denying the reports on his 'arrogance'. This strategy of appealing to psychological dispositions was not possible for Lawson – it would be implausible to claim that all the journalists in the room had faulty memories. What he does instead, in the parliamentary exchange above, is to readily admit that, not only were the journalists in agreement, but that, also, a record of the conversation exists in the form of shorthand notes. He then follows this with a claim that the interpretations of the briefing reported in the media were erroneous, because the journalists, under pressure to come up with a 'good enough story', subsequently colluded to construct a different version of events – recollection was wilfully distorted by institutional forces. Now, the point of this is not to say that Lawson's version of events is any more or less accurate than that of the journalists, but rather to understand how these rival versions are constructed and the rhetorical and political work that they do.

Discursive psychology, as developed by Edwards and Potter, is noteworthy because it insists on the considerable interactional skills of ordinary people. In tune with Fivush and Nelson's call for the study of autobiographical memory as a 'critical developmental skill',[53] discursive psychology rejects a 'deficit model' of memory in favour of highlighting the complexity and subtlety of the social acts that we all accomplish, from a very early age, when we make claims about the past. For Edwards and Potter, psychology ought to be principally concerned with social development and enactment of these abilities. Psychology loses its way when it appeals to a concept of 'mind' (and private 'cognition') as an explanation of action, without having first grasped the situated, contextual nature of the activities such as remembering:

Mind can be studied as intrinsically social and contextualised; it makes sense to begin with no a priori separation of person/mind from its embodiment in communicative practices. It is both possible and fruitful

The expanded view of memory 37

to pursue the study of action itself – accounts, versions, constructions – as discursive activity. Rather than offering us a window upon the workings of something else called 'mind', discourse can be examined for how speakers orient themselves to notions of mind, using these as resources in conversation (such as in framing accounts of truth and falsity, accomplishing blamings and excuses, mitigations and accusations, explanations of why people do what they do, and so on). Our recommendation is to let go of a commitment to mind as a pre-existing, independently knowable explanation of talk and action.[54]

Despite a high degree of common cause with experimental approaches on matters of context, pragmatics, function and reconstruction in memory, Edwards and Potter 'recommend' that the central organising concept in the cognitive-experimental tradition – mind as the engine that drives action – be 'let go'.[55] Perhaps unsurprisingly, when Edwards, Middleton and Potter repeated this recommendation in an article in the *The Psychologist*, a parade of eminent experimental psychologists lined up to unequivocally reject the idea in no uncertain terms.[56]

Asking a cognitive psychologist to give up on the idea that there is a cognitive basis to memory seems rather akin to expecting turkeys to vote for Christmas. However, the (wish)bone of contention is a little more specific. The 'standard model' of cognition is one where mind creates internal representations of the external world, which are then subject to processing, all of which is treated as ultimately reducible to neural activity. For many cognitive psychologists, memory is essentially a brain-bound process. As Tulving put it:

> [Memory] has a home, even if it is still a hidden one, in the brain . . . An event happens, a person experiences it, memory traces are laid down representing the event, the past vanishes and is replaced by the present. The memory traces of the event continue to exist in the present, they are retrieved, and the person remembers the event. This, in a nutshell . . . [is] how memory works.[57]

It is possible, however, to have a meaningful debate about the place of cognitive processes within remembering if we focus on externally derived representations and meanings rather than internally generated representations. As work on autobiographical memory has demonstrated, the events that tend to be remembered are those that have some significance for us as social beings.

38   The expanded view of memory

From this, it follows that the 'memory traces' that are laid down of those events will most likely be constituted using culturally specific modes of symbolisation and signification, rather than some private language for encoding.

For example, Sue recalls the break-up of her first significant relationship by telling of how she could not stop crying as she struggled to say the words at that moment and the miserable time she spent at home in her pyjamas over the next few days. Here, the uncontrollable tears are memorable because they are cultural markers of 'real emotion', and the description of the aftermath follows an instantly recognisable cultural script. Although, undoubtedly, the memory 'belongs' to Sue, the work of producing it has not gone on solely within her head. It is an activity that occurs by virtue of her participation in a particular cultural and historical setting and involves matters as diverse as: the immediate interactional context in which Sue recollects this event; its relevance to the people to whom she tells it; what Sue feels right now about this 'first love', and what this tells her about herself; what implications this may have for current and future personal relationships; the cultural representations of 'romantic love' that Sue draws upon, etc.

If we take this latter description of Sue's act of recollection as seriously as Tulving's initial description, it suggests the activity of remembering extends beyond the brain. This is not to say that the neurological activity is irrelevant. For example, if Sue has found herself telling this story while drinking a little too much on a blind date, there are clearly social consequences that can be indexed to her particular brain state. Although neurological activity clearly contributes to Sue's capacities to remember, her memories are not 'in' her brain, nor are her recollections reducible to what she does with her neurons. David Manier captures this with a rather lovely analogy to bird flight:

> We humans engage in acts of remembering of a certain sort because we have brains of a certain sort. But the brain, or a particular configuration of neurons within the brain, is not a potential memory, any more than a bird's wing is a 'potential flight'. Wings of a certain sort make it possible for birds to fly, and brains of a certain sort make it possible for humans to remember. But memory is not in the brain any more than flight is in the wing. Without a brain, a human could not remember, just as without a wing a bird could not fly. But wings are not the only body parts that birds use in flying, and brains are not the only body parts that humans use in remembering.[58]

A bird cannot fly without a wing, but a wing alone cannot produce flight. It only contributes to that activity when it becomes connected to a series of parts that together make a whole, of which flight may be said to be one of its emergent properties. What we need, then, is a better sense of how our embodiment – including our brains – is coupled with a broader set of 'parts' that together constitute remembering.

From minds to settings

If cognitive psychologists such as Tulving appear to be trenchant in their defence of 'in the head' explanations of psychological phenomena such as memory, then this reflects the origins of the approach as an explicit rejection of the 'empty organism' dogma of behaviourism[59]. The term 'cognition' – much like 'behaviour' before it – was initially adopted as a catch-all category for labelling very diverse processes associated with mind.[60] This inevitably meant that, as cognitive psychology has matured, considerable time has had to be spent disentangling some of the many processes to which it has laid claim – for example, the conscious and the unconscious, cognition and emotion, single-track and parallel processes. The situation resembles that of a nineteenth-century imperial power that discovers it has no map adequate to survey the territory it claims to govern. However, much has changed in the past two decades. Cognitive psychology may be moving towards what we might metaphorically term a 'post-colonial' era.

An important moment in this shift is the landmark paper by the philosophers Andy Clark and David Chalmers.[61] In their short piece 'The extended mind', Clark and Chalmers argue that cognitive processes are coupled to, and in some cases driven by, external entities and their associated processes. They claim that the resources that the brain offers may be either augmented or replaced in part by external resources, without fundamentally changing the nature of cognition. In their thought experiment, there is no functional distinction between Inga, who believes she knows the location of the New York Museum of Modern Art based on her personal recollection, and Otto, who suffers from Alzheimer's disease, but nevertheless arrives at a similar belief based on a notebook in which the information is written. Clark and Chalmers characterise Otto's belief as 'extended cognition' – a mental state that is as much determined by external resources (e.g. the notebook) as it is by internal resources (e.g. brain states).

40 The expanded view of memory

The 'extended cognition' thesis marks out a middle territory between cognitive science and the sort of constructionism found in discursive psychology. It adheres to the idea that there are 'intra-cranial' cognitive processes involved in activities such as remembering, but proposes that these processes can be hooked up with external processes that complement, extend and transform what mind can do. John Sutton and colleagues refer to this as 'complementarity' of resources,[62] rather than simple addition. Together, these 'transcranial' couplings of resources make new transactional systems with supervenient properties that are irreducible to any of their individual components. Empirical support for these ideas comes from work, such as Ed Hutchin's studies of naval navigation,[63] that shows that the knowledge and skills to accomplish the overall task are 'distributed' across the system formed by humans and technology, and the studies of 'situated cognition' by Jean Lave and colleagues that demonstrate how the use of cultural tools enable the contextual development of cognitive capacities.[64]

Consider, for instance, a student writing an essay.[65] Teachers often like to imagine students sitting in quiet contemplation, planning out their answers in their head, before settling down to craft their answer, sentence by sentence. The reality is typically a bit messier. A student will open up a blank word-processing document and then immediately open a web browser, search for key terms and cut and paste material. They might then go to their institution's virtual-learning site and extract bullet points and headings from a lecture they attended. Simultaneously, they may be dropping in and out of social media, messaging peers working on the same topic, taking and posting 'selfies' and writing status updates ('bored', 'idk wat im sposed 2 b doin') to communicate how they feel about the task in hand. Now, which bit of this distributed cognition is the 'real' or 'core' operation of remembering, and which bit is 'supplementary'? Following Clark and Chalmers, we would say that all of this is 'memory'. The work of calling to mind something said in a lecture does not differ in kind from jointly attempting to reconstruct its meaning with a friend, or from searching and finding the same phrases on a lecture slide, or else just googling the words online. Each individual act draws on a rich mixture of cognitive, technological, communicative and cultural resources. No one act bears the 'mark of the cognitive', as Fred Adams has it, more than any other.[66] Taken together, they make for an interlocking, 'transcranial' programme of activity that ultimately delivers on the task.

One of the obstacles to immediately hailing this kind of complex, distributed activity as remembering is the technological dimension. Surely memory is a human accomplishment, for which technology is a mere prosthetic addition? However, it is possible to tell the 'history of memory' – that is, what memory means and how it is enacted across different cultural and historical settings – precisely from the perspective of technology. Frances Yates's much celebrated work *The Art of Memory* shows how social technologies of memory – mnemotechnics – have been at the heart of how European cultures have considered remembering.[67] More recently, Matt Matsuda's *The Memory of the Modern* has updated the story, with details of how modern institutional practices of record keeping, visualisation and commemoration gave rise to the 'storehouse' model of memory from which cognitive psychology has only recently broken away.[68]

Histories such as these make it clear that technology and techniques are intrinsic to what we traditionally think of as 'human' or 'psychological' capacities. The philosopher Michel Serres has written extensively on the history of science and technology as a cycle where humans and things appear to 'exchange properties' with one another through their ongoing interactions.[69] Our sense of ourselves as 'subjects' who differ from 'objects' comes from our ongoing engagement with the material environment. For example, the 'rouge test', used by developmental psychologists to establish that the child can recognise its own image, can be thought of as a marker of internally driven cognitive development.[70] However, a more fitting description would be that it is a technically mediated accomplishment between a human and an object, where the reflective properties of the mirror enable the child to stabilise a self-image.[71] For Serres, agents and their material environments, subjects and objects, co-exist through interdependent mixtures. That mixture can change significantly – other people can offer the reflective properties of the mirror to the child – but it cannot be homogenised. Without objects, we cease to be subjects.

Serres refers to this exchange of properties in mixtures as 'translation'.[72] It is the mutual transformation of elements through their relational coupling. For example, the basic structure of communication places a sender and a receiver in a relation where they together differentiate themselves from background noise. To speak or to listen is to enter into a relationship that gives both parties a new status with respect to one another and differentiates them from their environment. It is also, for Serres, a fundamentally embodied matter. Perception and communication are not processes where an external world gets 'inside' the subject, but are rather activities of mixing, where, through the medium of sound or touch, bodies come together to form complex, shifting

42 The expanded view of memory

arrangements.[73] Even vision can be considered as a form of mixture. The eye allows an organism to 'parasitise' information about its environment, via the medium of electromagnetic radiation, such that it is able to physically place itself optimally with regard to its environment.[74]

We can draw upon the principles of distributed cognition – that remembering is enacted by a system rather than purely 'in the head' – along with the idea of translation to draw out the interdependency of people and things in memory. Take the following example discussed by Middleton and Brown, drawn from Buchanan and Middleton's study of elderly people participating in a reminiscence group session:[75]

Example 3 (from Buchanan and Middleton, 1995)

Vera: my mother used to wear erm (.) sack apron (.) cos years ago they used to make the aprons out of a (.) sack bag hadn't they

Doris: [ooh that's right

Enid: [you could buy [the sack bag (. . .)

Vera: [can you remember (.) I can remember [my mother (.) and she used to-

Jean: [yes (.) yes (.) used to make aprons out the sack bags or a black one (.) and you'd go and change after dinner and she'd put (.) you know (.) a new pinafore and a clean dress or something like that

Enid: we used to buy ours from the Beehive

Vera: ye:s (.) I can see my mother (.) she used (. . .) sack bag y'know (.)
[of her back and her front-

Jean: [yeah (.) that's wash day

Here, Vera is recalling her mother, with support and elaboration from Doris, Enid and Jean. What interests Middleton and Brown is the direction this recollection takes. Vera is not describing any particular episode; she focuses instead on an item of clothing, a 'sack apron'. Together, the women begin to unpack various facets of the sack bag – when it would be worn, how they were made, where the materials would be purchased, etc. The world inhabited by the mother gradually emerges, a time when women would 'make do' with garments fashioned from cheap materials while engaged in domestic labour, but would also change into fresh clothes in the evening. Out of the mass of possible versions of the past involving Vera's mother, the women jointly stabilise or fix this particular 'habitable world', with its own moral universe and relations between people and artefacts. The past is then worked up and shaped in the present as the speakers situate themselves and their personal histories through their mutual orientation to the features of particular objects and places.

Middleton and Brown's argument is that objects do a crucial job of lending form or 'punctualising' memory. They do this by translation, through exchanging properties with the people who are recollected – the mother's qualities (her resourcefulness and modesty) are passed into the sack apron, whose material form lends shape to the mother in turn (a grounding in the local, the moral order of changing for dinner). There is a mixing together of people and things here that are, in turn, recollected by situating oneself in relation to that mixture. This is not a purely 'in the head' operation, but one that requires either a direct engagement with the things themselves, or – as in the example above – a collective effort at communicatively reconstructing that material environment so that it can be 'felt' in the present. The objects are not 'cues' to memories that are beneath the skull. They are constituent parts of the material–communicative–neural process that, as a whole, enables the past to be mobilised in the present, and that is irreducible to any of its individual elements.

This leads us towards a bold claim. Remembering of this type is performed by a system, a functional mixture of people and things in a particular material environment, rather than isolated individuals. Put more bluntly, remembering is a setting-specific operation. An implication of this is that what a given individual can remember depends upon the settings in which they participate. In the above example, doubtless Vera can offer recollections of her mother across a range of settings, but this specific recollection of her mother as a moral being in relation to the sack apron is, we would argue, a specific accomplishment of this particular group setting. If this is so, then it makes little sense to say that we carry within us a set of memories of the past that are recollected when we encounter the right cues. It would be better to say that participating across a range of settings (families, groups, institutions, media) gives us access to the specific remembered accomplishments of those settings, out of which we reconstruct a personal life. We are not claiming that there is nothing at all 'in the head', but instead that what is there only becomes relevant to us when it is engaged with the setting-specific processes that deliver 'remembering'.

A further implication to be drawn from this is that settings perform different kinds of remembering, and, therefore, what we are able to do as participants in these settings ought to be subject to particular local evaluative criterion rather than global judgements. Take, for example, a woman whose claims to have been a victim of prior CSA result in her having to act as a defence witness in the trial of the man accused of being her abuser. Our argument would be that what is recollected in a court of law is an accomplishment of the setting as a whole, using a mixture of statements, narratives, evidence and procedures that are subject to criteria of accuracy and reliability. Now, although it is a necessary feature of the way that the law operates that judgments are then made about individuals, following the logic of distributed cognition we would have to say that the 'memories' to which these judgments refer are not the properties of individuals. In other words, what is really being judged here are not the personal memories of the individuals concerned, but rather the setting-level collective remembering of the court in which the various persons have participated, which are then deemed to be sufficient for legal judgments to be arrived at that attach to persons as legal subjects.

All of this only appears paradoxical if we remain committed to the fallacious view that remembering is primarily located 'in the head'. For example, Elizabeth Loftus has done much to criticise the idea of 'recovered memory', where adults recall CSA despite having been either previously unable to do so, or having only very incomplete memories.[76] For Loftus, memory is very much a personal property, whose major attribute is its accuracy or otherwise. This means that, if an individual recollects different versions of their past on different occasions, or in different settings (such as while in therapy), this must indicate a distortion or an error occurring during the course of 'in the head' processing. Loftus has set out to prove how this can happen by demonstrating that, under certain very specific conditions, it is possible to engineer personal recollections that can be falsified.[77] However, if we begin from the idea that the kinds of remembering that concern Loftus – such as claims about past sexual abuse – are setting-level accomplishments, then contradictions between occasioned recollections are by definition to be expected.[78] Courts of law that are deemed to be 'working properly' are able to collectively generate versions of the past, with the participation of witnesses, such that they can make legal judgments. Therapeutic encounters that follow principles of 'best practice' are able to collectively produce versions of the past that have implications for the client. If these two settings arrive at accounts of the past, in relation to the same individual, that appear to be contradictory, this does not mean that we can make a global judgement as to the 'unreliability' of that individual's memory. On the contrary, it merely demonstrates that what we can do with our memories is interdependent with the settings through which remembering occurs. Any judgement that attaches to the person in relation to memory ought to be a strictly local one that adheres to the evaluative criterion of the setting concerned (i.e. given standards for good testimony, at the end of the legal process, ought this person to be judged a 'reliable witness' to their own past? Following best practice for discussing disclosures of CSA, at the end of the therapeutic encounter, should this person's version of events be supported or challenged?).

The biases and errors in memory that Loftus claims to find are artefacts that result from the conflation of setting-specific memory with global judgements about 'in the head' processing. We do, however, agree that it is necessary to arrive at judgements in relation to recollected versions of the past, including, on many occasions, those that involve criteria of accuracy and reliability. However, these are local judgements that concern the accomplishments of particular settings, which draw upon established procedures maintained within those settings. Although these judgements subsequently attach to individuals as subjects within these settings, they do not technically have global purchase on them as persons, because the recollections on which they were based were setting-level accomplishments. Put more simply, if a court decides that a woman's testimony of prior sexual abuse is not sufficient to convict the accused, this does not mean that the account of abuse produced during therapy is 'wrong', because that account is subject to very different local procedures. Nor does it mean that there is something necessarily biased about this woman's memory.

The task for us here, then, is complex. If we are to view memory as extending into the world, and beyond the skull, we must seriously consider the relationship between local setting-level accomplishments (what and where we are now) and the more 'global' way in which we think about ourselves as persons (how we relate to and through others, and to things in the world). One of the ways in which we would like to think through this complex array of relations is to examine how minds extend into activities that occur in particular time–space relations, involving interdependent actions between persons and things and minds and bodies. These relations, we argue, constitute the extended perspective on the life-space of the person, where settings 'mark out' and 'afford' past, present and future possibilities for action. In the chapter that follows, we begin to speak to the way in which these relations are formed in the spaces that persons occupy. Furthermore, this will involve examining the fundamental role of affect in managing accessibility to the past – and what this means for not just memory, but forgetting also. Finally, our task must also be to account for the ongoing moral or ethical activities that constantly interweave processes

46 The expanded view of memory

of remembering and prompt reflections on what kind of a person we have been, are now and can be in the future.

Notes

1 Nelson, 2006.
2 Ebbinghaus, 1885/1913.
3 See Danziger's (1990) classic history of early experimental psychology.
4 Baddeley and Hitch, 1974.
5 Craik and Lockhart, 1972.
6 Bartlett, 1932.
7 Neisser, 1982.
8 Neisser (1981) terms this 'repisodic memory' – memory for the actual meaning of an event at that time, rather than 'literal accuracy' or overall 'gist'.
9 See Bruner, 1986, 1992.
10 Loftus and Ketcham, 1996; Loftus, 2003.
11 See Tulving, 1983.
12 Tulving, 1985a.
13 Tulving, 1985b.
14 Tulving, 1983.
15 Tulving, 1985b: 10.
16 Conway and Pleydell-Pearce, 2000.
17 Conway, 2005.
18 Conway et al., 2004.
19 Conway et al., 2004: 500.
20 Conway and Jobson, 2012.
21 Nelson and Fivush, 2004: 507.
22 Fivush, 2011.
23 Ibid.
24 See Wood et al., 1976.
25 Fivush et al., 2011: 323.
26 Nelson and Fivush, 2004; see also Nelson, 2009.
27 Fivush et al., 2011.
28 Fivush, 2011.
29 For an overview of this kind of sociocultural work in psychology, see Valsiner and Rosa (2007).
30 Vygotsky, 1978.
31 Markus and Kitiyama, 2010.
32 Fivush, 2008.
33 Fivush et al., 2011.
34 See Conway et al., 2004.
35 Ibid.
36 Haaken, 1998.
37 Wood and Middleton, 1975.
38 See Edwards and Mercer, 1987.
39 Edwards and Goodwin, 1985.
40 See the partial translation in Halbwachs (1925/1992).
41 Middleton and Edwards, 1990: 42.
42 One of the student participants at the time was our colleague, the critical psychologist John Cromby.
43 Edwards and Middleton, 1986a, 1986b.

The expanded view of memory   47

44 See Coulter (1979) for a full argument.
45 Edwards and Middleton, 1988.
46 Gilbert and Mulkay (1984). For a detailed – and very funny – account of this history see Ashmore, 1989.
47 See Brown and Locke, 2008.
48 See Edwards and Potter, 1992a.
49 See Edwards, 1997.
50 Edwards and Potter, 1992a.
51 Edwards and Potter, 1992b.
52 Ibid.
53 Fivush *et al.*, 2011.
54 Edwards and Potter, 1992b: 211.
55 We cannot resist noting that these scholars of rhetoric have here used a phrase that, in British–English, can also refer to making an employee redundant – 'I'm sorry but we're going to have to let you go from the company'.
56 See Edwards *et al.* (1992) and the accompanying responses.
57 Tulving, 2002: 20, cited in Manier, 2004: 252.
58 Manier, 2004: 259.
59 See Richards, 2009.
60 See Danziger, 1997.
61 Clark and Chalmers, 1998.
62 Sutton *et al.*, 2010; Harris *et al.*, 2014.
63 Hutchins, 1995.
64 Lave, 1988; Lave and Wenger, 1991.
65 We derive this example loosely from Crook and Dymott, 2005.
66 Adams and Aizawa, 2010.
67 Yates, 1966.
68 Matsuda, 1996.
69 See Serres, 1982.
70 The rouge test involves placing a coloured mark on the face of an infant or a primate in a place that is unlikely to create any stimulation of itself. The human or non-human participant is then shown their image in a mirror. If they move to rub the coloured mark on their own face, this is taken as evidence that they recognise that the image in the mirror is their own self-image and, hence, have some concept of 'self' as distinct from 'others'.
71 In a similar example, Serres (1995c) argues that ecological consciousness only really began to properly emerge once humans saw photographs of Planet Earth taken from space.
72 Serres, 1982.
73 Serres, 2008.
74 See a similar discussion in Clark and Chalmers (1998: 11).
75 See Buchanan and Middleton, 1995; Middleton and Brown, 2005: 145–9.
76 Loftus, 1994; Loftus and Pickrell, 1995.
77 See Garry *et al.*, 1996.
78 This also gives us some purchase on how experimental demonstrations of false memory work. They too are setting-level accomplishments. Persons who are recruited into the operations performed in these settings can indeed be made to say things that are technically 'inaccurate'. However, the production of that inaccuracy is an accomplishment of the setting as a whole – it is the joint product of what experimenter, participants, technical procedure, material artefacts etc. have done together. To then re-attribute the 'false memory' back to the participant alone is most peculiar.

Chapter 3

Memory and life-space

Affect, forgetting and ethics

Previously, in the textile factory

Kurt Lewin, the founder of action research, tells the following story:

> A woman stands at the loom in a big noisy factory, next to the last in the eighth row. A thread is broken. She is about to stop the machine to see what has happened. It is shortly before the lunch hour. She has accomplished very little during the morning. She is annoyed . . . She has been married for three years. For a year and a half, her husband has been unemployed. The 2-year old child has been seriously ill, but today seems somewhat better. She and her husband have been quarrelling more and more often recently. They had a quarrel this morning. Her husband's parents have suggested that she send the child to them in the country. The woman is undecided what to do about it.[1]

This is a slice of everyday misery. In a gigantic factory, ringing with the relentless noise of machines, a woman is having a terrible morning. Nothing seems to be working. Not the machine, which keeps stopping, nor her life, dominated by the illness of her child and problems in her relationship with her husband. She is caught twice over, by the drudgery of her working life and the difficulties of her home life. What to do?

Psychologists have been getting better at grasping the way that the travails of daily life shape our thoughts and feelings. The idea that depression, for example, is a product of how we interact with our local environment, rather than a simple predisposition, is now broadly accepted.[2] Some of this thinking can be traced back to Lewin, who famously claimed that, 'every psychological event depends upon the state of the person and at the same time the state of the environment.'[3] He even suggested that this could be represented by the formula $B = f(PE)$.[4] In the story above, we can say that the frustration the woman feels with the broken thread is a product of both the stresses of working in the factory and the anxieties created by her family situation. Psychological events (such as becoming annoyed) are the product of an interaction between our lives and the settings in which we live.

We need to think carefully about what is meant here by 'interaction'. Historically, psychology conceptualised environments as an array of stimuli that produced responses from the person. On this basis, behaviour is seen to be under the control of the environment; it suffices to simply deduce which stimulus is chained to the response to explain its occurrence. The 'cognitive revolution' had its origins, in part, in the observation that certain kinds of phenomenon could not be explained in this way. Persons draw on mental resources, not least an active memory of past events, that shape how they perceive and react to stimuli. Behaviour is the interaction between 'external' events and 'internal' processes. This sets up a dynamic mental topography where inside and outside are shaping one another. We would then say of the example that the reason the woman becomes so annoyed with the breaking thread is that the quarrel with her husband in the morning has left her in a state where she interprets what would otherwise be seen as minor frustrations as potential catastrophes.

This topographic description of psychological life establishes some clear boundaries. Mind is 'within' us, as persons, in the same way that our bodies are 'in' space. However, as we described in the last chapter, contemporary work in both cognitive and discursive psychology has troubled the 'container' model. Mind seems to overflow the boundaries of the brain, drawing upon resources beyond the skin and folding them into extended or distributed actions. What is happening 'in the head' is but one part of an activity that is not just 'in' space, but seems to be threaded entirely into the spatial distribution of activities. Lewin was interested in this kind of interaction that appears to undo common-sense boundaries between person and world. He proposed studying it as 'life-space'.

What kind of a space is 'life-space'? It is fundamentally a space that is defined by relations rather than metric properties. These relations appear to overspill divisions between mind and body, persons and things, and even space and time. For example, the scene that opens Lewin's story is very narrowly defined – a thread breaks on a loom, which annoys the operator. However, in order to understand this properly, Lewin suggests that we need to gradually expand the focus, first, to the extraordinarily unpleasant conditions of factory life, then further to the life problems of the female operator, and then perhaps further still, to the social and economic conditions that might result in her having to send her child away to the countryside. It is rather like a camera being pulled back from a close-up scene in a movie to reveal a broader landscape in which it is embedded. In this way, the space in which we observe some act occurring – the factory – is interconnected with many other spaces – the home, the country – through the relationships the actors have with others. Lewin argues that these relationships have an effect on the psychological event in question (the woman's anger): they are 'quasi-social' causes that lend form to what happens. Life-space is the set of connections that links the immediate scene to other spaces and actors, which are crucial to understanding any given psychological event.

Relationships 'outside' work can then be said to have an effect on and shape the woman's conduct 'inside' the workplace. We might say that the quarrel, which happened earlier that morning, is still, in a sense, ongoing. It has been prolonged into the day, where it forms part of how the woman manages the problem of the broken thread. This is a somewhat strange way of thinking – how can events that are spatially and temporally remote have a direct effect on what is happening right now?[5] Surely, if there is an effect, it is intermediate and marginal, with the argument with her husband changing the woman's mood, and that then being the reason for her overreaction to the broken thread. However, to explain things that way is to create an artificial distinction between past and present. If our ongoing life experience resembles a flow rather than a disconnected succession of moments, then what is past is still intimately connected to present action. As she operates the machine, the argument of that morning is still ongoing. The woman may be imagining other things she might have said, or perhaps is finding new things to be angry about in the words her husband spat at her. The past is still acting on the present, through the work of recollection.

This 'active' role of the past in the present is at work throughout the scene. In order to fix the broken thread, the woman will have to stop the machine. This will interrupt the productivity of her section of the factory floor. There will undoubtedly be consequences. It may be the case that her section is already under management scrutiny because of the number of previous stoppages. This is just the wrong time for this to happen. It may even be the case that management is considering automating this particular process, because of the

Memory and life-space   51

large number of human errors. Stopping the machine gives them one more reason to dismiss, not just her, but all the operators in that section.

In both cases – the significance of the argument and the meaning of the interrupted workflow – past events continue to act in shaping current actions. Lewin refers to this kind of action-at-a-distance as 'quasi-physical' causes. Things that are not immediately present nevertheless contribute their force to shaping matters at hand. Just as spatial remoteness is less important than relationships, so temporal distance is less important than the ongoing degree of connectedness between past and present events. His point is that current action needs to be inserted into a sequence of events, which have an ongoing relevance to understanding the present moment. We might see this as akin to the montage sequences summarising the plot of past episodes that are sometimes used in television dramas: 'previously, in the textile factory . . .'. Remembering does not simply allow us to bring additional information to bear in our actions, it is part of the way those actions are woven into the continuous unfolding of experience.

The last sense in which life-space is primarily a space of relations is with respect to the future significance of our actions. Again, a common-sense view would be to say that as, by definition, the future is what is yet to happen, it has no influence over the present. However, once more, separating action from its consequences may be premature. For example, at the very least, we know that the fact that the woman will likely have to miss out on her lunch break to investigate the problem with the machine is a probable factor in her anger. The anxiety over what will happen to both her and her colleagues when management learn about the stoppage may also be a very real concern. It may be that the woman is projecting forwards still further – presumably, if she loses her job, then the decision to send her child away may become forced.

Our actions do not simply bring about states of affairs in the present; they also realise or 'make actual' future possibilities. We may be more or less aware of these possibilities in the course of our acts, but they are nevertheless active in shaping what we do. Lewin uses the term 'quasi-conceptual' to refer to this anticipation of the future in the constitution of life-space. If the woman sees in the broken thread the 'tipping point' that will very soon put her on a railway platform desperately wiping away her tears as her child's tiny face grows smaller still, while the train to the country pulls away, this creates a different kind of relationship to the future than the one that existed in the moments before the thread snapped.

It is not just 'us' — the individual actors — who do this work of projection. If remembering may be viewed as a work of 'distributed cognition', so we may also see anticipating future events as collectively realised. The workers in the factory, for instance, together know what it might mean for the looms to fall silent (knowledge that is probably exploited by their managers to increase productivity). What the woman does next when the thread breaks will go neither unnoticed nor unremarked by her co-workers. Projecting into the future is also done formally, through organisational processes. It is the subject of meetings and reviews performed by supervisors and managers. The future is realised, on a daily basis, through numbers and observations that are automatically entered into spreadsheets and reports. Just as 'memory' is as much in diaries and archives as it is in brains and conversations, so constituting the future is an activity distributed in the relations between people, artefacts and technologies. Both remembering the past and projecting possible future are setting-level accomplishments.[6]

Life-space is relational space. Describing the complexity of the relations that make up the space is the means to understanding the activities — such as remembering — that are distributed within it. One way to understand this is to compare the life space of human experience with that of organisms who have a more restricted space of activity. Gilles Deleuze discusses the example of a small arachnid, a 'tick':

> Concretely, if you define bodies and thoughts as capacities for affecting and being affected, many things change. You will define an animal, or a human being, not by its form, its organs and its functions, and not as a subject either; you will define it by the affects of which it is capable . . . Take any animal and make a list of affects, in any order . . . For example, Jakob von Uexküll will do this for the tick, an animal that sucks the blood of mammals. He will define this animal by three affects: the first has to do with light (climb to the top of a branch); the second is olfactive (let yourself fall onto the mammal that passes beneath the branch); and the third is thermal (seek the area without fur, the warmest spot). A world with only three affects, in the midst of all that goes on in the immense forest.[7]

The tick exists in an 'affective universe' defined by just three sets of relations: climb upwards towards light, fall downwards towards mammal smells, position yourself at the spot of maximum heat and bite. This is a highly functional

Memory and life-space   53

account of what a tick is, rather than one based on notions of its biological structure or genus. However, Deleuze finds in it also a weird kind of phenomenological description. What it is like to be a tick is produced by these three sets of relationships (the play of light, the wafting smells, the zones of warmth). Now, the 'affective universe' of Lewin's loom operator is far more complex, but it too can be explored through descriptions of the relationships (even if only partially) that constitute her life-space.

In what follows in this chapter, we will be taking forward the idea of remembering as a form of distributed cognition that is accomplished in a relationally constituted life-space. This will lead us to focus on the crucial role played by affect and by practices of managing accessibility to the past, or 'forgetting'. The ethical questions that become apparent once we engage in this functional or 'weirdly' phenomenological description of remembering in life-space will become apparent as we proceed. Before doing so, we need to say a little more about relational approaches to space.

Spaces of memory

What is the relationship between space and memory? It seems unlikely that we will be able to produce an interesting answer to a question posed in such bare and abstract terms. Better, perhaps, to ask: how should we begin to think jointly about 'space' and 'memory'? We have discussed Lewin's proposal to rethink the psychological in terms of life-space. Some more qualification is now needed.

The approach to the psychology of memory that Ulrich Neisser worked out in the 1980s and 1990s is a good starting point. In 1978, Neisser, a founding figure for the cognitive approach, had made a surprising and extraordinary evaluation of the experimental studies of memory – 'If X is an interesting or socially important aspect of memory, then psychologists have hardly ever studied X'.[8] His claim here is that laboratory studies blind researchers to the 'real-world' dynamics of memory. This rather placed the onus on Neisser to come up with a viable alternative, which he did by pointing to the utility of naturalistic data in the John Dean study.[9] He also began to develop an 'ecological' model of remembering, which drew heavily on the work of his colleagues, J.J. Gibson and Eleanor Gibson, on 'direct perception'.

Direct perception is a curious position in psychology that has attracted few supporters. The key idea is that perception involves the 'extraction' of information from 'invariant' features of the environment, without the need for much additional cognitive processing. For example, texture gradients, such as the furrows of a ploughed field, remain constant as observers change position in relation to them. Although observers shift perspective, they can 'read off' all the invariant information provided by the environment (the 'non-change that persists during change'[10]) that is required to grasp what they are seeing, without the need for further processing. By contrast, a traditional cognitive approach would hold that whole series of mental processes are required to transform light patterns hitting the retina into 'inner' cognitive representations.

Texture gradients are instances of relatively simple invariants, but there are other 'higher-order' invariants, called *affordances*, that are considerably more meaningful.[11] An affordance is a possibility for action that the environment offers to the organism. Water, for example, offers the possibilities of drinking or swimming, depending on the organism concerned. Fire offers warmth, but also the danger of burning. The sorts of higher-order invariants, or affordances, that an organism can 'pick up' from its environment depend upon both its complexity and prior experience. So, in the example discussed previously, there were three affordances (go to light, fall to smell, seek warmth) that defined the tick's relationship to its environment. Humans are able to engage both with infinitely more affordances and also with those of a relatively 'higher grade' (e.g. a forest affords the possibility of communing with nature or of a gathering a stack of raw materials for fuel, building or commerce).

Neisser uses Gibson's notion of affordance to argue that the perceptual 'inputs' into memory come via direct perception of environmental invariants. In this way, our self-knowledge is grounded in what Neisser calls an 'ecological self'.[12] However, Neisser goes on to assert that interactions with others, along with personal autobiographical memories, allow us to expand upon direct perception.[13] We elaborate upon and augment the information offered by the environment through our personal communicative and mnemonic capacities.[14] What is interesting about this 'ecological' approach to memory is that it underscores the role of place. However, at the same time, Neisser does not really break with an 'in the head' notion of cognitive processes. Place is rendered as meaningful by 'higher-order' forms of internally generated self-knowledge, rather than treated as directly affording significance in and of itself. By contrast, we can view the environment as always already shaped by the kinds of communicative relationship we have to others, and by the social and cultural practices that are locally relevant. The higher-grade invariants or affordances we perceive in our immediate world are produced through an intertwining of the social and the material. If we experience forests as places to retreat to nature, that is not just because of the feeling of being among the trees, but also because of the long human history of 'domesticating' wooded spaces and the rich cultural mythologies through which we understand the forest as a particular kind of space (e.g. as a liminal space of freedom and danger).[15]

Consider, for instance, the memorial to the 2005 London bombings located in Hyde Park in London (see Figure 3.1). When a visitor first encounters the memorial, it is not altogether clear exactly what this site is. There are a number of large (3.5 metres tall) stainless-steel pillars (or 'stelae') situated together in a clearing surrounded by trees. As you approach the stelae, it feels like entering into a packed space, where one is sheltered by the sheer size of the steel pillars. It becomes apparent, as you move among them, that they are grouped into four loose clusters (commemorating victims of each of the four bombings – Aldgate, Edgware Road, Kings Cross/Russell Square and Tavistock Square) (see Figure 3.2). If one chooses to count the number of stalae – which is difficult, because, with the exception of the text noting location, they are not otherwise named, numbered or regularly spaced – there are fifty-two overall, one for each of the victims. Looking closer at the steel surface, one discovers that every stelae has individual features that make it somewhat different from the rest. The overall effect is to create a sense of the loss of fifty-two unique

Figure 3.1 Hyde Park memorial to 2005 London bombings
Source: Photo © Maurice Savage/Alamy

56 Memory and life-space

Figure 3.2 Location text
Source: Photo © Colin Underhill/Alamy

individuals, whose lives happened to coincide at the tragic moment of the bombings, but who are not to be defined by that fate (the size of the pillars making it difficult to appreciate the full details of each).

This is a space of memory that is deliberately designed to facilitate a particular kind of reflective relationship to the past.[16] The design and placing of the stelae function as an affordance that creates a feeling for and an empathy with the individuality of the victims. This stands in stark contrast to sites such as First World War memorials, which are typically emblazoned with explicit references to nationhood, courage and sacrifice, and where the persons being commemorated are reduced to one name among others.[17] In fact, the Hyde Park memorial does list the names of the victims in a separate plaque, alongside the stelae (Figure 3.3), but this is a supplement rather than the main focus of the site. And even here, care has been taken with the form of the memorial, as the typographic system, the font, used for the lettering was designed to be reminiscent of the styles historically used in London street signs. The shape of the letters communicates an idea of 'London-ness'.[18]

The example of the Hyde Park memorial demonstrates that knowledge derived from our situated actions in place is already shaped by communicative and cultural practices. However, Neisser's ecological approach remains of interest because it emphasises that our experiences are not purely 'in the head' matters. They arise through the affordances of place. For many British people, for example, memories of the 2005 London bombings are a rich mixture of recollections of place and time, emotions and felt relationships to London, conversations and stories, media images and coverage, and broader notions of 'terror', 'war' and 'victimhood'. The elements in this mixture reciprocally shape one another, and continue to do so over time.

Figure 3.3 Names
Source: Photo © Jeffrey Blackler/Alamy

Space is not a container in which individual and collective memorial activities simply occur. Rather, space is actively shaped by practices that transform material features of the environment into memorial affordances. Maurice Halbwachs, from whose work the notion of 'collective memory' was derived, spoke of how, under a feudal system, tenants could perceive the qualities of the lord of the land in the very landscape around them:

> Such an assemblage of lands, forests, hills and prairies has a personal physiognomy arising from the fact that it reflects the figure and history of the noble family that hunts in its forests, walks through its lands, builds castles on its hills, supervises its roads.[19]

The feudal lord and the noble family 'engrave their form' on the land they own, through the way they shape and manage the space. In turn, something of that environment becomes imbued with their personal characteristics. The power of the feudal lord appears as stable and well entrenched as the castle he builds or the roads he has cut into the landscape.

Memorial activities 'mark' space. They may do so in a highly visible and public manner, such as through the construction of a monument, but marking also occurs in the routine, informal activities of according memorial significance to the environment around us – the arrangement of treasured objects on a mantelpiece, pinning photographs to a wall, a favourite mug in the break room at work. Relationships between people and objects are stabilised and rendered durable by the marking and arranging of the material features of the environment.[20] In this way, a relationship to a long-departed colleague persists every time the mug is used, which was a symbol of the crafty cigarette breaks we took together. Lighting the oil burner on the mantelpiece, smelling the citrusy fragrance, connects us to that particular holiday. And the feudal lord is still there, just, in the ruins of the crumbling castle on the hill, for those who are able to read his presence.

Reavey discusses this kind of 'spatial marking' in the context of memories of CSA.[21] She argues that difficult or distressing activities mark out the settings where they occur, and this marking or spatial ordering of relations can persist over time and across different spaces. For example, in Sylvia Fraser's autobiographical work, *My Father's House*, there is a passage where the adult Sylvia describes an episode that occurred during an affair she had with a childhood friend's father (Paul): 'Paul opens the door wearing a white terry robe. His grey hair wet and tufted as if from the shower. My daddy sits on the bed in his undershirt'.[22] Here, the physical similarities between her adult lover and her father, his mature grey hair and position sitting on the bed, make the complex, abusive relationship with her father present at that moment, encapsulated in the childlike utterance 'daddy'. As Reavey puts it, 'the man sitting on "the bed" is a concrete, visible marker of the connection she makes between past and present'.[23]

A restricted view of memory would view Paul's posture as a 'trigger' to personal memories. The 'real action' goes on inside Sylvia's mind, with the space being merely a stimulus to internal cognitive events. However, if we follow Lewin and suspend the distinction between inside and outside, mind and environment, we can see instead that the spatial organisation, marked by the prior experiences, affords or proposes the relationship to the father. Paul's sitting on the bed lends form both to the relationship of father and daughter and to the spatial ordering of power and agency that was enacted in that relationship. The arrangement of Paul/father and bed is a higher-order invariant, or affordance, that makes the memorial properties of the relationship to the father travel across time and space. This is a properly expanded view of memory that treats remembering as an activity distributed between persons, spaces and 'things' (i.e. the bed).

It would be better to say that Sylvia's experience of time and space here is constituted by the Paul/bed/father invariance. This is an approach to thinking time and space together (or 'space–time') that has gained ground in contemporary social science, notably, human geography. Nigel Thrift, for instance, argues for a view of place as 'a knot tied from the strands of the movements of its many inhabitants . . . life is a meshwork of successive foldings . . . in which the environment cannot be bounded and life is forged in the transformative process of moving around'.[24] The properties of particular space–times – the forms of connection, the spatial ordering of agency, the possibilities for action, the relationship between presence and absence – are not simply givens. They are generated from the tying or knotting together of relations and movements. Sylvia's affair with Paul constitutes its own space–time where her now deceased father and past scenes of abuse are 'folded into' the present, with implications for her sexual agency. Understanding settings as 'relational spaces' requires an analysis of how this folding together is accomplished through practices of remembering, to constitute a space–time with its own specific temporal rhythms and properties of transformation, connection, continuity and discontinuity.

Lewin argued, in 1936, that then-recent mathematical developments in topology could provide a conceptual toolkit for thinking about what we would now call relational space. Topology is a branch of mathematics that is concerned with continuous transformations in spatial figures.[25] In particular, it is concerned with the qualitative properties of a figure that are preserved (i.e. invariant) through processes of deformation. The most famous example of this is transformation of a figure of a coffee cup into a doughnut. Although the two figures clearly look very different, they remain three-dimensional surfaces with a single hole. In this sense, they are topologically identical or 'homeomorphic'. We might say of the passage in *My Father's House* that it is a transformation between the space of abuse and the space of the affair that retains the key invariance of the Paul/bed/father relation, with its accompanying spatial ordering of agency.

The difference between a topological conception of 'life-space' and the container model of space and action (or 'Euclidean' view of space) can be grasped by considering how measurement is performed in each. A Euclidean procedure consists of placing external co-ordinates around a figure. Here, the relationship between two points within a geometric figure is measured by the superimposition of a scalar grid. A topological analysis transfers the co-ordinates directly on to the figure itself:

> Topologists thus treat figures as manifolds – spaces whose coordinates are not extrinsic, as in a line embedded in a Cartesian grid, but rather intrinsic to the surface itself – and focus on what aspects of a figure remain constant (such as the figure's dimensionality or number of edges) when the surface is bent, stretched or rotated, but not cut or augmented.[26]

The difference here is between putting an object into an external space of measurement versus transferring the measurement system directly to the figure itself (which is referred to as a 'manifold'). For example, co-ordinates between points can be directly plotted on to the surface of a sphere – or indeed a coffee cup, doughnut or any other figure. Psychologists often implicitly rely upon Euclidean or Cartesian procedures of applying external measures and scales. This is why human perception is conceptualised in terms of stimuli that are 'near' to us rather than 'far' away, and memory is traditionally seen to be better for 'recent' rather than 'older' events. However, near and far, along with recent and old (or present and absent), are relations that are relative to the topological properties of the space under consideration. As we saw with Lewin's example of the factory worker, people and events that we might consider as remote can actually be integral to a particular event.

Experience, for Lewin, is the ceaseless unfolding of life-space. In our ongoing relations with others, we are continuously co-constructing life-space. Living consists of passages between a multiplicity of life-spaces, each with their own particular topological properties and specific rhythms of timing and spacing. As she enters the room with Paul on the bed, Sylvia passes into a particular form of spatial and temporal ordering, with its own specific 'logic'. When the woman at the loom stops the machine, she may participate in the transformation of life-space from one topological form – where her child stays at home – to another – where he is sent away because she is sacked for interrupting production. Our actions serve to deform our life-space in relation to its invariances and properties, leading to passages and boundary crossing between one space and another. Lewin's great achievement was to see this folding of life-space as of greater importance for psychology than externally imposed measures of space and time.

To study remembering, we need to ask what kind of life-space is being constituted on any given occasion. We can look at how invariant features – or affordances – of life-space mark out or propose an ordering of relations and their properties. We can explore the 'logic' of this ordering and situate acts of remembering with respect to its emergence. In this way, we can say that the 'setting specificity' of memory as a distributed activity depends upon the topological features of the life-space in question. Courts of law are different kinds of space to therapeutic encounters. The social topology of the home is not the same as the social topology of the workplace (although there are points of passage between them). We will, then, expect remembering to work differently in each of these spaces.

Affect and life-space

As we noted earlier, the life-space of the tick described by Deleuze is constituted by three invariant features in relation to light, smell and warmth, which afford different but intersecting planes of action. However, in the passage, Deleuze speaks of these affordances as 'affects'. What does this mean? The term affect has been of enormous interest in contemporary social science.[27] There are numerous bodies of work that have converged on the term, ranging from psychoanalytically informed approaches to the psychosocial,[28] to work building on Silvan Tomkin's theory of a biologically based fundamental 'affect system'.[29] There has been considerable debate as to how the term 'affect' is to be defined in relation to cognate terms such as 'emotion' and 'feeling', with many commentators feeling that the long history of research in these areas has been ignored by the recent 'fashion' in cultural studies for natural science-sounding

62 Memory and life-space

terms.[30] Indeed, there is plenty of evidence to suggest that the prevalence of the term 'affect' in contemporary social science is in direct, inverse proportion to the meaning it conveys.

Nevertheless, Deleuze has two very specific philosophical points of reference that qualify his use of 'affect'. The first is Spinoza's *Ethics*.[31] In this dense seventeenth-century work, Spinoza accomplishes the remarkable feat of offering a political philosophy alongside a practical ethics of existence, wrapped up in an overarching metaphysics of being. To do this, Spinoza is compelled to redefine basic philosophical distinctions. Since the time of Plato, Western metaphysics has separated human experience from a timeless, transcendent realm of knowledge that surpasses what we can hope to perceive or understand. Spinoza sees this as both a philosophical error, as it creates a black hole in our ability to reason, and a political problem, as it places the ultimate source of knowledge and truth beyond democratic reach, opening the way for despotism. By contrast, Spinoza offers a materialist and immanentist philosophy, where there is nothing in principle 'outside' the relations that constitute our world, no 'God's eye' perspective that the despot may claim to be channelling. Knowledge is a practical matter, available to all who seek it, which comes from grasping the best (most 'adequate') way to order worldly relations.

The hope of 'democratisating' knowledge leads Spinoza to reconsider Descartes's dualism of body and mind. Descartes famously fissured human experience into pure thought and embodied perception. Thought becomes a disembodied matter that is internal to the subject, cut off from the material world. As we have discussed, this Cartesian/restricted position on cognition is a very peculiar and limiting view of thinking that contemporary psychologists have only just recently been able to overcome.[32] Spinoza anticipated these difficulties at the time and proposed that the division of body and mind be treated instead as a matter of perspective – we may feel that our thoughts are distinct from our bodies, but in fact they are two aspects of our material existence. What this means in practical terms is that, as the ordering of ideas should parallel the ordering of bodies, given that they are in some sense 'the same thing', adequate knowledge can be developed through exploring our embodied relations to other bodies:

> The mind and the body are one and the same thing, which is conceived now under the attribute of thought, now under the attribute of extension. The result is that the order, *or* connection, of things is one, whether Nature is conceived under this attribute or that; hence the order of actions and

passions of our body is, by nature, at one with the order and passions of the mind.[33]

'Affect' is the term for the 'actions and passions' our body experiences in relation to other bodies. A 'body' can be defined here as an organic or inorganic thing that acts upon us and upon which we can act.[34] To put it in Gibson's terms, we might say that affect is the 'feeling' of affordance – our sense of the ways in which we might engage with some other body, what it offers, what we can do with it and through it, and what it might do to us. And, in the same way that Gibson claims that environmental invariants do not need to be 'thought' in order to be acted upon, so we can say of affect that it is experienced without necessarily being part of explicit, reflective cognition.

The second reference point for Deleuze is the later philosophical work of A.N. Whitehead.[35] Like Spinoza, Whitehead offered a grand metaphysical system that was unique in its creative reversal of philosophical *doxa* and also rejected a transcendent source of all knowledge. However, Whitehead's materialism was able to take advantage of the quarter millennium of natural science that separated him from Spinoza. In *Process and Reality*, Whitehead drew upon the view of a 'quantum universe' emerging from the physics of his time, to replace Spinoza's language of bodies with a more nuanced account of how provisional assemblies of actual entities, nexuses and societies are extracted from energetic flows. Although the complexities of Whitehead's metaphysics are often highly challenging for readers outside philosophy, his work supports an 'expanded' approach to psychology, where thinking, remembering and feeling are forms of experience that cut across the division between subject and environment.[36] Take, for example, the overarching concern with the strictly defined 'truth' or 'falsity' of recollections that dominates the 'restricted' approach to memory. How can the truth of what we say be established? In analytic logic, a proposition is a statement whose truth or falsehood can be established either through deductive principles or by the action of an observer checking the statement against empirical facts. Thus, the statement 'the child lives with his grandparents in the country' is either true or false, based on either its *logical* or its *psychological* determination. However, for Whitehead, both methods are faulty, because they do not account for the 'actual occasion' – that is, the contingent material assembly – in which the proposition comes into the world. The statement 'the child lives with his grandparents in the country' emerges from a very particular arrangement of people and things and a distinct set of subjects for whom it is a meaningful

64 Memory and life-space

proposition to think. In a sense, we might say that the proposition requires the 'actual world' of the factory, workers, families and town/country to be afforded as possible 'datum' for thought. When the machine breaks down, the woman does not imagine her child's future through an internal conscious reflection on what has just happened. Instead, she feels the force of a proposition that is afforded by the life-space of the factory:

> A proposition . . . is a datum for feeling, awaiting a subject feeling it. Its relevance to the actual world by means of its logical subjects makes it a lure for feeling. In fact many subjects may feel it with diverse sorts of feelings.[37]

The proposition is a 'lure for feeling' that 'awaits a subject' who is capable of embracing it, by virtue of their particular relationship to the part of the world where it emerges. A proposition – a thought-datum awaiting a subject who can be lured into feeling/thinking it – is an environmental affordance that is not fundamentally different in kind to the three invariants of the universe of the tick, but is of sufficiently 'higher grade' that only a complex organism could feel it. For Whitehead, the 'truth' of the proposition will depend upon what the subject who thinks it does next. The woman will herself bring about the circumstances where the proposition can be either verified or falsified through her actions, such as stopping the machine or ignoring the broken thread. We make propositions true or false through the way we take them up and act upon them. Therefore, what is especially important about propositions is not, in principle, their truth or falsity, but rather what kind of world they make possible for us in being thought:

> The fact that propositions were first considered in connection with logic, and the moralistic preference for true propositions, have obscured the role of propositions in the actual world . . . In the real world it is more important that the proposition be interesting than that it be true. The importance of truth is, that it adds to interest.[38]

There are echoes here of Frederick Bartlett's famous observation that the main function of remembering is not to establish the truth of 'what really happened', but rather to bring about a novel relationship between the organism and its environment:

> An organism which possesses so many avenues of sensory response as man's [sic], and which lives in intimate social relationship with numberless other organisms of the same kind, must find some way in which it can break up this chronological order and rove more or less at will in any order over the events which have built up its present momentary 'schemata'. It must find a way of being dominantly determined, not by the immediately preceding reaction, or experience, but by some reaction or experience more remote ... We must, then, consider what does actually happen more often than not when we say what we remember. The first notion to get rid of is that memory is primarily or literally reduplicative, or reproductive. In a world of constantly changing environment, literal recall is extraordinarily unimportant.[39]

Humans can feel a wide range of propositions from their life-space, because it is exponentially expanded by memory. Remembering deforms life-space and exposes us to affordances that free us from being tied to a limited conception of the here and now. It allows us to 'swim upstream' in the flow of experience. Affect plays as central a role here as the feeling of affordance, our sensitivity to the relational possibilities of the particular space–time contours of the life-space in which we act. However, the feelings that are lured by affordances are rarely unambiguous.

Consider, for instance, the use of video and CCTV images in media reporting of cases of child neglect and abuse, such as Baby P. In this tragic case, a 17-month-old child died of physical injuries and neglect inflicted by his primary carers (including his mother). After their trial and conviction, 'home-video' footage was repeatedly broadcast showing the young infant smiling, set in what appeared to be the family kitchen. What makes this footage so difficult to watch is the range of feelings it affords. The dominant ones are horror and disgust at the contrast between the happy child in the video and the awful suffering that would befall him. We wonder if we, or anyone, might have saved Baby P if we had known what would happen. At the same time, there is the sense of comfort in seeing the child appearing to enjoy being filmed, that he had known happiness in his short life. From this, we naturally wonder who took the footage and assume it was most likely the carers responsible for his death. Here, there is a contrast between the actions for which they were convicted and their behaviour at the time when the video was taken. In seeking to record the child's life, they are demonstrating both familial care and anticipating a future family life together, where this video would have some meaning as a document of their shared past and the child's early years.

How can this normative image of a happy family possibly be reconciled with a reality of child neglect and abuse? The video seems to afford a proposition – 'this is a happy family' – that we know to be both true and false. We are sent upstream and downstream, to the life of Baby P before the video footage and to the awful outcome that we wish we could prevent, but are powerless to do so. Ambiguity, rather than clarity, is key to the 'diverse sorts of feelings' that this proposition invites us to take on.

The feelings that watching the Baby P video evokes are not strictly speaking 'within us'. They are properties of the relationship to the world that the video affords. If we say, building on Deleuze, that affect is the 'feeling of affordance', then those feelings do not 'belong' to us – they are 'intensive' relational properties that are constituted through our engagement with the life-space that the video opens up. Considered in purely physical terms, an intensive property is made up of a balance of forces. Temperature and pressure, for example, are measurable intensities. Intensive properties differ from extensive properties (such as mass or distance) in respect to how they can be divided. If you split an extension roughly in half, by say finding a point equidistant between Westminster and Haringey, you have two parts of equal measure, but dividing a room at a temperature of 20°C into two smaller units does not result in two spaces at 10°C. The division of an intensity results in an overall transformation, rather than a simple breaking into equivalent parts. If affect is a relational intensity, then attempting to evaluate what we are feeling is likely to change the experience.[40]

Nick Lee and Steve Brown provide an analysis of a case that is useful here. They discuss a report of a small child – Morris – who was so scared by a performance of *Peter Pan* that his parents subsequently sued the producers for 'stress and trauma' suffered by their son.[41] The performance was a dramatised version of the children's novel by J.M. Barrie. The original text is certainly rich in potential terrors. As Lee and Brown note, the text involves the transporting of a group of children to an unknown world, where they encounter a vicious pirate – Captain Hook – whose enthusiasms include kidnapping infants and drowning people. The details are then as follows:

In 1996 the 3-year-old boy Morris, his grandmother, parents, and 6-year-old cousin Chloe went to see a performance of the play. Grandma had booked the tickets early for her sixty-first birthday treat. We have seen how the play sounds scary. This production in particular capitalized on scariness. Peter Pan wore a dramatic cloak of black feathers. Wolves circled the stage. A crocodile character was huge and imposing. Morris was scared and, within minutes of the curtain going up, sobbed 'Get me out . . . Get me out!'. According to his mother, Morris was 'absolutely petrified'. This was bad enough in itself. One would hope that once his parents had gotten Morris out, Morris would be able to leave his terror behind him. But the family's troubles continued. Morris did not leave his terror behind him. He had nightmares about the play. The events also distributed relationships within the family: 'My own grandson now calls me "Nasty Granny" for taking him to the theatre . . . I'm distressed that I took him to see something so frightening.'[42]

The theatrical production is meant to be scary for the audience. Lee and Brown describe the theatre on that day as an 'assemblage' designed to generate collective emotion. Through a combination of the costumes, set and lighting, coupled with the heightened dramatic tension of the plot and acting, the production created a very particular kind of emotional intensity for the audience. Morris's fear was then constituted relationally through his family's participation in the theatrical event. For many of the children in the audience, the combination of watching 'imaginary danger' while in the comforting presence of their family was probably highly exciting. The collective affect was constituted by joint forces of reality/imagination and safety/danger that were arranged in such a way to invite the audience into the life world mapped out by the play. In this respect, Lee and Brown note, the theatrical assemblage worked like other related assemblages, such as roller coasters or scary movies, where the experience is simultaneously terrifying and controlled.

However, something happened to change all of that. Morris began to cry 'Get me out . . . Get me out'. What was, up until that point, an ambiguous and exhilarating experience, an intensity that combined terror and comfort, resolved into something else. The moment Morris demanded he be taken out, the assemblage became a group of actors behaving in a menacing way towards children, with potential moral and legal consequences for all involved. The theatre or the roller coaster only generates ambiguous intensities as long as everyone involved participates. If, for some reason, either is halted, there is a qualitative transformation in the experience. For Morris, this was a little like the moment in a children's game where the music is stopped: he became 'it'. Morris was no longer participating, not part of the game anymore. He was

68 Memory and life-space

forced to 'own' or subjectify the ambiguous collective affect, which he did as 'fear'. This resulted in a rearranging of his family relationships, notably with his unfortunate grandmother.

The story of Morris and *Peter Pan* draws together our thinking around life-space and affect. Life-space is relational space that stretches beyond current circumstances through our capacities to remember and our shared memorial practices. The relationships that constitute life-space have many and varied potential properties. These potential properties present themselves as affordances, or possibilities for action. We 'feel' these affordances as *affect* and 'think' them as *propositions*. Affect, as the intensive property of relations, is characterised by ambiguity. We experience it as something like the 'atmosphere' of life-space, an invariant mixture of forces in combination. Our actions, including recollection, serve to deform life-space, thereby realising some possibilities according to the particular logic of timing and spacing constituted by the particular life-space in which we currently act. We realise the truth or falsity of propositions through our actions in the same way that we resolve affect by 'owning' or 'subjectifying' it as distinct emotions. Realising a proposition or subjectifying an affect momentarily transforms life-space by breaking invariance. Instead of possibility and ambiguity, we have circumscribed actions, emotions and consequences.

Active forgetting

Remembering situates us within a flow of experience, which lends shape to life-space. Significant, distressing events in our past mark out space and show themselves, in the present, as invariance. They link the upstream to the downstream, carving a chreod where what happened then appears as directly relevant to what is happening now, with implications for how we understand our capacity to act, our current agency. The use of the metaphor of flow is important here. The early psychology of memory was, by contrast, attracted to metaphors of solids and permanence. Richard Semon, for instance, conceived of memory as the creation of 'memory traces' or 'engrams' within the organism through its efforts to retain the impact of external stimuli upon it.[43] Once etched upon the organism, these traces served as the basis for subsequent recall. However, the traces left by stimuli might not be particularly durable. Like the shattered stone face of Ozymandias in Shelley's sonnet, so human memory was thought of as prone to eventual decay and erosion over time. Writing in 1913, Philip Boswood Ballard pointed to the 'tendency towards oblivion' or *oblivescence* in memory, which could only be forestalled by the activity of reminiscence.[44] Only those who sought to rehearse and practise their power of recollection could hope to delay the inevitable.

The metaphor of solids sets up an opposition between the 'active' power of recall or retrieval and the 'passive' tendency towards forgetting and oblivescence. Given the foundational role played by this root metaphor, it is scarcely surprising that a great deal of the contemporary psychology of memory places a firm moral value on recollection and, in particular, veridical recollection. This is increasingly so given the issues raised by an ageing population, where a decline in the ability to recall is taken as the beginning of a dissolution of social and personal identity. However, the opposition between memory and forgetting has not always been accorded the same values. In his wide-ranging 'history of forgetting', Harald Weinrich demonstrates that the idea of having a 'good memory' has often been seen as a vice rather than a virtue, as it turns the person away from pressing current concerns towards a trivial and bookish obsession with the past.[45] In his *Essais*, Michel de Montaigne recommends that, when engaging a tutor, the quality of their thinking rather than the quantity of what they can recall is more desirable: 'I should like you to be very careful to choose a tutor for him whose head is well made rather than well-filled'.[46] In a similar vein, Nietzsche famously associated a tendency toward 'historicism' with political conservatism and argued that the 'vice' of history would choke life and engulf the present.[47] However, the prescribed treatment for this vice was not, for Nietzsche, the destruction of memory, but rather a measured setting aside or suspension of the past.[48] This 'creative forgetting' would free space for the living present.

To promote the role of forgetting as an 'active' effort to alter the relationship we have with the past is to invite suspicion. Paul Connerton, for example, in a deliberate professional 'in joke', lists seven different uses or types of forgetting.[49] Some forms of forgetting, he argues, may serve as social goods, such as when the parties to a political settlement agree to set aside their former historical differences to work towards a new future.[50] This can also occur on a smaller scale when marriage partners tacitly agree not to dwell upon previous relationships for the sake of building a new life together. However, many of the forms of forgetting that Connerton identifies are either imposed upon civil society, such as when authoritarian regimes seek a 'repressive erasure' of the past to silence political alternatives, or when the very means of recollection is itself destabilised through the ordering of remnants of the past in such a way as to make them difficult to coherently narrate, or through their near complete destruction.

Scholars such as Pierre Nora or Rafael Samuel have theorised modern Western societies as driven by the desire to 'stockpile' the past as a source of potential value to be sold as 'heritage', thereby negating a lived connection to the past.[51] Connerton, by contrast, sees modernity as expressing a 'will to forget' that is permanently in thrall to 'the new' and the future and that can see in the past only a source of deficiency or political threat.[52] It may be that both positions are essentially correct. In *Archive Fever*, Derrida offers an analysis of the logic of archiving, based on a deconstructive reading of Freud.[53] Any archive that has the aspiration towards completion through a comprehensive organisation of the materials it stores will find that the cost of this aspiration is paid by an endless repetition of its own status, such that the desire to archive becomes more important than what is actually archived, which becomes, in a sense, forgotten.

The problem here is that the root metaphor of solids encourages us to initially view memory as a 'thing' that needs to be preserved against the forces of erosion, and then subsequently to commodify that thing as something that requires auditing and safeguarding. In this way, we proceed from placing intrinsic *moral value* to explicit *exchange value* on the contents of memory. However, this creates a paradox. If everything is equally of value, then how do we establish scales of moral worth in relation to what we ought to remember? Does the task of preserving the past then actually prevent us from living well? As Halbwachs pithily put it, an obsession with the past can make history resemble 'a crowded cemetery, where room must be constantly made for new tombstones'.[54] And, although stockpiling and 'selling' the past has great commercial value – as evidenced by the trade in memorabilia and vintage items – the logic of capital drives at the wholesale destruction of the past in pursuit of profit derived from 'change' and 'innovation'.[55]

Things become even more difficult when we consider distressing autobiographical memories. What is their particular value? Should they be preserved from erosion, along with other memories, simply because it is of unalloyed moral importance to remember rather than forget? Or do these particular kinds of memory really impair the ability of she or he who recalls them to 'get on with their life'? Is there any exchange value in telling these kinds of story? There is currently a buoyant market for books and films that recount painful autobiographical experiences, such as the bestselling books by Dave Pelzer.[56] This genre of work, disparaged as 'misery lit' by its critics, raises questions about the motivation of those who tell their stories in this way, along with the veracity, especially when commercial gain is involved. However, the practice of overcoming past distress by putting it into a narrative form has widespread support across a range of therapeutic traditions.[57] It could be further argued that selling a narrative of past distress might be the best way to have done with it, to actively forget it as a pressing life concern by transforming it into an object of exchange value.

Some of these difficulties in thinking about the relationship between recollection and forgetting are circumvented by using the metaphor of flow. Rather than treat memory as eroded over time, we can say instead that time places us further downstream from past events to which we remain perpetually connected. Recollection is the acknowledgement of that connection, that a pattern, a flow, can be traced from where we are right now, back upstream to past events. Their influence upon us comes from the chreod, the direction, the particular way in which our experiences have been accorded meaning in the course of that passage downstream. It is in this sense that people who have suffered distressing life events may speak of them as defining their subsequent life, such as in Primo Levi's reflections on his experiences at Auschwitz.

How can we then think of forgetting, from the perspective of the flow of experience, if it can no longer be seen as erosion? Henri Bergson posed this question during an invited address at Oxford University in 1911:

> If we take into consideration the continuity of the inner life and conse-quently of its indivisibility, we no longer have to explain the preservation of the past, but rather its apparent abolition. We shall no longer have to account for remembering, but for forgetting.[58]

Bergson argued that, if experience – which he termed *duration* – was akin to a continuous flow rather than a stringing together of instants, then there was no need to explain memory as a 'special faculty' whose purpose is 'to retain quantities of the past in order to pour it into the present'.[59] The past is automatically preserved within the duration, in the same manner that something of the upstream passes to the downstream. The issue instead is to explain how it is that we are not overwhelmed by the totality of the past at every moment. If Ballard saw reminiscence as the defence against natural erosion, Bergson saw forgetting as protection against the dominance of the past over the present. Forgetting is selective 'canalisation' of the past, such that only those aspects of our past that may inform our current actions are retained at any given point.

However, because duration, as flow, is 'indivisible', the past in its entirety is never erased; it remains permanently accessible, much as the tributaries of a river can, in principle, be navigated, starting from the downstream main stem.

Based on the root metaphor of flow, we may treat forgetting as a selective orientation towards particular aspects of the past. However, although Bergson saw active forgetting as informed by current needs – as indeed does much contemporary psychology – vital memories do not seem to be governed by this kind of logic. What purpose does it serve to hold on to memories that are painful and that appear to be corrosive of agency in the present? The kind of active, selective forgetting that goes on around vital memories can be characterised as a form of *displacement*, an effort to redirect the flow of experience while retaining the connection. This can be thought of as resembling a distributive river system, where a main stem bifurcates into a number of streams. Although these streams follow the direction carved out by the chreod of the main stem, they break the overall velocity of the flow and create new patterns, such as delta formations.

The active forgetting that goes on around vital memories is an effort to break the direct flow of a distressing past into the present. Frances Yates reintroduced the term 'art of memory' to describe the history of mnemonic practices.[60] She traces this history back to Cicero's story of how Simonides discovered the method of loci.[61] However, as Weinrich points out, there is another side to this story. Having gained repute for this 'art of memory', Simonides offered to teach the practice to the Athenian military leader Themistocles:

> Themistocles replied that he did not need any art of memory. Rather than learning how to remember everything, he would prefer to learn how to forget everything he wants to forget . . . According to another version of the anecdote Themistocles curtly replied that he was not interested in an art of memory (*ars memoriae*) but rather was interested in an art of forgetting (*ars oblivionis*).[62]

Presumably, as a soldier, Themistocles has seen much that he would rather not remember. For him, an *ars oblivionis*, or 'art of forgetting', is of far greater use. However, Themistocles does not want to forget everything – he wishes to set his own terms for defining the things 'he want to forget'. Practising an effective art of forgetting is key to living with a distressing past.

However, envisaging what such an 'art' would look like in practice is not entirely straightforward. Umberto Eco mulls over this difficulty when repeating the story of a 'joke' hatched with a group of friends for an imaginary university, which would be composed of fantastical departments, including historically impossible sciences (e.g. 'Aztec horse racing'), self-contradictory disciplines (e.g. 'nomadic urban studies') and studies of utter uselessness (e.g. 'the art of cutting broth').[63] One of the disciplines they considered was *ars oblivionis*, or practices of forgetting. However, Eco and his friends were unable to conceive of how these practices might function as intentional acts (rather than as, say, accidents or physical impairments). To illustrate, Eco notes that *ars memoriae* typically use method of loci techniques such as building imaginary 'memory palaces', where a visual space is conceptualised in which the material to be remembered is placed. This works according to semiotic principles, where one sign, such as a location in a house, stands in relation to another, such as the line of a sonnet that the speaker wishes to subsequently recall. However, semiotic techniques such as this would not help at all with forgetting, because 'semiotics is by definition a mechanism that presents something to the mind and therefore a mechanism for producing *intentional acts*'.[64] In other words, efforts at intentionally forgetting something are likely to produce precisely the opposite effect – such as in the instruction 'Do not think about a white bear' – because they work by making ideas present rather than absent. How then can one ever *intentionally* forget anything? Eco suggests that the only way to do this is by overloading the system. If one attempts to associate many different things with the same sign (for instance, placing all the lines of the sonnet in the same location within the 'memory palace'), it is possible that one idea might become confused with another. Although this might not result in the actual forgetting of the idea, it might, for all practical purposes, make it difficult to recover.

Eco invokes the ancient art of concealed writing, or *steganography*, by way of illustration. Steganography involves the sending of a message hidden within another form, such that it is not immediately apparent that the 'secret' communication is occurring. For example, in the TV drama *Prison Break*, the central character, Michael, conceals the architectural plans to a prison, in order to assist his brother's escape, by having them transformed into a highly elaborate tattoo that is inked across his entire upper body. This secret message is hidden in 'plain sight', as no one, except Michael, has knowledge of what it actually means. This suggests that one might effectively render something as 'forgotten' or 'inaccessible' by embedding it within a broader pattern, such that it could only be decoded under very specific circumstances. A version of this idea forms the central plot device of the film *Memento*, where the protagonist, Leonard, uses a complex system of externalised memory, including body tattoos, a journal and annotated photographs, to overcome his anterograde amnesia (the capacity to generate new memories) in searching for the man who murdered his wife. However – spoilers! – this system is actually an elaborate deception that Leonard has designed to conceal his own role in his wife's death, wherein he becomes increasingly unable to disentangle his own past from the information contained in this prosthetic memory.

The practice of actively forgetting vital memories can then be studied by looking at the ways persons displace their relationship to painful or distressing events by embedding their recollections in other kinds of experience – a kind of 'managed accessibility'. As we will discuss later on, victims of the London bombings and their relatives have developed sophisticated strategies for mixing their recollections with other kinds of experience. In doing so, they do not erase their recollections of what happened to them, but they do make those memories flow into distributary channels of experience that offer new possibilities for action and agency. This typically requires collaboration with others. It is very rare for selective forgetting to be accomplished by individuals on their own. If memory is intrinsically social, shaped by the categories and forms of intelligibility that are shared by local groups and communities, then forgetting is almost always a collective practice too. Forgetting is as much a matter of distributed cognition as is remembering. This is powerfully demonstrated by recent experimental work on socially shared, retrieval-induced forgetting that has shown how forgetting can be facilitated through interaction with others.[65] To this, we would add that such interaction may be entered into with the explicit aspiration among some or all parties of selectively displacing a given aspect of the past.

This collective dimension brings an additional layer of complexity to the ethical issues around forgetting. Where there are knowledge asymmetries in relation to the past events between group members, or superordinate relationships of care, one person may feel that they are responsible for ensuring that another does not recollect some experience that may be difficult for them to manage. In Chapter 5, we will meet adoptive parents who are highly concerned that their adoptive children will remember very problematic early experiences before the point where they will have sufficient maturity to deal with them. These parents are not just custodians of their adoptive children in the usual legal sense, they are also custodians of their memories, because they know details of events that their adoptive children may only be able to vaguely recall at present. They are also painfully aware that the 'truth will out' at some point, and that they will be accountable at some future point if they decide to deliberately withhold access to those memories. As we will see, this makes for a very challenging set of practical decisions about how to support and steer children's memories.

Robyn Fivush has done much to clarify how parents support the memories of their children through conversational practices, as they develop greater linguistic and interactional competencies.[66] Parents tutor children in strategies for making the past relevant to present actions ('Don't you remember when . . .?') and offer tools and techniques to preserve the past, from a birthday card kept safe to a disposable camera bought for a school trip. What adoptive parents make very clear is the need for adults to manage what might be potentially difficult recollections. This can similarly range from conversational tutoring ('Oh, let's not think about that right now . . .') to practices aimed at preserving, while displacing, the past (e.g. hiding particular toys, making explicitly mock or inauthentic photographs to prevent children from obsessing about their origins). We need to learn how to actively forget, just as much as we need to learn how to recollect.

The ethics of memory

In *The Moral Demands of Memory*, Jeffrey Blustein rejects the notion that remembering is itself always an unalloyed good. He sympathetically cites Nietzsche's notion of 'critical history' – that the past must be continually re-evaluated with regard to our current needs, values and interests. On this basis, one can say neither that remembering is always the right thing to do, nor that one should always strive to overcome the past. Persons should be evaluated on the basis of 'the sort of balance they have achieved or are trying to achieve between remembering and forgetting'.[67] The actual goods and obligations that are attached to memory are those that are relevant in the here and now, which may include righting some wrong in the past. As such, these goods do not constitute a primary virtue, but instead need to be compared with competing social goods and obligations of other kinds, which may require the intervention of political judgement. The simple exercise of memory is not, by itself, a sufficient means of realising the good life (and, indeed, we can easily think of instances where a surfeit of memory or an obsession with the past is corrosive of other virtues).

76 Memory and life-space

However, for Blustein, it is creditworthy to use one's memory to 'take responsibility' for past events and experiences in which one's agency is implicated. This is relatively straightforward in cases where one is to blame for harm caused to others. To acknowledge one's agency is to accept the 'reformative implications' of such an admission, which can lead to changes in one's character and conduct that are themselves morally worthy, along with the possibility of performing reparative actions to ameliorate the past harm. Conversely, to refuse to recognise that one is 'bounded by the past' or subject to 'moral constraints' as a consequence of ones' actions is to risk developing faulty self-conceptions. For Blustein, this has normative negative implications for the development of identity – refusing the past will not lead to a well-developed identity. To this, we also need to add that Blustein does not see the reparative function as necessarily the most important aspect of 'taking responsibility' for the past:

> Taking responsibility for one's past, I propose, centrally involves this as well: looking back and over how one has lived one's life not merely from the standpoint of a disinterested curiosity but with a view to actively taking up the past and annexing it to and integrating it with the present. That is, taking responsibility for one's past is an activity that connects and binds us to ourselves through time. One makes past acts or portions of one's past one's own by *appropriating* them, by enlarging the field of one's agency to include them and laying claim to them.[68]

When one takes responsibility for some aspect of the past in which one is involved, this results in the expansion of the domain of one's sense of agency, irrespective of whether or not one is actually culpable for some past harm. Taking responsibility is then, normatively, a means to the good life, because it is expansive of our sense of agency, which carries implications for our future development. However, this is premised on an apparent choice between either appropriating or rejecting the past. In the case of vital memories, no such choice exists. The adult survivor of CSA, for instance, is not in a position to be able to speculatively entertain whether or not to 'enlarge the field' of their agency. It is more usually the case that they feel their own current sense of agency is thoroughly interdependent with past events – it is they who are being appropriated by the past, so to speak.

For Blustein, autobiographical reconstruction is a source of both obligation and virtue. Being able to tell a story about some past event that narrativises either our agency in those events or our connection to that event in ways that we now deem as relevant to our current sense of agency will, in a normative sense, enable us to be better than we currently are. Blustein here emphasises the importance of constructing continuity in memory, of putting things in order. It may well be that the events we recollect have been upsetting, offensive or directly harmful to us – this does not matter. What is crucial is that we recognise that we were active participants in the fate that subsequently befell us. For Blustein, 'hiding from one's agency' is more problematic than misattributing agency where we, in fact, had none. This is based on the argument that expanding the remit of agency 'backwards' into the past has positive effects on our capacity to define our personhood, irrespective of whether that attribution of agency is justified or not.

Taking responsibility here amounts to constructing a good story. If identity is defined in biographical, rather diachronic terms, then what we are is dependent on having a narrative in place that clearly and unambiguously locates us in agentic terms with respect to some past event or experience. Once again, this normative ethical framework appears rather at odds with how vital memories are narrated. As Sue Campbell describes, one of the major issues that survivors of CSA face concerns the gaps and discontinuities in their accounts of their own experiences.[69] To experience sexual abuse at a young age is to be forced to live a life that runs counter to established narrative milestones that define many other autobiographical accounts of childhood (the 'first times' that make up the reminiscence bump for most people are not things that survivors necessarily wish to recall). Things do not add up, events do not sit in the right order. It is extremely difficult to tell a normative story about experiences that are utterly corrosive of the culturally espoused norms of family life. And, as Janice Haaken has described, even when CSA becomes a 'master narrative' in itself, it tends to significantly degrade the narrative structure of recollections.[70] (Incidentally, recognising these two processes gives us significantly more purchase on the so-called 'false/recovered memory' debate than any effort at establishing an internal criterion for truth in memory.) Blustein's ethical framework then seems insensitive to the gaps, discontinuities and ambiguities that may be present in memory, a point that Haaken and Reavey point to in their work on recollection and CSA.[71]

Doubtless this is related to an unwillingness on Blustein's part to make distinctions between different kinds of recollection. It is significant that there is only one mention, as a footnote to Chapter 2, where Blustein engages with memories of sexual violence. In the course of a discussion of 'unwarranted

78   Memory and life-space

self-blame', Blustein observes that a blurring between 'what has happened to oneself and is the product of one's agency' may occur when 'the past is appropriated, but it is appropriated improperly, because one attributes agency and responsibility where they do not belong'.[72] Unfortunately, Blustein does not spell out how the propriety of agency attributions is to be established, but we may assume, based on his general argument, that it is the role of external, historical accounts to supply this evaluative bedrock. Footnote 44 then adds:

> Examples include the rape or incest survivor who holds herself responsible for the earlier violation despite having been only a passive victim. Taking responsibility for the rape or act of incest in this way compounds the original harm and is an all too common phenomenon among its victims.[73]

We may find it in ourselves, perhaps, to forgive a philosopher for their gendered use of language. Throughout the text, Blustein typically uses the pronoun 'him' in his examples, doubtless to convey the supposed universality of the cases. Here, he makes the exception by implicitly defining 'rape' and 'incest' as specifically female experiences that are, following the logic of his syntax, related to 'violation' and 'passivity'. One can only assume he has in mind a scene of sexual violence the guiding narrative of which is the penetration of the passive bodies of women and girls by active male penises. To say that this is a rather limited understanding of the range of acts between women, men, adults and children that are (correctly) grouped under the category of 'abuse' is somewhat of an understatement. Moreover, Blustein appears to suggest that 'taking responsibility' here is just a simple category error: the survivor should simply not take responsibility, but often does. However, this shies away from the knotty ethical dilemmas that Blustein claims he wishes to address – what does it mean, in ethical terms, for a survivor to identify with an experience of abuse? How does 'enlarging the field of one's agency' work when it appropriates problematic memories? Must we see recollections of abuse as necessarily subordinate to establishing responsibility before we can ask ethical questions around the memorial work that survivors do? Blustein's approach leads to an ethics that is allergic to the messiness and ambiguity of recollections situated in the engagements between embodied persons.

What seems to be required is an ethics that is instead grounded in the particularities of living, including the specific affective experiences that accompany having a particular kind of embodied relation to the world. Spinoza's ethics offers precisely this kind of radically specific, affective and embodied ethical treatment of memory. For Spinoza, bodies and minds are attributes of a single immanent field – which Spinoza refers to as 'God or nature' – that gives rise to different aspects of our experience as we encounter others. Thinking and feeling may appear to be distinct to us, but they are not distinct in nature. They are, so to speak, simply two sides of the same coin. Our encounters with other bodies simultaneously afford both 'ideas' and 'affects'. Note that, because body and mind are not divided 'in nature' (as they are in the kind of Cartesian dualism that is foundational for many version of psychology), there is no need to theorise how they can be sewn back together. Ideas and affects are two parallel, interconnected modes for experiencing any given encounter.

Living, for Spinoza, is a matter of organising encounters in particular ways. This is guided by our fundamental drive for preservation that he terms as 'endeavour to persist in being' or simply *conatus*. We are all, at base, a society of simple or complex bodies that combine with other bodies through encounters. Successful encounters increase our powers to act, and hence our ability to 'persist in being', whereas unsuccessful encounters diminish our powers. This means that expanding our personal powers to act (which is, at the same time, an expansion in the possibilities of being acted upon) leads to a greater expression of conatus. The central ethical precept of Spinoza's system is the maximisation of this expression of the endeavour to persist. However, persistence does not here mean maintenance of a steady state of being, but rather the continuous modulation and transformation of what we are and our personal powers – the homeorhetic movement that Deleuze refers to as 'becoming'.[74]

Spinoza argues that the means to increasing our powers is via the ordering of our relations with the world in such a way that we maximise successful encounters and minimise unsuccessful encounters. We experience the former as 'joyful affects' and the latter as 'sorrowful affects'. However, as ideas are intimately connected with affects, good encounters give rise to 'adequate ideas' and bad encounters to 'inadequate'. What Spinoza means here by 'adequate' is similar to the way that Whitehead treats propositions as either 'interesting' or 'uninteresting'. An adequate or an interesting idea is one that enables us to think differently, to realise new and emergent possibilities in the world around us. Note that, for both Spinoza and Whitehead, our ideas are afforded by the world, rather than originating solely from within our minds. Our thinking is, then, thoroughly grounded in historical and material contingencies. Moreover, ideas are to be judged, not with reference to some external criterion of truth or falsity, but rather in terms of the situated manner in which they transform our relation to the world. The pursuit of 'adequate' or transformative knowledge is, at the same time, the experimental exploration of 'joyful' or expansive affects.

If we apply this ethical scheme to the approach to memory we have developed so far, then we can say that, if remembering involves the folding together of relations, these can be evaluated in terms of how far they give rise to 'joyful' affects and 'adequate' ideas. For example, an adoptive parent arrives home to discover that their adopted child has placed a large picture of a foster parent on their bedroom wall. Although this is troubling ('Why are they still thinking about them – are they not happy here?'), the parent can see that, in placing the picture, the child has increased the number of 'caring adults' who are visible to them on a daily basis, thereby affirming that they are a person who is deserving of love and attention. For the child, the photograph produces a 'joyful affect', because it expands their felt engagement with the world. However, it only does so under these very particular conditions of adoptive parents who have the self-confidence to not be threatened by the act of placing the image on the wall.

Remembering is an ordering of encounters accomplished by folding the past into the present. Whereas Blustein seeks universal principles that will determine the moral worth of acts of remembering on any given occasion, here, we treat such judgements as highly contingent. Good and bad are not subject to universal judgement but are radically specific to what is good or bad for me right now, given the relationships in which I am currently involved. Establishing whether a recollection is 'joyful' or not depends upon what it does to the person at that particular point in their life (e.g. as embedded in a secure adoption placement), the relations that define their current life-space (e.g. how tolerant the adoptive parents are of the child remembering former carers) and the overall composition of relations that is realised through remembering (e.g. what it does to join together the current family with the former foster family). It is extremely difficult to predict in advance how things will turn out – quite what remembering particular events will do to and for us in our current life-space. And, indeed, it is not as simple as trying to remember 'nice things' and forgetting 'bad things', as goodness and badness are defined by the capacity of a memory to transform the present. This is, then, one of the fundamental reasons why people cannot simply have done with difficult pasts – the vital memories that they give rise to continue to have both a relevance and a transformative capacity in the present. However, much depends on whether it is possible to find elements that may expand one's current engagement with the world among the distress of painful experiences.

To take the example of recollections of CSA, this version of ethics would suggest that we first of all recognise that past harm is correctly experienced as 'sorrow' because it was then, and continues to be, a diminution of powers to act. We must also recognise that what brings about the sorrow is the relation, rather than the individuals involved. In this sense, it may not assist the survivor to struggle to attribute moral qualities to either themselves or their abuser in any definitive sense. Reconstructing the event in more than one way – which a survivor might wish to do to increase her or his overall capacity to act in the present and future – is then a matter of primarily attempting to *feel* the encounter differently. Being sensitive to the range of relations present within the encounter, which are likely to include relationships, not just to the abuser, but also to other people and material surfaces, is one potential way in which to read that past and to render matters of ongoing agency as more expansive and, hence, more active. Let us make absolutely clear that we are not suggesting that the abuse be discounted – far from it – but rather suggesting an opening up of other affective routes to the encounter. This will likely take the form of an ambiguity or ambivalence, where a range of emotions might join together but also potentially collide to produce a more ambivalent, and thus flexible, recollection. This may involve engaging with aspects of love, pleasure, connection to constitute an enlarged version of the encounter, along with experiences of pain, hurt and betrayal. Out of this affective atmosphere, it may be possible to express affects that were grounded in one's active engagements, rather than pure passivity. In this sense, we are with Blustein in his claim that there is value in engaging with the past, even if it comes at some cost. Where we differ is in seeing this engagement as one that proceeds from affective embodied relations, and in making the contingent relation, rather than the subjects or the events, the matters of moral evaluation.

There is also a historical dimension here. What we can feel is, of course, shaped by the wider conditions within which a body exists. Moira Gatens frames this point precisely:

> Differences between one human individual and the next may amount to qualitative as well as quantitative differences in power. This would be one possible way in which one could describe differences between men and women . . . historical and socio-political conditions can, and do, affect the range of capacities and powers that women and men are able to express.

> A person's capacity to affect and to be affected are not determined solely by the body he or she is but also by everything which makes up the context in which that body is acted upon and acts. When the term 'embodiment' is used in the context of Spinoza's thought it should be understood to refer not simply to an individual body but to the total affective context of that body.[75]

We cannot think of any single body outside the dense networks of encounters they inhabit. There is a social, cultural and historical specificity at work here. Under certain conditions, bodies are organised in such a way as to inhibit their powers. We can, through a critical historical account or genealogy, trace histories of these modes of organising and how they engender passive rather than active affects. We can also say, from the perspectives of the communities of embodied persons involved, that these arrangements are clearly wrong, because they do not allow for the full expression of the capacities to act. In this sense, reconstructing our own personal pasts along affective lines necessarily engages with a broader historical account of the sorts of person we are and the place we have in the social conditions that we inhabit. An ethics of memory – as the effort to mobilise the past through affective engagement – then necessarily opens out on to moral and political judgements based on genealogies of the arrangements of bodies.

Spinoza uses the term 'common notions' to refer to the kind of knowledge that we can collectively develop through our affective relations to one another. When bodies form 'joyful encounters', they jointly express a power to act that is supervenient upon that relation – it is a quality that emerges from the relationship itself, rather than being produced in an additive fashion from the component parts. A common notion is the idea that is formed of this novel, emergent power to act. For example, a common notion is realised when adoptive parents and children discover together that there is a way of holding on to a relation with former carers that actually enhances rather than threatens the stability of the current family unit. Remembering facilitates the experimental production of new forms of identity and social relations when it enables us to articulate common notions, or ideas of collective transformations in life-space.

In the chapters that follow, this work of engaging with the messy, affective sprawl of relations through memory is realised in the empirical accounts we provide of the studies outlined in Chapter 1. To 'do justice' to these accounts, we present analyses of a range of experiences, channelled mostly via verbal and visual materials. The rich contours of these wonderfully complex memorial narratives are then read with a view to expanding upon a more nuanced understanding of how memories are constantly woven through the affective and ethical engagements individuals have with their past – in the multiple and multifarious ways in which they confront their capacities to act, and to become.

Notes

1 Lewin, 1936: 22–3.
2 See Brown and Harris's (1978) classic. For more on recent 'critical' approaches to mental health, see Cromby *et al.* (2013).
3 Lewin, 1936: 12.
4 B = behaviour; P = person; E = environment.
5 For a very readable account of how ideas such as this, derived from quantum mechanics, can be applied to the human sciences, see Plotnisky (2002).
6 Bob Cooper's work explored this theme of folding together past and present through organisational processes – see, in particular, Cooper (1992, 1993, 1998).
7 Deleuze, 1988: 124–5.
8 Neisser, 1978: 4.
9 Neisser, 1981.
10 Gibson, 1966: 201.
11 Gibson, 1979.
12 Neisser, 1993.
13 Neisser, 1988.
14 See Neisser, 1994.
15 See McCarthy, 2006.
16 See Allen and Brown (forthcoming) for further discussion of the Hyde Park memorial.
17 See King, 1998.
18 Allen and Brown, forthcoming.
19 Halbwachs, 1925/1992: 123.
20 See Serres, 1995a.
21 Reavey, 2010b.
22 Fraser, 1989: 171.
23 Reavey, 2010a: 316.
24 Thrift, 2006: 141–2.
25 Jänich, 1995; DeLanda, 2002.
26 Martin and Secor, 2013: 4.
27 See Brennan, 2004; Clough, 2007; Greco and Stenner 2008; Thrift, 2008; Gregg and Seigworth, 2010; Davidson *et al.*, 2011; Wetherell, 2012. The texts that arguably opened up the topic to broad appeal – 'Shame in the cybernetic fold: Reading Sylvan Tomkins' and 'The autonomy of affect' – can be found in Sedgwick (2003) and Massumi (2002), respectively.
28 Walkerdine, 2010.
29 Sedgwick, 2003.
30 In particular, the thoroughgoing critique offered by Leys (2011). See also the introductory essay to Greco and Stenner (2008).
31 Deleuze, 1988, 1992; Spinoza, 1677/1996.
32 See also Brown and Stenner, 2009.
33 Spinoza, 1677/1996: 71.

34 Deleuze draws on the work of Antonin Artaud to argue for treating speech as the production of 'sonic bodies' – see Deleuze (1990, 1998).
35 Whereas Deleuze wrote extensively about Spinoza, he made very few explicit comments on Whitehead (see Deleuze, 1993, chapter 6). However, the influence of Whitehead on Deleuze had been proposed by Isabelle Stengers (2011b) and Steven Shaviro (2012). Stengers has gone so far as to describe Deleuze as fundamentally a 'Whiteheadian' (personal communication).
36 See Stenner, 2008, and Brown and Stenner, 2009, chapter 2.
37 Whitehead, 1929/1978: 259.
38 Ibid.: 259.
39 Bartlett, 1932: 203–4.
40 See DeLanda, 2002.
41 See Lee and Brown (2002). The case was originally reported by *The Guardian* newspaper in 1996.
42 Lee and Brown, 2002: 262.
43 Semon, 1923.
44 Ballard, 1913: 1.
45 Weinrich, 2004.
46 Montaigne, cited in Weinrich, 2004: 44.
47 Nietzsche, 1997.
48 As Weinrich points out, this 'setting aside' is helpfully already contained in the German term for forgetting, *vergessen*, which combines the old German/Scandinavian term for 'take aim' (*gessen*) countered by the prefix *ver-*, suggesting a turning away. Thus *gessen/vergessen* make an opposition in the same manner as *kaufen/verkaufen* (buy/sell). See Weinrich (2004: 1–2).
49 Connerton (2008) is playing here on the well-known formula 'the magic number 7 plus or minus 2', which George Miller (1956) offered as an estimate of the units of information that could be retained in short-term memory. This 'magic number' recurs through academic and commercial attempts to exploit memory, as with Heinz's supposed '57' varieties of soup, which was chosen simply for the memorable qualities of the numerals '5' and '7' – see Brown (2008).
50 Connerton, 2008, 2011.
51 Nora, 1996; Samuel, 2012.
52 Connerton, 2009.
53 Derrida, 1995.
54 Halbwachs, 1950/1980: 52.
55 Harvey, 1990.
56 Pelzer, 2004.
57 The best known being White and Epston's (1990) formulation of 'narrative therapy'.
58 Bergson, 1933/1992: 153.
59 Ibid.: 153.
60 Yates, 1966.
61 In brief, the story goes that Simonides was interrupted and called outside during the peformance of a victory ode at a banquet. In his absence, the roof collapsed, killing all the guests. Simonides was called upon to identify the mangled bodies, which he was able to do by matching the remains to what he recalled of their positions at the banquet table. According to Yates (1966), this use of spatial ordering to organise information in memory gave rise to the technique of using a 'memory palace'.
62 Weinrich, 2004: 11.
63 Eco, 1988.
64 Eco, 1988: 259.
65 See Stone *et al.*, 2012.

66 Fivush, 2007, 2008.
67 Blustein, 2008: 14.
68 Ibid.: 69.
69 Campbell, 2003.
70 Haaken, 1998.
71 Haaken and Reavey, 2010.
72 Blustein, 2008: 89.
73 Ibid.: 108.
74 See Deleuze and Guattari, 1988, chapter 10.
75 Gatens, 1996: 131.

Chapter 4

Feeling an ambivalent past
Survivors of child sexual abuse

Trapped between labelling Woody Allen a child molester or his daughter a liar

In an article published in the newspaper *The Observer*, Victoria Coren Mitchell reflects on the accusation made by Dylan Farrow that her legal father, the film director Woody Allen, sexually assaulted her when she was aged seven.[1] The accusation was initially made around the time of the alleged assault in 1992. An investigation at the time rejected the claim, and no prosecution was pursued. In 2014, Dylan repeated the accusation in an open letter to the *New York Times*, in response to the nomination of one of Allen's films for an Oscar award. In the piece, Coren Mitchell reflects on the dilemma presented by the case. Clearly, no person should be labelled an offender in the absence of any legal proceedings. However, she goes on to observe, it is widely acknowledged that there are huge numbers of victims of CSA whose cases are never pursued, and, as a consequence, there are 'a vast crowd of abusers who walk free across the planet'.[2] The difficulty appears to lie with either labelling Allen an abuser when he has never faced prosecution, or labelling Foster a liar while recognising the shockingly low figures of successful prosecutions of CSA.

Is there a way to avoid being caught between these positions? Coren Mitchell notes some of the contextual details. At the beginning of the year in which the alleged incident happened, Mia Farrow, Dylan's legal mother, had split from Allen after learning that he had been conducting an affair with Soon-Yi Previn, Dylan's sister. Mia Farrow and Woody Allen had acted as parents to both girls since their relationship began in 1980 (when Soon-Yi was aged eight). The affair came to light in 1992, when naked photographs of the adult Soon-Yi, taken by Allen, were discovered. It is in this context, Coren Mitchell argues, that we need to situate the allegations made by Dylan:

Seven-year-old Dylan is adjusting to a world where her parents have split up and her father's having sex with her sister. In all meaningful ways, when it comes to what it feels like for the family, he is committing incest. Technically, no. Emotionally, yes. To her mother, it must also feel like child abuse. All the definitions of all the relationships have been disrespected and are crumbling apart. Now that Mia Farrow knows it's possible for Woody Allen to feel a sexual interest in her children, at any age, she is fighting for sole custody. So, Dylan is dealing with a father who's having sex with her sister and a mother who is trying to protect her from him. In this context, Dylan does not want to be touched by him. That means being touched by someone who's become frightening, who is not the innocent father she believed. She has been stroked, kissed and told she is beautiful by a monster who's been casting his sexual eye around the family. It's sinister. She does not want it. She may not understand the detail, but everything has turned horrible and weird . . . The family boundaries were transgressed. The caresses became sinister. The memory of them felt dirty and shameful. Wherever Woody Allen did or didn't put his hands, these are the feelings of child abuse. So, even with Allen's innocence of a crime presumed, there is no version where Dylan Farrow is lying. Either way, her father brought sex into her childhood consciousness, mixed with family life, in a way that left psychological scars. Either way, her development was compromised by something disturbing and wrong. Either way, she remembers unwanted touches; was a victim and is a survivor.[3]

What happens to us takes its place within a flow of experience. Dylan's life has taken a 'horrible and weird' turn. Her family relationships have been turned upside down. Her father has become, in her eyes, a sexual predator, and her mother is now her protector. What might have previously felt like attention and displays of love from her father now become 'sinister'. Her recollections of their life together up until that point cannot now be disentangled from the shocking revelation of her father's sexual interest in her sister. In this context, physical contact with her father is 'frightening' and unwanted. If that is how the experience may have felt at the time, then the successive 20 odd years leading to the repeating of the allegation, during which time Dylan was estranged from Allen, doubtless deepened the sense of 'shame' over 'unwanted touches'. A chreod has formed where Dylan's memories of her family life flow through and from 'feelings of child abuse'.

Coren Mitchell's argument has two important implications for our understanding of vital memories. The first is that judging the veracity of memory cannot be done in the abstract. If we wish to take a position on whether the allegations are based on 'true' or 'false' memories, then we need to situate ourselves within a particular practice where we can specify the criteria that will be used to establish the judgement. In this way, there may be legal, therapeutic or moral 'truths' that can be accorded to a given recollection, depending on the way it is constituted and deliberated in particular settings. There is no superordinate or 'disinterested' position from which the 'real truth' of any matter can be confirmed.

Psychologists such as Elizabeth Loftus have heavily promoted the idea that it is, in principle, possible to establish the truth or falsity of recollections.[4] They typically do this through the curiously asymmetrical reasoning of arguing that, if one can demonstrate possible sources of 'bias' (e.g. prior discussion of the recollection with a vested party such as a therapist), then claims to 'truth' can be discounted.[5] Here, however, 'truth' is seen as simply the absence of external inputs. Left to our own devices, we would remember more or less correctly. The presence of others puts us on the road to falsity. This kind of asymmetrical reasoning leads to the disqualification of Dylan Farrow's allegations, because they became entangled at the time with the divorce proceedings between her mother and father. She was clearly encouraged or even coached in her recollections, the argument runs. The assumption here is that 'natural' (i.e. accurate) recollections are not shaped through our interactions with others. And yet, the vast majority of autobiographical memories, especially those that originate in childhood, are shared, discussed, shaped, reformulated and subject to possible contestation, as part of the ordinary course of family and close relationships. As practically all memories of the kind recollected by Dylan are relationally afforded, the question is not whether they can be disqualified by pointing to alleged bias, but rather, given this relational basis to memory, does the recollection meet the professional standards set by specific practices of legal, therapeutic or moral evaluation to be judged as requiring redress?[6]

The second, and for our purposes more important, implication is that recollections are woven into life-space. When we remember, we do so in place, in context, through the relationships that afford our capacity to reconstruct the past through recollection. What we recollect connects us to prior life-spaces, which become folded into the present through our memorial work. Our memories are marked by, and bear the traces of, the material and relational conditions through which they are afforded. If we wish to understand the place a given recollection has within the unfolding experience of a person, rather than to seek to arrive at an *in principle* judgement as to its veracity, we ought instead to attend to the folding together of life-space through memory, and how this acts to distribute a sense of agency and identity.

It is in this sense that Coren Mitchell can claim that there is 'no version where Dylan Farrow is lying'. The recollections Farrow has made public have a place in her ongoing flow of experience, which runs from past to present. They provide a connection between the spaces of her childhood, with the 'weird and horrible' feelings they afforded, and her present adult relationship to her father. This flow follows the course of chreod cut out around a common invariance. Her father was, and remains, for her, the transgressor, the person who destroyed her family life and sought to conceal his 'sinister' sexual desires. She feels herself to be a victim of that transgression, which retains ongoing significance for what is currently possible in her relationships to her father, sister and mother. Her present agency and identity flow, in part, from the persistence of that particular aspect of her past in the present.

We can understand agency here as the relational possibilities for action offered by life-space. Rather than treat agency as something of which we are either possessed or dispossessed, we may say that agency, as what we feel we can and cannot do, is always a matter of degrees and perpetually in flux. Our actions involve others, clearly, whose own actions reciprocally shape our own. More importantly, the setting itself, including its material features, offers up affordances, possibilities for feeling, understanding and acting. Memory expands or dilates our sense of agency by deforming life-space, connecting the present to other kinds of space. Agency is then a relational effect of the unfolding of life-space through recollection. It depends upon the particular ways that the past comes to matter in the present.

In this chapter, we will look at issues of past and present agency in relation to recollections of CSA.[7] We will consider how materiality is part of the very fabric of memories, in terms of establishing agency and in deciphering responsibility and blame. Central to this analysis are questions relating to the positioning of agency and its associated ambivalence within these accounts. It is important to state that the accounts that we analyse here have been provided by participants who have already engaged with therapeutic and legal practices. The veracity of what is recollected is already settled. What concerns us here is the place of these vital memories in establishing matters of agency and identity.

Agency and ambivalence

A crucial issue for many survivors of CSA is how they account for their own past actions in relation to the abuse they have previously suffered. There are subject positions – that is, ways of representing self in relation to prevalent cultural narratives – that fit better with established notions of a 'good victim'.[8] Typically, these involve either an absolute dispossession of agency ('There was nothing I could do') or complete passivity ('It was not my fault'). These subject positions in the past stand in relation to the current subject position adopted by the survivor. To speak from the perspective of an 'innocent child', rather than as a sexually active or rebellious adult woman or adolescent, typically attracts greater support for the narrative. This can leave female survivors who do not appear to fit with conventional models of femininity (notably sexually proactive and non-heterosexual women) with considerable difficulties, as their recollections may be doubted on the basis of their current (unacceptable) sexual/social actions.[9]

Creating a narrative consistency between past and present agency can then be a major task for survivors (and, indeed, a search for this kind of narrative organisation is a goal in some therapeutic interventions).[10] However, this may come at some cost. Janice Haaken has spoken in some detail of the kinds of problems that may emerge when survivors simplify experiences of abuse to literalist adult interpretations of childhood powerlessness.[11] Emphasising past passivity can create a narrative framework that constitutes the adult survivor as similarly lacking in agency, a victim rather than an actor in their own unfolding life experience. Haaken argues that recollections of abuse may contain within them multiple layers of meaning and explanation. These may include testimonies of pleasure as well as pain, feelings of love and hate towards an abuser and other such ambivalent emotions. Rather than seek to subordinate these often contradictory meanings and feelings within an overarching 'master narrative' of passivity, Haaken calls for interpretative flexibility, where these contradictions might be treated by the survivors as resources for different kinds of narrative, which might facilitate better versions of agency in the present. Ambivalence, then, sits at the very heart of survivors' accounts of their past, as questions relating to who was responsible for abusive encounters and relationships may not always appear straightforward to survivors, especially when relationships contain positive, as well as negative. elements.[12]

Although Haaken's perspective provides a highly important counterpoint to the cultural demand for adult survivors to conform to notions of 'good victimhood', her approach is strongly grounded in narrative and looks to the capacity of survivors to find the means of telling better stories about their pasts. From our perspective, the past does not require narrating to come into being, because, if experience is continuous and indivisible, we are always already connected to our personal histories. The past persists in terms of both the ways it has directed our experience – the chreods that become worn into lives – and the kinds of invariance and affordance that fold together in life-space. Ambivalence around past agency certainly does offer narrative challenges, but it is, at the same time, a felt matter that is grounded in the materiality of invariances that 'mark' memory. We saw in Chapter 3, how the Paul/bed/father invariance was central to Sylvia Fraser's felt sense of the link between her present sexual agency and the past abuse that she suffered. If affect can be considered as 'the feeling of affordance', then our felt relationship to our material circumstances is accompanied by a sense of what we can do, of the possibilities for action that are afforded. What we are capable of is rooted in this felt engagement with the world and the way the world is acting upon us. In survivor accounts, there are numerous examples of feelings, such as shame, guilt, terror, fear. But there are also feelings of joy, pleasure, excitement and warmth. All of these different configurations of feelings appear to feed into agentic actions and their associated ambivalence. We can tie these feelings of affordance to the material spaces and objects themselves, to demonstrate how certain material features of the memories propose 'settlements' of agency.

The relational assembling of people and things within life-space does a particular work of distributing the intentions of the actors in these memories (more potently, the deliberate and negative intentions of the abusers). This is crucial for managing and dispensing with difficult feelings of ambivalence that continue to generate confusion and guilt in the present experiences of survivors: for example, the way an abuser appears to choose from the various kinds of action afforded within the space, 'marks out' their intentions in one way or another and settles – even if only provisionally – feelings of ambivalence. Judgements about past intentions are then rooted in the felt relation to life-space – 'He did this when he could have done that'. In this way, the spaces and objects that provide the scene for survivors' memories are not simply peripheral, but contribute to reducing or disposing of ambivalence around agency.

The first example comes from an interview with a woman who had experienced sexual abuse at the hands of her best friend's father. She was 8 years old at the time the abuse started. In the following extract, she talks about

92   Feeling an ambivalent past

a particularly special place (the wall) where she and her friend often hung out. The wall was quite high, but they were usually able to climb up and down by themselves:

> Extract 4.1
> I couldn't forfeit the important relationships in my life, just to stop this abuse happening, so it carried on for about a year . . . I mean I can remember one time we were sitting on top of this wall, and he came out, and he lifted his daughter down, sort of like you do with a child . . . and he lifted me down, and he looked over his shoulder and he put his hand between my legs . . . he didn't have to lift me down like that. It was that that made me realise the lengths he would go to, I don't know why I put up with it and that's when it stopped.
>
> (Bella, 37 years old)

It is apparent from this example that agency forms a major part of this memory. Bella asserts that she 'couldn't forfeit the important relationships' in her life, so the abuse continued, until the time of the episode described above. Clearly though, Bella is struggling to accept why she 'allowed' the abuse to continue, which is a major concern for her throughout the interview. One partial resolution comes through her acknowledgement that her childhood home life was impoverished, which is why her friendships played such a major part in her life at that time. Her agency was affirmed through her ability to maintain one particular friendship, even if at great cost.

The space of this particular encounter with the abuser is important to these relationships in a number of ways. This is a space of pleasure, a place of connection with a cherished friend. The space is thus integral to feelings of active agency in the world. And yet, midway through this description, something alters dramatically. The change occurs through the way in which her encounter with the abuser (her friend's father) unfolds, and the manner in which this is mediated by the wall. As the wall is high, Bella and her friend accept help from the abuser. Bella's status as a child, therefore, is reaffirmed by the height of the wall and her smaller physical scale. The wall acts as an affordance, which establishes the relation of adult provider to child in need of support. Her physical limitations (in finding it difficult to get down from the wall) are brought to the fore, and her agency in the situation is called into question and repositioned. The wall *condenses* and *simplifies* the dynamics of power. It offers up the proposition of a powerless child and more powerful adult. Engaging with this proposition is clearly distressing, as it requires Bella

Feeling an ambivalent past   93

to negate the sense of agency that her and her friend's interaction with the wall previously afforded. In this sense, the recollection turns from one where the features of the space initially afforded agency to one where it is precisely those features that led to agency being denied. Furthermore, pleasure turns to feelings of shame, as what happens next becomes directed by the abuser – the turning of his head to look over his shoulder and the abusive act of putting his hand between the child's legs.

The shift in subject positioning – from active to passive – is relationally accomplished through the girls/wall/adult arrangement of the life-space. It becomes an invariance in Bella's recollection, around which she rehearses the different possibilities that might be afforded by that relationship. Bella contrasts what happened with normative, 'usual' relationships, where adults would respond to the need of the child to be lifted off the wall – that is, with kindness, rather than abuse. The actions around the wall, therefore, mark out the intentions of the abuser, and his contravening of 'normal' adult/child relations:

and he lifted his daughter down, sort of *like you do with a child* . . . and he lifted me down, and he looked over his shoulder and he put his hand between my legs . . . he didn't have to lift me down like that. It was that that made me realise . . .

It is at this particular point that the chasm between her relationship to the abuser and her friend's apparently 'normal' relationship to her father is rendered concrete. She appears struck by how adults can and 'ought' to behave and captures a glimpse of the abuser as a loving father who behaved in a protective manner towards his own daughter. Furthermore, the usual thrill and rush of being lifted down from a high place is displaced by the shame evoked by the actions of the abuser. A potentially positive affective moment is redirected by the actions of the abusive other and is transformed into an unequivocally upsetting and destabilising one. Her position as an abused child, therefore, becomes visible through the girl/wall/adult invariance, which distributes and simplifies the position of each of the actors within their mutual relationships to one another.

The power dynamics that are in play are afforded stability through the child's relationship to this concrete object and her inability to prevent the man taking this as an opportunity to abuse her. In her recollection, the actions mediated by the wall are precisely the point at which she becomes clear about the powerless position she finds herself in more generally. Not only this, in his

94 Feeling an ambivalent past

'looking around' to see if anyone is watching when he performs this abusive act, a visible sign is provided to Bella that his act is indeed intentional, which in turn reaffirms his position as the knowing wrongdoer. Her assertion of will then shifts from the preservation of her relationship with her friend to stopping the abuse.

The feelings of affordance

Particular arrangements of people and things in a relationally defined space of possible actions (i.e. life-space) constitute higher-order invariances, or affordances, around which the flow of past to present is structured. Arrangements, such as the girl/wall/adult invariance, offer a range of possible actions. They can be sources of pleasure and excitement, as well as abuse, anger and shame. For each particular arrangement, we can explore how it constitutes an 'affective universe' through mapping the feelings and various senses of agency that it affords. Clearly, this can give rise to complex and ambivalent experiences, because, as we saw with Bella, it is possible to feel both the potential pleasure and distress that are afforded by the arrangement.

The arrangement also gives rise to what Whitehead called a 'proposition'. This is a statement that arises from the relational ordering of people and things that we are 'lured' into thinking by our engagement with the affordance. A proposition might also be termed a 'conceptual affordance'. In Bella's case, the girl/wall/adult arrangement invites her to think of her friend's father in a particular way – 'He is a loving father'. Bella can feel this statement in the way he responds to his child being perched high on the wall. However, she can also feel the negation of the statement in the covert way that he seizes the opportunity to abuse her. In this way, just as the affordance gives rise to ambivalence, it can also provide the means to settle or simplify matters. Whitehead argues that propositions are neither inherently true nor false, rather that we affirm or deny propositions through how we act upon them and engage with the world they help to realise. In Bella's case, by focusing on how her abuser engages with what the arrangement affords, she is able to reject the proposition and put a stop to the abuse (he could have used this space to demonstrate his capacity to be a caring adult, but instead he has shown that even here, in public, in front of his daughter, he will take the chance to abuse me).

In the following extract, a similar movement from engaging with ambivalent feelings and propositions to an eventual provisional settlement can be seen. Lorna describes being abused as a child by her older brother. She focuses, in

Feeling an ambivalent past 95

particular, on one particular aspect of her brother's behaviour, his locking of the door to the bedroom where the abuse took place:

Extract 4.2

Lorna: It was my brother, we I would think that when he started, it was, er curiosity, but I think, erm . . . one thing I tried convincing myself of, that that he was naive and he didn't know what he was doing was wrong, but he used to lock the door to to, we didn't have key locks, he used to take the handle and take out the bar.

[later in the interview]

I'd say the main problem there is is, the guilt for enjoying what he did, and that can really tear me up sometimes, and I think that's been, big problem, actually specifically before I realized the the feeling of confusion, and what I should feel about enjoying this. I do feel guilty about writing it down, cos it makes it solid, it makes it er, it's evidence and it's just . . . like I say, it makes it, it makes it real, which of course it was, but some of me wonders how much of it was real . . . but there's a big part of you that wants to be believe he didn't know what he was doing, but I don't think I can convince myself of that, like I say, going to the extent of locking the door . . . by the time he got to 15, he must have known, he must have done . . . I think so . . . but it would have been nice if he didn't.

Interviewer: Would it make a difference?

Lorna: Yeah because of the way I feel about him, because . . . because if it was basic curiosity, if if, and, rather than actually knowing that it was wrong . . . he must have known how it would affect me.

(Lorna, 28 years old)

The act of abuse clearly still holds some ambivalence for Lorna. The memory contains a mixture of emotions and sensations (e.g. pleasure, confusion), as well as a set of dilemmas around how to name her experiences as abusive. Such feelings also provide her with a means to reading accountability within the situation, as pleasure indicates to her a certain kind agency she must have had at the time. But what is centrally at stake in this passage is the constitution of Lorna's experiences as incidences of curiosity or else as her having fallen victim to malicious, intentional acts carried out by her brother. In terms of the space of the bedroom, this comes down to establishing who is acting on the space and who is being acted upon. If the latter can be established, then the 'effects' of these acts can be more readily understood, and the identity of Lorna as a survivor becomes secured. The intentional awareness of her brother is also at stake in the setting up of Lorna's agency – there is interdependency between his and her agency. If his intentions were to do with mere 'curiosity', then it is more likely that her own 'curiosity' would be called into question. Hence, Lorna is attempting here to manage emotional ambivalences in the recollection. If ambivalence can be displaced, a more 'solid' ground for trusting that the abuse was real and harmful can be advanced.

The propensities of the door clearly play a key role in the constitution of agency in this recollection. Locks on doors 'close' rooms against uninvited visitors and delineate between public and private spaces. They also afford a particular ordering of the sexual relations that take place behind those closed doors. The intentions of the actor become translated and stabilised in relation to the door itself. The person who can lock (and unlock) the door is recognisably in charge of the situation. The stability of the victim/perpetrator binary is produced through the participation of the objects (handle, lock, door) that make up the setting. Together, they form a sister/door/brother arrangement that defines the relational possibilities of the life-space centred on the bedroom. So long as the door remains unlocked, the scene retains its ambivalence. The brother is sexually curious and demonstrates that he does not know that what he is doing is wrong by being apparently unconcerned that they might be disturbed. But the locking of the door is taken to be a clear sign of the intended malice behind the act, which subsequently lends weight to the attribution that he must then have been knowingly damaging her sense of self. Her brother, through locking the door, not only tries to hide the act, but also demonstrates a willingness to cause present and future harm to his sister. By locking the door, he communicates a lack of care around her emotions, as he must have known 'how it would affect' Lorna. His ability to alter the course of her emotions over time becomes stabilised in this physical act that transforms the space from an accessible room in the house to a space of abuse and negative affect. As Lorna laments:

> It makes it, it makes it real, which of course it was, but some of me wonders how much of it was real . . . but there's a big part of you that wants to be believe he didn't know what he was doing, but I don't think I can convince myself of that, like I say, going to the extent of locking the door . . . by the time he got to 15, he must have known, he must have done.

The judgement of the brother's sexual agency is not based on the exercise of his sexual desire per se (because curiosity would have been more acceptable); it is directed at his ability to forfeit that desire to protect his sister. The brother's agency thus feeds into Lorna's own, with the matter settled by the locking of the door. The state of the door (locked/unlocked) serves here to settle things in the moment and allows Lorna to proceed with a causal narrative of damage. The intention involved in taking off the handle to lock the door – an act that requires notable effort and thought to accomplish – demonstrates to Lorna that ambivalence over her brother's agency can be provisionally placed to one side, making it possible for future attributions (by her and others) concerning her willing participation in this event to be displaced. Moreover, any memory of pleasure, desire, arousal or associated bodily states alluded to in Lorna's memory must be disattended to and essentially forgotten, to sit in a kind of acknowledged yet humiliated silence.[13]

The life-space of the child

One of the consequences of adopting Lewin's topological definition of life-space is that spatial and temporal remoteness does not negate psychological significance. Put simply, if we are relationally connected to something or someone, it does not matter how far away they are from us right now, in terms of space or time. The relationship continues to structure the possibilities we see for our actions in the here and now. Our current life-space unfolds around invariances that connect past and present. The material propensities of those invariances (such as the height of the wall, the locking/unlocking of the door) shape our conduct, irrespective of whether they are directly present to us. We feel what they afford, they bear the 'marks' of a putative distribution of agency. Our current experiences, right now, are situated in a flow, a chreod, that has been directed, pointed out, by past affordances.

Recollection is not simply a matter of bringing to mind, or of speaking about, some past event. It is an expanding or unfolding of current life-space to include past spaces. This affords a peculiar kind of experience. The adult survivor of CSA, in this case, feels the past space in relation to both what it afforded as a child and what it now affords as an adult. In engaging with the recollection, the survivor does so as both the child-who-was-abused and as the adult-who-survived-abuse. In this way, survivors display both awareness of how the space felt at the time, along with recognition of other possibilities within the space. This can expand the sense of ambivalence survivors

98   Feeling an ambivalent past

experience in relation to past abuse and abusers, when the abuse occurred in spaces that afforded care as well as neglect. In the following extract, Theresa describes being locked in her childhood bedroom by her father during the periods where he sexually abused her:

> Extract 4.3
> And what he did was locked me in the bedroom, didn't give me anything to eat, until I basically gave in, or I was a good girl, in his terms . . . we . . . and that was really frightening, and the memory I had, but he took all the bedding and all the clothes out of the room . . . and I remember, the chest of drawers looked like a monster because the drawers weren't there, it'd got this mouth, which was strange.
>
> (Theresa, 40 years old)

In this extract, the relationship between the father and child is marked out and stabilised by the act of locking the door, removing the clothes and drawers and leaving the child alone in a familiar place, altered through the violation of familiar objects (e.g. the monstrous chest of drawers). The space of a child's room is of a piece with the ordering of familial relations within a household.[14] It contains markers of security and care, such as a bed and clothes. A bedroom is a private space, where a child can express her or his own agency, to some degree, without parental intervention or interruption. Being sent to one's room as a child is an established way for particular moral lessons to be learned, including learning how to follow parental rules. Teaching moral lessons in this way turns the privacy of the bedroom on its head. The child can only really feel a sense of agency in their bedroom if they are able to freely enter and leave. There is little agency to be had if the bedroom is a prison.

In Teresa's recollection, the private space of her childhood has been transformed. The father has taken away all traces of comfort from her familiar surroundings; he has usurped her bedroom. Not only has her bedroom become a prison, but much that made it into 'her space' has also been removed. The things that afforded comfort and care have been transformed into markers of her lack of agency and of the demand that she submit to her father's will. The central object here is the chest of drawers. Previously, this contained Teresa's clothes. Now, with its drawers taken out by the father, it resembles a 'monster', the empty spaces in the front looking like a strange 'mouth'.

Why is the disfigured chest of drawers so memorable? Beyond the sheer oddity and strangeness of its appearance, it seems to be doing a considerable amount of work in the way Teresa connects her past and current life-space. Teresa recollects her father as both an abuser and as a kind parent. He is the parent who abused her, but also the man who expressed love and was experienced by others as a caring individual. In her recollections, Teresa engages with this duality, which even extends to the pattern of abuse. His practice of locking her in her room is a dreadful perversion of the normative parental practice of 'teaching lessons', in the service of his own sexual interest, rather than completely inexplicable and alien behaviour. The chest of drawers that becomes a monster mediates the complex relationship between Teresa and her father, translating it into a more culturally recognisable plot, involving an inhuman villain. The father's behaviour can be displaced on to the objects in the room, which punctualise a whole complex of relations that Theresa has had to endure with her father, who is both a caring parent and an inhuman villain. It is via this 'monster object', which frightens and breaks the will of the child, that Teresa can hold together the duality of her father and parent and abuser, while clearly experiencing her lack of agency at that time, objectified through the mediation of the grinning chest of drawers.

Ambivalence can then be translated into a concrete set of relations by the punctualisation of recollections around the central object. In Teresa's recollection, she can engage with both the stark, concrete reality of fear she experienced as a child, and her adult's awareness of the duality of her father. The relational propensities of the chest of drawers provide the possibility of holding these potentially ambivalent experiences together. The lack of drawers that makes for a 'mouth' acts as a sort of materialised 'generative grammar'. It provides the possibility of seeing the abuse as a monstrous transformation of family life. Her childhood space was irrevocably subsumed into abuse.

In the following extract, from Martha, we see a similar deformation of child space into the space of abuse by adults. However, in Martha's recollection, that deformation is not complete:

> Extract 4.4
> It was my place [her bedroom], my zone of comfort. Even though he had reign over it when he did what he did to me, it was over before you knew it and what I was left with was my fucking room, with my stuff in it and I protected it with my life, no one was allowed to enter, because without any of that, I had no sense of who I was, where he finished and I began.
>
> (Martha, 29 years old)

In this passage, Martha refers to her bedroom as a space that is her own and, despite the horror of the abuse, a comfort zone containing her treasured possessions. Martha constructs her sense of agency through the mediation of a privatised space (her bedroom), ensuring that her father's reign is temporary, rather than constant. Her respite comes from her ability to reassert her agency in the private zone of the bedroom, which she protects by prohibiting entry. Her agency is clearly compromised by the intrusion of the abuser into her private zone, and yet she discusses the regaining of boundaries and her sense of 'who she is' when he exits, resulting in the reclaiming of her territory. Agency is afforded by the boundaries that are marked out in the space itself and through Martha's (partial) ability to defend it. Although this certainly has a physical demarcation (the bedroom and the outside), agency is a thoroughly relational effect (bound up in her relationships with others in the home) of Martha's way of inhabiting her bedroom. The defence of the private speaks to the success of Martha's abilities to maintain her sense of self and agency, which is dependent upon her separation from the abuser, outside the times when the abuse is taking place. Without such an ability to defend and prevent others from entering her protected private world, her ability to sense 'who she is' is impaired, and the line separating her and her abuser, blurred and inchoate.

This sense of gaining control over the private world of the bedroom is common in survivor testimonials. In connecting adult and child life-spaces, survivors can articulate how important it was to them at the time, and to them now, to have this sense of agency affirmed through maintaining spatial boundaries. Children may also leave the privacy of their own rooms to visit their abusers, so that, once they return to their room again, they can better retain a sense of boundaries, safety and sleep.[15] These bounded places can operate as potential sites of agency, registering areas where women held some form of control over the boundaries between self and other, and some investment in their own pleasures and activities. Agency then, to an extent, can appear to be organised around the boundaries of private spaces.[16]

Privacy boundaries were certainly not available to all survivors, especially those who recollect less defined domestic households or those who did not have access to an exclusive privacy, such as a bedroom. Children who have stepped into the shoes of an absent mother, expected to fulfil traditional female duties, such as washing and ironing and providing for younger siblings, are particularly at risk of having no definable private territory.[17] The 'parentification' process involves the child occupying adult roles, but with contradictory and unstable consequences. Even when the role of the adult mother is performed, the tasks can feel demeaning and denigrating, not only because the task is associated with gendered inequalities in the production of domestic labour, but also because the child feels decidedly 'out of place' in the domestic sphere.[18] The spaces associated with childhood pleasures are, therefore, neglected, disrupted or severely compromised. One survivor, Sukie, describes how her abuse by a family friend at the age of nine was facilitated by the lack of privacy she encountered at home, wherein she was required to carry out all sorts of domestic duties, as a result of her mother's absence. In order to gain space and a sense of individuality, she would regularly visit a relative's house, where the abuse subsequently took place:

Extract 4.5

When I told my mum about the abuse, she didn't believe me and said that I must have done something to provoke it. I don't think she wanted to see me as a child though I was responsible for pretty much everything . . . I was all and sundry's babysitter, it was more forced than it was anything, so I used to go and visit my aunty everyday and I loved it there, I really loved it, I think I actually preferred over my mum because there were no demands on me there. At home I wasn't actually allowed to lock the door, so I used to just lie in bed pretending to be asleep.

(Sukie, 26 years old)

Sukie's account signals a wider set of issues that go beyond her mother's rejection of her account of sexual abuse, including conflicts between mother and daughter. Sukie's lack of agency is represented through the confines of the domestic space and the complex set of familial relations that occupy that space. She has no room to call her own and, as a result, pretends to be asleep, because of the lack of a bounded space (e.g. a private, locked room). Conversely, Sukie asserts agency by spending a significant proportion of her time with her aunty, who fills the emotional void created through parental neglect and provides her with a childlike space, with no adult demands to be met. As an adult connecting with her childhood life-space, Sukie reflects on the lack of boundaries, both at home and in the more public settings of her aunty's, where visitors were constantly passing through. This resulted in the merging of adult and child roles, which in its turn partly facilitated the abuse, as it pushed her towards the more open space of the aunty's house. The difficulty for the adult Sukie, is to know whether she could be considered to have been a child at all.

Again, we see how connecting together childhood space and adult life-space surfaces considerable ambivalence, which becomes mediated by the materiality of the space itself. Moving between home and the aunty's house involves a transition from being a child-treated-as-adult to being a child who is sexually abused. In each place, the adult Sukie can see herself as 'not being treated as a child', in terms of either age-appropriate roles or sexual experiences. And yet, there was a kind of privacy at her aunty's house that was not possible at the mother's house, centred on being able to lock the door. The ambivalence surrounding why the child Sukie would want to visit a place where she was abused is handled by reading off the affordance of being able to shut away demands.

The affordance of 'choice'

For survivors to recollect themselves as having no agency in the past in relation to their experiences around sexual abuse is problematic. Although it might allow for a survivor to offer a coherent, socially sanctioned narrative of 'good victimhood', it forecloses on the range of other feelings and possibilities that childhood space also affords. And, when current life-space folds itself around that of childhood space, a lack of agency in the past might appear to mark out the present as repeating that passivity. As we have seen in all the extracts we have discussed so far, the material propensities of objects in childhood space afford ways of connecting to experiences of abuse that both disrupt and (partially) settle questions of agency and intention, both on the part of the child and the abuser. What we have called the material 'generative grammar' of relations between people and things in childhood life-space also helps to establish a rough moral order. Reflecting on how these arrangements afforded patterns of action – what could be done, what could not be done – allows the adult survivor to map out a set of moral evaluations – what was right, what was wrong. We see this clearly in the last extract:

Extract 4.6
I can remember, having been crossed over the road by my grandma, standing at the gates of this house, and thinking, I don't want to go here, because I knew what was going to happen, but, and I also knew that there was a playground, a bit further down, and there were swings and things, which was also very exciting, and I, I can remember wondering whether I could actually go to the swings instead of going and seeing this man,

and em, and em, I think that I've always felt . . . why didn't I make the choice, and part of me knows that if I'd gone to the swings my grandma would have found out, one, she would have been extremely angry, and she would have told my mum, and my mum would have been extremely angry, em, too, my grandma would have been terrified, if I wasn't where I'd ought to have been . . . my therapist used to say there wasn't an option, because er, I didn't have an option because I was a child . . . but I can't can't deal with that.

(Sara, 34 years old)

The concrete character of the spatial relations described here objectifies a moral order and a set of dilemmas that the child is faced with. The adult Sara connects herself to the child Sara, who stands at the gate to a house, having been escorted there by her grandma (who mistakenly thought that the child would be safely cared for by her neighbours). This is the place where she was repeatedly abused. She recollects thinking, 'I don't want to go here'. She also recollects feeling the pull of the potential excitement of going to the playground, a space of pleasure and freedom. She could go there instead of 'seeing this man'. In this way, her agency and associated feelings are starkly concretised — obey your mother, go through the gate and risk being abused, or ignore your mother, turn down the street and play on the swings. The adult Sara is then confronted with a complex moral dilemma. It was the right thing to do, going through the gate, but it resulted in an enormous wrong inflicted upon her, which she is still disentangling. It would have been the wrong thing to do, at that moment, to have turned towards the park, but what a better life it might have turned out to have been, if she had only gone that way.

The difficulty here is that the arrangement of house/child/park has become an invariance in Sara's recollections, around which her supposed 'choice' can be evaluated. The 'road' in particular becomes a stable feature of this narrative, in that it dramatises the inevitability of the choice to go to the abuser's house — she has to cross the road because her grandma has escorted her there. However, in her doing so, it is as if the 'choice' to be abused has been made. If expectations had not been met (i.e. the child staying in the man's house), severe consequences would have to be faced. The invariance is the lynchpin around which this complex order is unfolded. She ends up crossing the road and so avoids a litany of negative emotions in others, such as anger, worry and terror. Her emotional actions are thus utterly interdependent with the

104 Feeling an ambivalent past

intentions, motivations and emotional responses of others. However, because they are mapped out in relation to the actions afforded by the house/child/park arrangement, Sara is prompted to view the actions she followed as an explicit choice.

It is common for therapists to point to the interdependence of children's actions with the intentions and emotions of (powerful) others, to persuade adults of their inability to have really made a choice as a child, and yet, as Steven Angelides argues, this imposition of a straightforward moral order contradicts the child's perception of having a degree of power or control.[19] Sharon Lamb similarly observes that children can recognise situations as fluid, dynamic and interactional, rather than as defined by clear intentions and moral sensibilities.[20] This mismatch between a purely adult account of the situation and the mixed experience of connecting adult and child life-spaces creates difficulties, because it requires the survivor to discount the range of feelings and sense of choice, however minimal or ill founded, that the child felt at the time. Sara, however, reflects on this ambivalence. In her account of the swings as *her* 'object' of pleasure, which she could have *chosen* to indulge in, she emphasises the reality of the child's agency and ambivalence that lurks in the shadows. Sara refuses to take the line (as her therapist encourages her to do) that children are not capable of choice and represents the reality of children's agentic capabilities and pleasures in the objects themselves. This account firmly departs, then, from the usual interpretation of Sara's narrative as a straightforward example of cognitive distortion that requires 'correction' through therapeutic engagement. We would argue that the fluidity of the account and the acknowledgement of a complex dynamics is not a distortion but a felt engagement between the world and the person that requires serious recognition, so that the forces of the entire material–subject assembly can be examined and, at the same time, normalised.

Jeffrey Blustein argues for the moral necessity of incorporating our past experiences into our current sense of self.[21] We must connect what we think we are to what we have done, what we have experienced. To not do so is to fail to submit one's life to reflective evaluation, to be a person who lacks proper moral standing. Yet, as we have discussed before, he is prepared to make an exception when it comes to experiences of abuse and sexual violence. 'What good can come of dwelling on these painful and unwanted experiences?', he implies. However, what runs through all of the survivors' recollections we have described in this chapter is the danger in ignoring the profound ambivalence that emerges when one attempts to fold adult life-space around the space of the childhood experience.

To dismiss ambivalence is to decontextualise unwanted and distressing experiences of sexual abuse from a range of other relations that obtained at the time. For Bella, for instance, abuse entered into the relationship with her friend, which had been a source of great pleasure and value. Similarly, for Sukie, abuse occurred in the course of her efforts to extricate herself from other kinds of demand. It happened to her in a place that she 'loved', because it allowed her to achieve some kind of privacy. There are, then, elements of the childhood space that are inextricably woven around the experience of abuse, but are nevertheless of value to the adult survivor. These can take the form of feelings or of a sense of choice, however limited, that can take on enormous importance, such as with Martha's struggle to maintain the boundary of her bedroom, despite the abuse that occurred within it. Indeed, as Sara's recollection demonstrates, trying to absolve survivors of the need to address the moral dilemmas that they feel are present in their recollections can be counter-productive, because it washes out matters of ongoing importance that may speak to an enhanced sense of agency in the present.

Blustein's moral philosophy puts a great deal of stress on the idea of owning our past, of taking responsibility for our experiences. However, working out these kinds of moral and ethical positions need not begin on the basis that our personal past 'belongs to us' in any strong sense. Memory emerges from a relational life-space. What we remember does not come entirely from within us, but is afforded, in part, by the arrangements of people and things through which our ongoing experiences are unfolded. Teresa's recollections of the duality of her father, as loving parent and abuser, for example, are translated by the chest of drawers. The materiality of that object lends its propensities to her memory. What she recollects bears the mark of, and necessarily includes, that object. In the same way, Lorna's memories turn around the sister/door/brother arrangement. What she recollects and its moral significance for her as an adult are interdependent with the past intentions of her brother, which are themselves marked out by the propensity of the door to be locked and unlocked. For Lorna, there is no 'pure' or 'true' version of past events that can be extricated from what this invariance continues to afford, as it shapes her recollections.

Sorting out matters of agency and intention is a serious moral business, which has enormous implications for adult survivors of CSA. The desire to provide a clear and unambiguous moral framework for survivors, such that they can be reassured of their blamelessness for the great wrongs that have been inflicted on them as children, is understandable. In certain evaluative settings, such as in courts of law, this may be entirely what is required to accomplish justice or reparation. However, outside these settings, when it is a question of how survivors incorporate their past into their current sense of self, matters are different. If a moral framework is used that requires survivors to prematurely dispose of ambivalence, to cut away at the range of contradictory feelings and relationships that are bound up with abuse, then this does not necessarily deliver 'good' outcomes, nor establish, of itself, moral worth in the present. What is required is an ethical framework that is sensitive to the multiple ways in which possibilities for expanding our sense of who and what we are can be derived. It is not a question of having or of not having agency, but rather of engaging with feelings of affordance, in the way that Lorna feels different versions of herself at stake in the locking/unlocking of the door, or that Sara feels by placing herself back at the crossing of the road. To feel the contingency of the way the past has flowed towards the present is, in an important way, a basis for situating oneself differently in relation to that past.

Notes

1 Coren Mitchell, V. (2014) My Woody Allen conundrum. *The Observer*, 9 February, p. 40. Extract reproduced with permission.
2 Ibid.
3 Ibid.
4 Loftus, 1994, 2003; Loftus and Pickrell, 1995.
5 See Latour (1988) for an extended analysis of symmetry and asymmetry in accounts. Also Potter (1996).
6 It is important to restate that, on the first of these grounds – legal standards – the allegation was judged not to have met this bar.
7 The material here was taken from a study conducted by Reavey (1998).
8 See Reavey and Warner, 2003; Reavey and Brown, 2007.
9 See Warner, 1996; O'Dell, 1997; Worrell, 2003.
10 See Herman, 1992.
11 Haaken, 1998.
12 See also Lamb, 1996.
13 Connerton, 2011.
14 Duncan, 1996.
15 Bass and Davis, 1988.
16 Duncan, 1996.
17 Baker, 2002.
18 Hall, 1996.
19 Angelides, 2004.
20 Lamb, 1996.
21 Blustein, 2008.

Chapter 5

Managing the memories of others
Adoptive parents and their children

Why are there no trousers?

'Diary of a separation' was a weekly column published in the UK newspaper *The Guardian*. It is an account of a relationship breakdown that provides almost forensic descriptions of the practical and emotional problems involved in separation and shared childcare. In an article entitled 'Where have all the trousers gone?', the author describes a frantic search for clothes for the children before school:

'Why are there no trousers?' I mutter. I kick aside an abandoned bag of swimming gear, damp and mildewed. 'Why are there no *trousers*?' I shout this time. The children ignore me. They are watching TV. The eldest looks up, momentarily, confused. 'What?' 'Why can't I find any trousers? How is it even possible that you have no trousers?' . . . X must have them all, I think, irritably. Of course, that isn't possible, really. The eldest can't be stockpiling trousers at his father's house. Common sense dictates that he must leave here, and return, with one pair. I frown. I suspect what's really happening is that he leaves here with what I consider a decent pair of trousers and comes back with something I don't: shorts, tracksuit bottoms with holes in the knees, trousers that only reach his shins. Nothing he can decently wear to school. I call X, trying to keep the note of complaint out of my voice. 'I haven't got any trousers for the eldest,' I say. 'Have you got them?' 'But . . . surely I can't have them all?' he reasons, correctly. 'That makes no sense.' 'No, I know, but . . .' I trail off. 'But somehow I don't have any decent ones. And last weekend he came back in his karate trousers.' Wow, I sound amazingly petty. 'Fine,' he says. 'You can come and get some if you need to.' He sounds appropriately bored by the discussion, which is, indeed, very boring. No one cares except me.[1]

At first glance, it may appear irrational or churlish to become upset by the disappearance of an object of clothing. Indeed, the author consciously reflects upon why exactly she is so upset with such apparently trivial matters. Surely, if one has been through the process of agreeing the separation of the 'big stuff', such as finances, housing and child custody, a missing pair of trousers ought to count for very little? And yet they do count. They provoke anger and suspicion about the inferred actions of the ex-partner ('X'). They lead the author to behave in ways that she herself sees as unreasonable and 'petty'. Lurking behind it all is a sense of lacking control in one's own daily affairs, and of sneaking, rising guilt at the shortcomings of one's newly single parenting. All of this arises from a missing pair of trousers.

What is of interest for us here is how the life-space of the family, populated with objects, is practically managed in relation to memory. Furthermore, our intention is to explore how relations between adults and children are worked out, through focusing on the life-space of the family, which includes the spatial and temporal relations constituting the family home, the affordances of objects within the home, and the field of possible actions that arise from these intersecting sets of relations.

In this chapter, we will be drawing upon a study we have conducted with adoptive parents where they discuss some of the issues that arise around maintaining 'life-story books'.[2] One of the requirements in the British care system is for adoptive parents to either create or update an existing life-story book on behalf of their child. The book is a chronologically organised narrative of the child's life. It does not have a fixed format, but typically consists of text produced by adult carers, photographs, drawing and other documents, which may be pasted into the pages.[3] A typical entry might be around 'first day at school' or 'when you first met your new foster parents' or 'your favourite pet'. The book is written for the child – both as they are now and as the person they will become – in such a way that they will be able to have access to past families, events and possessions. Given the complexities and changing circumstances of the lives of children who enter into the adoption process, which can involve having been taken into protective custody by local social services, these details of their early lives might otherwise be easily forgotten. The life-story book is a way of preserving the personal history of the child, so that they are able to build a story of their life, both now and in the future.

The life-story book is a vivid example of a more general work that adoptive parents do in relation to their children. They are responsible for the vicarious management of children's memories. The term 'vicarious memories' comes from the work of Marianne Hirsch on the transmission of the memories of Holocaust survivors and Jewish European refugees within their families.[4] She notes that children in these families feel both a responsibility towards the preservation of their parents' memories and also a sense of ownership, because hearing these stories of the past being told is such a vivid part of their own childhood memories. Hence, others' memories may be 'vicariously' one's own. However, vicarious memories may also be troubling, as there may be a tension between the work of sharing and preserving the stories and what they come to mean for the successive generation who feels obligated to hold on to them. This is most piquantly demonstrated in a beautiful essay written by Hirsch with Leo Spitzer, where they describe taking Hirsch's elderly parents (Lotte and Carl) back to the Czernowitz ghetto that they escaped in 1941:

> For Lotte and Carl – the first generation – the crossroads [at Czernowitz] is a site of nostalgic return because it confirms their good fortune while highlighting their decisiveness and agency. It grounds the enabling moment that set a direction for their subsequent lives in a physical space . . . And for us, in the postmemorial generation, this crossroad is – paradoxically an index for our ambivalent and rootless nostalgia. It is less location than transitional space where the encounter between generations, between past and present, between nostalgic and traumatic memory, can momentarily, effervescently be staged.[5]

The return to Czernowitz serves as something of an affirmation of agency for Lotte and Carl, but proves to be strangely unsettling for Marianne and Leo, because they find it difficult to absorb this place into their current life-space (a problem that is intensified when some of the geographical features of the ghetto raise questions about certain aspects of the story of Lotte and Carl's escape).[6]

For adoptive parents, the situation is reversed – they are the ones charged with preserving the history of the child – but the problems and possible sources of ambivalence remain broadly similar. Parents are faced with considerations about what to include and what not to include in the life-story book. They must confront both present and future concerns about their child's ability to cope with some difficult materials. What can they deal with hearing right now about their biological parents? What might they want to know in the future? How can that be phrased appropriately, so that the child can understand it now and then? In the absence of much by way of formal guidelines, adoptive parents develop practical strategies to manage their child's past. This can involve placing and displacing particular toys from previous families at certain times, editing photographs where deemed necessary, and managing the presentation of factual materials, including case-report information, that might contain difficult details about neglect and abuse.

This process of managing adoptive children's memories is complex in that it requires parents to make judgements about what children can and should know about their past, as well as encouraging their child to forget certain aspects, at least for the present time. This involves a delicate and ethically motivated arrangement of the family life-space, such that the space is marked out so as to provide the possibility for positive actions between family members (including future actions). As we will see, sometimes, engineering affordances that are intended to support a positive life story for the child can come at a cost to adoptive parents. They may be forced to engage with aspects of the child's past that they find emotionally difficult, or that they see as threatening the stability of the family as a whole. Adoptive parents also live with the ongoing ethical concerns that their child may hold them accountable, either now or in the future, for either withholding information or for the particular way they chose to manage family memories.

We approach the adoptive family as an assembly of spatial and temporal relations that is in flux. Processes of remembering and forgetting fold children's memories into the life-space of the family, but, in doing so, they open the family up to other relations and forces – such as biological parents, episodes of abuse or violence, felt life trajectories – that can serve to destabilise family relations. It is useful, perhaps, to think of this folding of life-space using Peter Sloterdijk's image of a 'bubble'.[7] We can think of an adoptive family as an enclosed sphere of intimacy and belonging, where adoptive children are constructed as having legitimate participation in the family, all of whose members share in a notion of a joint future. One tendency is to narrow the 'bubble' to constitute a place of love, safety and belonging. However, accomplishing the incorporation of the adoptive child involves an apposing tendency to widen or dilate to include other relations that may be important to adoptive children, such as with former carers, biological parents or perhaps entire cultural or ethnic lineages, either real or imagined. Blood, love and memory intertwine in opening out the family to other forces and relations.

Sometimes, this can prove unsustainable altogether, the enclosure dissipates, and relations come apart. The tendency towards producing the family as an enclosed sphere of intimacy and belonging is then opposed by the tendencies towards over-expansion and dissipation. Our question then becomes that of the role that practices of remembering and forgetting play in condensing relations into the 'bubble' of the family.

Folding the life-space of the child

Photographs have a central place in the constitution of life stories.[8] Arranging photographs, whether in albums, on social media or in physical displays, is an activity that is traditionally associated with reminiscence and story-telling. It can also serve as a means for adults to scaffold the memories of children, through practices of making inferences about what can be 'read' from photographic images ('You look happy there', 'That was a nice day wasn't it?', 'Do you remember when we saw that horse?').[9] As Robyn Fivush notes, this kind of informal tutelage tends to begin very early in childhood and is a critical resource in the development of autobiographical memories.[10] Hence, many adoptive parents choose to place photographs throughout the life-story books they maintain for their children.

However, there is a difficulty to be negotiated within this practice. Although adoptive parents typically have a great many photographs that have been taken post-adoption, there are often few photographs available from before adoption. If photographs do exist, they are likely to have come from former carers. This can create a fear on the part of adoptive parents that the child might still be overly attached to these former carers and, therefore, reticent to fully commit to their new family. Other photographs may have been taken for official purposes, such as in the course of assessment by social services or the police, and may show children in states that are all too easily readable as neglect, or worse. As we discussed earlier in the example of the Baby P video, these kinds of images offer propositions that are difficult to entertain and emotionally unsettling. In both cases, adoptive parents are placed in the position of being torn between the desire to preserve for the child the past that was legible in the photographs, and the corresponding need to manage and 'tame' that past within a narrative and practice of building a 'new home'.

Harder still are cases where photographs simply did not exist, leading some parents to specially construct new images to assist in filling in the gaps, sometimes at the behest of the child. For example, one participant in our

112   Managing the memories of others

research described how she and her partner had posed for a photograph outside the hospital where their adoptive child had been born, holding a baby doll. Their child was perfectly aware of the artificial nature of this specially constructed (and factually impossible) image, but nevertheless wanted something to fill in the initial pages of their life-story book. This gap filling is explicable in relation to the range of institutional practices that set up certain narratives about what it means to be a 'normal family'. For example, many of the parents complained bitterly about their children being asked to bring baby photos into school. This is a standard practice in many UK schools and is typically done with 'early years' children as part of lessons about personal development and family relationships in the National Curriculum. Not having these photographs, or having to supply an additional explanation alongside whatever photographs do exist, sets children apart as being different from their peers:

> Extract 5.1
> C: (Inaudible) that day when we go to school and we have to bring in pictures of them when they are a baby
> A: Oh you've done that haven't you?
> B: (Inaudible) It's the system (inaudible)

Anxiety is shown by the use of phrase 'that day' to describe an event that is anticipated and dreaded. The comment by B that 'It's the system' may be heard as a formulation that constitutes a degree of powerlessness on the part of an adoptive parent whose child is not part of the accepted norm, and also serves to ward off the potential implications in A's comment 'Oh you've done that haven't you' that B is conforming to this explicit norm by agreeing to send the photographs into school. Baby photographs are clearly a difficult issue for adoptive parents to manage, as they make the adoptive family visible and unusual against a normative expectation of continuity in child development, as represented in the preservation of a continuous visual record.

Adoptive parents have what appears an immediate pragmatic problem – how to provide a visual record of the early years of their child's life. However, what is really at stake here is the expectation of continuity of development coupled with continuity of care. Assuming that a continuous visual record exists also assumes that: (a) current carers/parents have been involved in these early years and can document this; (b) there is a coherent narrative of child development that can be evidenced visually; and (c) the child is both capable of and comfortable discussing her or his identity with reference to a narrative of continuity, which the child is invited to construct around the baby photographs. However, both adoptive children and parents not only may not have access to such a narrative but also may have good reasons not to tell it. The problem then, is not simply the lack of photographs, but rather a difficulty with the sort of narrative that children are encouraged to tell around such images.

It is within this context that we can understand the importance adopters place on having photographs from their child's pre-adoption past, as shown in the following extracts:

Extract 5.2

A: We don't have photos of the parents.

B: We do now. They seem very, sort of not great photos but then one of those files is lost and unavailable.

A: Yeah yeah (laughter) um. So she was there for 6 months and so yeah there were these few photographs and there is (pause) somehow we got hold of one photograph of a contact session between the parents and the girls so there's a photograph of both of the parents and there's a couple of other photographs of the birth mother, aren't there?

W: Well, we've got, we've actually got a lot of photographic evidence of you know from 5 months on haven't we?

In the first part of the extract, A and B, who are partners, discuss the relative absence of photographs they have of their adopted daughter. They have managed to acquire more photographs over time, although the use of the phrase 'somehow we got hold of' suggests that this was accomplished through an informal rather than formal process. Although they now possess the photographs, these are considered to be 'sort of not great photos', because what they depict were scenes that occurred during institutional 'contact sessions', after the child had been separated from her birth parents. The staged nature of this interaction means that the resulting photographs look very different from the kinds of incidentally taken snapshot that populate many family albums. W's contribution at the end – that her family has 'a lot of photographic evidence' – is interesting, because it sums up the work that many of these pre-adoption photographs are required to do. If children enter the adoption process at a young age (as is the case with the children discussed above), then any photographs that do exist depict birth parents and other adults about whom the children actually remember very little, if indeed anything at all. However, as the child grows, the photographs can act as devices ('evidence') around which inferences can be made about the child's past and subsequent development.[11] They can act as a means for parents to help the adopted child fold their past into the life-space of the family by jointly creating plausible narratives of the child's life journey. To be able to see oneself as a child with a birth parent is to be able to imaginatively construct both what one was and what one will become – 'I have her eyes', 'She smiled a lot', 'She loved me but she wanted me to have a better life'.

In Extract 5.2, the problem parents face is dealing with gaps and absences in the past of their adopted children and anticipating the difficulties this might cause the child in the future, if they are not able to construct a story about their origins (hence the effort A and B invested in securing photographs of their daughter). However, there can also be difficulties with managing a past that is, in some sense, 'unwanted', that is to say, with a *lack* of gaps. For example, one parent described a situation where she received letters intended for her son, sent from his birth mother:

Extract 5.3

C: I've never hidden anything from my adopted children and, but it was quite difficult because um, I mean, those letters would come, we were still in contact with the social worker. The social workers would come with these letters from her, but we needed to explain to him that this is, this is not true and that this is symptomatic of the reason why he's with you, not a reason why he should not be with you.

C reports the difficult decision here to share the letters with her adopted son on the grounds of 'not hiding anything', despite what she feels are the potential risks. She states that she has been forced to tell her son that she believes the claims in the letters to be 'not true' and has gone further by pointing to the letters as evidence of why her son is better off in his adoptive family than with his birth mother. This is clearly a high-risk strategy, as it places the child in the position of having to choose which of these two adults (the birth mother and the adoptive mother) he ought to believe. However, for C, this difficult situation is preferable to that of not passing on the letters, which might result in her son accusing her, at some later date, of having withheld important information. C chooses to jointly confront the past with her son, rather than attempt to shield him from it. However, C appears to make a very different choice in relation to her adopted daughter U:

Extract 5.4

C: Yeah, um, so we, that was that. With, with U nobody really had anything. She, she came with two or three photos, for T they managed actually to get quite a few photos and things. With U, um, U's birth parents were chronic alcoholics and they hadn't, they actually didn't exist, the photos didn't exist. We have a couple of, because she was in quite a poor way, the photos are not very nice and I don't show them to her because a, a couple of photos of her as a baby but does look in a poor way and it's not something I want her to have to see, um, but there were photos of X hospital where she was born and um, her foster carers took a picture on the day she came and there's, there's that sort of stuff but it isn't really a life history book.

In this extract, C compares the pre-adoption photographs she currently possesses of her son T and her daughter U. Although there are 'quite a few photos' of T, unfortunately 'nobody really had anything' for U. The reason given for this absence is that U's birth parents had an extremely unstable lifestyle, and, it is assumed, they had either not taken any photographs of their daughter, or the photographs had been lost before the baby had been removed from the family by social services. There are, in fact, 'a couple' of photographs, but these were taken by social workers during the process of U being taken into care. They show U in a state of physical poor health, which is presumably due to neglect and poor domestic circumstances. In contrast to the way she has managed the letters arriving from T's birth parents, here C has decided not to show U these images, despite them being one of the only remaining material links to her very early years.

Why are these photographs handled in a different way from the letters, especially given C's espoused commitment to 'never hiding anything' from her adopted children? There may, of course, be a range of very specific reasons to do with C's relationships with these two adopted children, but we can nevertheless make some observations. The text of a letter serves as an account – it typically consists of a mixture of descriptions of events, claims, attributions of intentionality, promises, etc. As such, it offers numerous points around which interpretations and counter-arguments can be explicitly mobilised, in just the way that C herself describes: 'we needed to explain to him that this, this is not true'. However, a photograph does not offer these rhetorical points of engagement; it is interpretively rich in other ways.

Photographic images can be read in terms of the cultural and historical details they contain, or with references to the context and framing of how the image was taken. However, as critics such as Roland Barthes and Susan Sontag have observed,[12] photographs also have a kind of immediacy, a sense of a displaced moment in time that draws us into a brief co-presence with the subject in the images, often concentrated in a striking detail that 'bites' at the viewer, which arouses our interest or pity.[13] Having been 'bitten' by the detail, we want to expand upon what we can see, to fill in the details and back story that would enable us to make sense of, or perhaps in some way 'tame', the power that the detail has over our attention. This is similar to the way that Whitehead describes 'propositions' – conceptual affordances that we are lured into thinking through our engagement with particular material arrangements.

If this is so, then these photographs of baby U looking 'in a poor way' contain details that 'bite at' or 'lure' the viewer into the proposition that 'this child is a victim of neglect'. They further invite the viewer to expand on these details and imaginatively fill in the gaps about the kinds of distressing event that must have led to this image being taken. C's problem is, we venture, with precisely this process. She is extremely wary of how U might read the image as clear evidence of neglect and go on to expand those details into a narrative of tragedy, which would ultimately be unhelpful because it might encourage her to ground her account of the direction of her life in the space outside the adoptive family. These are images – and a past – that need to be tamed, because they are profoundly disruptive of the story of care and accomplishment that C wants her daughter to share in (hence the deliberately downgraded claim 'the photos are not very nice', which manages the unpleasantness of the images in a discourse of polite approbation). We encountered similar examples in the research where adoptive parents described how adopted children came to believe that their very early experiences with birth parents had destined them to a life of misfortune or criminality, owing to their 'bad blood'.[14]

Adoptive parents are also wary of how children might invest in pre-adoption images and be tempted to construct idealised narratives of their early lives. The following extract describes the power and fascination of photographs for some of the adopted children and the role they play in enabling the past to intrude into the present:

Extract 5.5

E: We were going up to visit the foster family and I realised that we hadn't talked about them for a little while, and you know, the tomes of photographs were gathering dust on the shelf, so I got out um, (. . .) one of each of the members of the family holding a baby (inaudible) um, you know on the back of the you know photograph and on the other side there were scenes from our very recent album, family members, people that are important to us (. . .) X (the speaker's partner) got really disconcerted by the fact that L just would not you know, move, move away from this. She wouldn't look at the stuff about us (inaudible) she was just like you know, fascinated by these people in the pictures and I said we'll just go with the flow, don't worry about it and so it was kind of on the wall for a while, you know the foster family's grinning out at us. I think X found this, you know quite irksome.

B: It can be slightly galling sometimes (laughter).

E: Yeah, yeah. Um, but I just said, look, you know it, it's important that if we go up to see them for a meal that she has them, so we've loads of stuff generally and actually as soon as we'd been there to visit them (. . .) she hasn't taken any notice of them since then um, and I, you know, I kind of like feel, again try with them, give it a stab.

W: Absolutely.

C: And then it kind of comes down again, because I went home the other day and found this giant A4 blown colour picture of her being held by the foster carer and I said, 'Oh where's that come from?' My partner had got it off the computer and blown it up, at, kind of at request, such is technology. Yes, yeah this picture was quietly sitting above her bed. Umm.

Here, the child – L – is described as being fascinated by the people of her past, who look out at her and the family from the wall, literally marking the space with their presence. The flow of family life-space becomes disrupted by these 'spectral' presences from the past that intrude into the present. The photographs act as extensions of past relations, creating their own significant tributaries that cause a disturbance in the downstream flow of the current adoptive family, through the child's fixation. The people staring out from the photos are an unwanted presence for the adoptive parents (as suggested by the terms 'grinning out at us' and 'irksome'). Although they are unable to make any direct claim on the present, as E notes in her account of the outcome of previous visits to the foster parents ('she hasn't taken any notice of them since'), they nonetheless appear to act from a distance via the photographs. This is particularly acute in the comments at the end made by C, who describes arriving home to discover a large photograph of a former foster parent having been placed, like a sacred relic or poster of a pop star, above her adopted daughter's bed.

The institutional practices of social work (in the form of the life-story book) and education (through the National Curriculum) require parents and children to use photographs and other visual objects to construct stories of normative trajectories of development. The life-space of the adoptive family needs to fold in either direct or mediated relationships to former carers and, where possible, birth parents. What this means, in practice, is that parents become the trustees of vital memories for their adopted children. These can take the form of either memories of early years that have been subsequently scaffolded by the use of photographs, or materials that might enable the child to vicariously reconstruct their past at a later date. It then falls to parents to make extremely difficult and emotional decisions about the best way to manage this responsibility, in terms of both their adopted child's long-term well-being and the current needs and demands of the family as a whole.

Spectral objects

Photographs are not the only material links that adoptive children bring with them to their new families. Many children have a small number of possessions – primarily clothes and toys – that they have acquired during their time with birth parents and foster parents. Clearly, these objects have considerable significance for the relationship between adoptive parents and their children, and yet they also appear to be ambiguous, difficult. Parents described some objects in disparaging terms, detailing their efforts at hiding them while feeling unable to actually get rid of them. How best to understand this complex set of meanings? What is the power these objects have over parents?

Over the course of a life, each of us typically accumulates a sizeable number of possessions. Some objects 'travel with us', becoming important markers of identity – a much loved and repaired jacket, a souvenir from a fondly remembered holiday, a small piece of jewellery that once belonged to a relative. These objects may be tied to particular periods of our life and can thus serve as the means through which the past can be recalled and put to work in the present. Alan Radley, for instance, describes how the act of rediscovering some forgotten and misplaced object can surface contrasts between past and present – 'a silver lighter from one's smoking days, a cribbage board from times when the family came round to play cards'.[15] This is particularly acute in circumstances where the contrast is between a desired past that is irrevocably foreclosed and a present that is dissatisfactory or found wanting, such as in Edward Said's description of the importance of objects as markers of a lost homeland in Palestinian homes.[16] The value of such objects lies in their ability to make that past present. Hence, when elderly people, faced with the move from independent to sheltered accommodation, are asked to give up or 'clear' a significant number of their possessions, this is experienced as a threat to memory, to the ability to narrate one's past.[17]

Recent scholarship on materiality and objects has grappled at length with the problem of the relationship between the symbolic and the material that is at work in cases such as those above: are objects a surface of the world upon which we project our own thoughts, or do they contribute to shaping the way we think and act?[18] Psychologists have typically taken the first view and seen objects as 'cues' or 'stimuli' to cognitive processes.[19] The infamous 'madeleine' cake consumed by the narrator of Proust's *In Search of Lost Time*, for example, can be treated as a 'trigger' that activates the recollection of the dense network of autobiographical memories that are recounted in the book.[20] However, as Middleton and Brown argue, this treatment renders the process rather mysterious – why did this specific object trigger the memories at this particular time? The answer surely has to be with the entangling of relationships around the object over time (as we saw with the relationships between the elderly people and the 'sack apron' in Chapter 2). If arrangements of people and things involve a translation of properties, then the reappearance of an object at a later date brings those relationships along with it.

Relationships to previous carers seem to inhere in the very materiality of the objects that adoptive children bring with them. As Steven Connor notes, some objects appear 'invested with powers, associations, and significances' that render them as 'not just docile things, but signs, showings, epiphanies'.[21] He coins the term 'magical objects' to refer to the affordances of such objects, and in particular to the appearance of unexpected possibilities for their use. In the last chapter, we similarly considered the material affordances of mundane and domestic objects, such as walls, doors, keys, wardrobes. However, whereas Connor suggests that the affordances of 'magical objects' are intrinsic to their material propensities, we have argued that the possibilities for action that objects afford depends upon the way they mark out life-space. The chest of drawers, for example, became a monster for Theresa because of the specific way it became entangled in the relationship with her abusive father.

We will use a slightly different term – 'spectral objects' – to refer to the relationship between objects and the vital memories of adoptive children. As we will see, the material propensities of the objects – the way they look and feel, what can be done to them and with them – are important because they become invariant markers of relationships and events in the past. Equally important, however, are the propositions, or conceptual affordances, that the objects lure parents and children into thinking. It is the interplay between material and conceptual affordances in marking out life-space that is of central importance. This interplay projects a sense of 'unfinished business' that can be experienced as threatening and requiring ongoing management. Spectral objects point the way to a difficult past, but do so in a way that renders that past as something that cannot be simply erased without considerable cost.

Our choice of the word 'spectral' arises directly from the way this term sometimes appeared in the talk of adoptive parents:

Extract 5.6

B: There was a great deal of fear about the father within social services and that permeated through all of the file and through all of the, um all of the discussions we had with social workers throughout there was this great spectre um and, and he remained a spectre didn't he I think until we got a letter from him.

Biological parents and former carers are clearly important figures in any account of the life of an adopted child. Yet they can also give rise to tremendous anxieties about how this early life can reappear in the present. This is particularly so when these figures are not directly present, but are experienced at a remove – such as through case-file details in the example above and in the traces of them that appear to be woven into the objects we will go on to discuss. Spectral objects, then, appear to have a kind of agency of their own that arises in part because of the residue of absent or phantom subjectivity left upon them by the actions or choices of former carers or birth parents. It is the displacement of the object from a past life and the precarious way in which they have survived to accompany the child that gives them their unsettling holding power. To dispose of such an object is to choose to break that fragile link to the child's past, however difficult it might have been.

In one of the very earliest discussions of collective memory, Maurice Halbwachs clearly articulated the role of object as markers of the shifting boundary between past and present within a community of rememberers.[22] If we consider the family as a particular instance of such a community, then our attention rapidly falls to the diverse range of memorabilia that adorns a typical family home, from treasured objects that have passed between generations to souvenirs of travel or important events and 'prized possessions'. The generic term 'stuff' seems best to capture the heterogeneity of these objects and the way in which they seem to point out constitutive relationships of ownership and experience – 'this is our stuff', 'she still has a lot of her stuff here', 'going through all that old stuff really reminded me of how things used to be'.

Adopted children move into a space that is already populated with objects that speak to a particular past. Entering this space means both a break with the past and incorporation into a new present. The delicacy of this transition can be handled in part by exchanging the properties of the child with the 'stuff' that they are travelling with. In the following example, C describes how contact with former carers during this transitional period was assisted by the movement of objects:

Extract 5.7

C: And that was really helpful. Um, because they were fostering other children and she went there and the bed that <u>had</u> been her bed was now somebody else's bed, somebody else's posters were on the wall and it, it really clicked with her that all <u>her</u> stuff was now at <u>ours</u> and, and that was it, you know, that, that, that was completed and the reason that she'd been there was as they had said, that she was waiting for a permanent family and um, that had happened.

Visiting her former home, the child sees that the space that defined relations of care has now been reshaped. What was her bed now belongs to someone else. Or, more properly speaking, the bed that she had thought was hers is now revealed as belonging to no one in particular, as a marker of a transitional space that is temporarily occupied by a string of fostered children in turn. What is permanent is 'her stuff', the objects that she has accrued in her life to date and that travel with her. They are now in place in the new family home and mark out life-space, such that they embody permanency. The sense of this home having stood there waiting to receive the adoptive child is communicated by the physical organisation of the home space as being receptive to the depositing of the child's 'stuff'. The space thus acts to provide the possibility of permanency.

This sense of the 'destining' of the child to be with the adopting family – the 'completion' of the transition to the 'permanent family' – is not straightforward. Permanent placements can break down through the rejection of the arrangement by the child, adoptive parents or other parties. Here again, 'stuff' can be referred to as the material token in which this complex affective atmosphere is registered. In the extract below, C describes another adoptive child who oriented to the placement process in a different way:

Extract 5.8

C: Um, and he, he was then told the judge has <u>ordered</u> him (laughs) to be, placed with us and he, he again got this image you know, that sort of out of the blue, um, he was picked up and carried off and he always sold his stuff and, and he, he stayed overnight with people on the streets without clothes, staying out all night. He always felt he needed to break free from us, because he feels we took him and imprisoned him.

The child here treats the boundaries between past and present as one reflecting the subordination of his own agency to the formal will of the law – a judge legally bound him to a future that was not of his choosing, and he was transported, much like a commodity, to a new home where he was 'imprisoned'. Interestingly, his rebellion against this supposed commodification takes the form of divesting himself of all the things that travelled with him and that he subsequently accrued in the new family setting – 'he always sold his stuff' and 'stayed overnight with people on the streets without clothes'. It is as though it is the stuff itself that holds him to the adoptive family, and, conversely, from the perspective of the adoptive parent, that it is stuff that expresses the relations of care that the child has rejected.

In the previous two examples, 'stuff' was comparatively undefined, referring to the heterogeneous array of materials that travel with the child. Although stuff is invested with a kind of spectrality – a residue of the past in the present that makes this boundary an ongoing concern – the particular things that we would characterise as spectral objects have more ambiguous and complex qualities. They have ambiguous qualities in the sense that they constitute a solid link with the past and must then at all costs be preserved, and never forgotten. In the following example, two adoptive parents discuss an episode in which a particular soft toy – Pooh Bear – is mislaid:

Extract 5.9

W: F has got a Pooh Bear

B: That she got from the foster parents

W: That she got from the foster parents, that is a true transitional object that we nearly lost in the woods once.

B: And we both nearly killed ourselves when we crossed the road searching for him.

W: Pooh's jumper . . .

B: She's asleep in the buggy

W: <u>Oh it's Pooh Bear, my god!</u> Ohhh

B: We found him, on the side of the road, just, life would not have been worth living . . .

It is worth pointing out that the parents here use the psychoanalytic language of 'transitional object' to refer to the toy.[23] However, this does not entirely capture the emotion that is generated around the possible loss of Pooh Bear. The child mentioned is an infant, one small enough to still need to be pushed in a buggy, and therefore one who might presumably have very little by way of memories of her life before adoption. Although it might be unfortunate to lose Pooh Bear, over time it might be replaced with other objects that become more important as durable markers of caring relations. However, this particular toy is not simply transitional. It is a link to a past – to the former foster parents – that is constitutive of the present. To have this object forgotten is thus considered entirely unthinkable.

Although this may now be the permanent home for the child, it cannot be formed on the basis of a rejection of everything that came before without the risk that, at some point in the future, this child may place importance on this early period. The past must then be accessible, it must be given a place within the adoptive family such that the family does not seal itself off in a way that would make a desire to connect with the past impossible to address. Pooh Bear is not a symbol of the past – it is that past made manifest in the material form of the toy, whose safekeeping is simultaneously the preservation of a conduit to an early past in the ongoing work of making the present of the permanent family.

The stakes involved in such safekeeping become considerably heightened when the past that is marked out by the spectral object is problematic. In the next extract, the parent F talks of a toy whose material state threatens to make a particular version of the past inescapable:

Extract 5.10
F: R, at three, she came with a tiny little white, like Snoopy Dog and that was from, that was from birth mother era and that has a cigarette burn on it, the same as she has a cigarette burn, she has, um, and then she paid no attention to it whatsoever. You know, they accumulate so many toys and things. I've always kept that in her room but it's hidden at the back of the pile.

The Snoopy Dog described here has been burned with a cigarette, which F compares directly to a similar injury inflicted on the child during the 'birth mother era'. In memorial terms, the past is unfolded from the burn mark. To examine the damaged toy is to be drawn immediately to the burning hot tip of the cigarette that inflicted the mark, the hands that held that cigarette, the action itself (intentional? incidental? a moment of fury? regretted? or enjoyed?). A whole set of deeply troubling worlds seem to spring from or grow out of the burn mark, in a way akin to the unfolding origami image that Proust offers in the famous madeleine example, or the worlding of the peasant's labour that Heidegger articulates in his analysis of Van Gogh's *A Pair of Shoes*.[24] And, if F can do this work, what is implied here is that the child might themselves also do the same work at some point in the future. So, why not simply throw away Snoopy Dog? Why not literally forget that it ever existed? Surely this will prevent any future distress caused by this knowledge of past abuses and allow the child to continue forward, enfolded within the loving life-space of the present family.

However, it is not that simple: like Pooh Bear, Snoopy Dog is a surviving link to the past, one that almost triumphantly survived the precarious transition from a problematic early life to the projected settlement of the present. To get rid of the toy is to break that link. If Snoopy Dog has survived the horrors that led to the cigarette burning, then so too will the child. That proposition needs to be preserved. However, Snoopy Dog must nevertheless stand waiting to do that – for now at least – from the relative solitude of being 'hidden at the back of the pile'. In other words, being literally at the bottom of the pile, in the material space of the family home, affords a temporary suspension of the past — a provisional forgetting that enables the child to feel the secure relations of their present, without being blighted by their past. Of course, parents acknowledge that this provisional forgetting cannot last indefinitely, as they anticipate a future where questions will be raised. Active forgetting in the present thus becomes steered by the ongoing flow of experience and the anticipated demands that are lurking downstream, in the future.

Spectral objects point a way to versions of the past that make manifest a range of figures and actions that are either already significant for the child or may yet come to matter. This work of attending to the boundary between past and present in which adoptive parents engage has its corollary in the concern to anticipate the future needs of the child. In our material, adoptive parents routinely describe their anxieties about how adopted children make sense of their past in relation to anticipated futures as they grow. For example, a child may report having witnessed acts of violence that they come to believe will inevitably recur in their adult life. Whether or not these memories are 'actual' in the strict sense matters less than the power of these images to indicate to the child and to adoptive parents the possible life trajectories that the child will live out.

In the following long example, we see how a particular piece of clothing is fraught with significance for these anticipated trajectories. Beginning with a mention of a play costume owned by her daughter, C articulates how the costume poses the risk of opening up a discussion of a particularly dramatic episode from her daughter's early life, when her birth mother accidentally started a fire in her home:

Extract 5.11

C: My daughter's obsessed with fire and um, we don't talk, we don't um, she's actually got a fireman's costume, a firefighter's costume, a firefighter's kit you know, age appropriate children's things but I don't talk about fires and there was, you now the New Town fire.[25] Of course we haven't mentioned it, haven't shown her pictures but, um, today she was out visiting a friend who has a younger child and doesn't realize how big ears she's got and talking about, you know, those explosions there and the sky so she's heard about it and we . . . and then um M had promised to show her a newspaper picture because she's obsessed with it it. She just . . .

B: Amazing what they take in, isn't it you know?

A: Its amazing . . . when she's three

126   Managing the memories of others

C: Yeah

W: It's quite unsettling

C: Oh, but also you sort of think its alright because there's this huge picture of like, like a mushroom and there's three um firefighters in the picture and the main interest was one didn't have his hat on! (Laughter) You have to think, you know

A: You're building this up, yeah

C: Well, it's like, well it's like, you know what do I do when she's, you know, talking to her about this, this sort of thing about what her mum did you know, I suppose it's quite hard to talk to her without having an example apart from the drugs, having pictures and things like that, you know that sort of thing, other sorts of scenarios but um, she will hear about that because siblings, you know will, will tell her. Anytime really, but anytime and it is so, and I know that I'm doing it myself, I'm sort of visualizing it and I know I have to talk it down, the fact that she wasn't an arsonist she had started a fire by mistake, you know, um it was the fact that she went much longer into distress, you know but the flat got burned down and the fact was she went to prison because of it and had a long sentence, so that's unfortunate but you have to sort of try to work out.

The firefighter's costume is a thoroughly ambiguous object. C reports that her daughter is 'obsessed with fire'. The costume is then, on the one hand, an 'age-appropriate' way of entertaining the child's interests. It is, we might say, a way of normalising these interests, of framing them as innocent childish concerns with the dangers of the adult world, in the same way that other children might be bought doctors' or soldiers' play outfits. However, what C is aware of is that this obsession has roots in an actual episode from her daughter's early years that the child is apparently unaware of. There is a secret – her birth mother's role in a fire – that will be revealed at some point, most likely by siblings. C has apparently spent some considerable time imagining or 'visualising' how this story will be framed, the kinds of image and resource that she will need to draw upon to do so. The firefighter costume then stands as the centre of a future effort to recapitulate a past that is continuously reiterated by the child's current obsession with fire.

It is the future revelation of this shared secret that is written into the costume. To refuse to allow her daughter to engage with her obsession would be for

C to stand accountable at some later date of having misdirected her daughter, of having deliberately steered her away from getting on to the path that would eventually lead her to a confrontation with this particular aspect of her past and her relationship to her birth mother. Allowing her to have the costume gives C the resource of being able to present herself as having merely delayed, rather than dismissed, the possibility of this confrontation. And, indeed, this choice appears to have worked to the extent that the daughter's interest in images of fire seems to be age-appropriately skewed (e.g. whether hats are being worn properly by firefighters, rather than on the consequences). The costume is, then, something akin to Poe's famous 'purloined letter', discussed by both Lacan and Derrida.[26] It is a secret or mystery whose quality is both intensified and managed on account of its being hidden in plain sight, a proposition that is encoded in a steganographic fashion. To stretch a metaphor, we might say that this future confrontation with the past is hidden in the folds of the costume, waiting to be unfolded and opened up at any point.

As spectral objects, what the firefighter costume and soft toys afford is a means for adoptive parents to anticipate a range of future life trajectories for their child. Some trajectories are the desired outcomes that follow from the child's integration in the new family. Other, less desirable trajectories are those where the child seems fated to return to the circumstances and kinds of life experience that dominated their early years. Spectral objects play an ambiguous role. On the one hand, they are a visible link to a difficult past, a material means by which that past continues to exert an influence over the present that threatens the effort to sustain a stable life trajectory for the child. On the other hand, they represent one of the few means by which an emotional link to the past can be sustained for the child, and by which she or he might, at some future date, be able to reflect upon and place that past in the context of their subsequent life. The spectral object is a threat and a promise, an affectively charged medium through which the past continues to act, and the means by which it might be tamed.

Telling the truth

We have attempted to show how parents manage the ongoing sets of dilemmas and ambiguities produced by the links between their child's past, present and future. Viewed from the perspective of a temporal flow, we can see this work as anticipating and working with the tributaries and distributaries of experience. Parents engage with the material and conceptual affordances of the images and

128 Managing the memories of others

objects that adoptive children bring with them. This may lead to literally displacing these material links, for the time being, in order to ensure that the life-space of the child is not marked out by a past that is corrosive of their current family situation. But how far should this 'managed accessibility' of the past be taken? Consider the following extract. Here, E describes a strategy that she has adopted to make up for comparative gaps in the life-story books of their two adopted children, V and W:

Extract 5.12

E: Yeah, um, our, our two were, V was 6 so he had quite a lot of history that he remembered (inaudible) although not always particularly nice stories about birth mum and um, when, they'd spent 18 months at, they'd been through a few placements, but they spent the last 18 months with foster carers who had done a bit of life story work, not, doesn't sound like the same kind of level as, as, as you were er, given, but they'd, they'd, got some photos of things and put some, a line under each to say, say where it was, like in Brighton, and so they both had Life Story Books but only V actually had any photos from, you know pre-foster care, so he had a couple of baby photos, um, which is a shame because (inaudible) W thinking that she missed out, so we tried to fill that gap by writing something in her life story book and I drew a couple of pictures of what she might have been like

In part owing to their ages, V and W have different connections to the past. V has some memories of his birth parents, although, as E points out, these are 'not always particularly nice stories', along with a life-story book that has been partially completed by previous foster parents. W, by contrast, has much less by way of material links, with no baby photographs. To address this absence, E has drawn some pictures of 'what she might have been like', which she has placed in the appropriate part of W's life-story book.

Clearly, these drawings are works of imagination, and yet they have been offered to W as part of the life-story book, which is a central resource for the child to reconstruct their own past. There are traditions within the psychology of memory that are especially concerned with questions of the veracity of recollections and the dangers of suggestibility.[27] Kimberly Wade's work, for example, has sought to demonstrate the power of 'fake' images in creating so-called 'false memories'.[28] From this perspective, creating a permanent record of a child's life that is, in some parts, deliberately invented raises significant ethical questions. Adoptive parents are indeed aware of the risks involved. B, for example, describes how she and her partner, A, have dealt with their adopted daughter's 'pre-occupation' with absent details of her birth parents:

Extract 5.13

B: Y's pre-occupied with, probably for the past year, is what did my birth parents look like and she's very aware that we have all that information for J (. . .) and began to realise that we had none of that information for her. Because we get support from lots of other X (Asian country) adopters we have some stratagems around that. We, we try to extrapolate from what she looks like and we say, 'Well, we don't know', um, but like you, C, we never say anything we're not sure of and we say everything we do know so, we say, 'We're not sure what your parents looked like, but they probably had' and we can go through some of her features, and, and suggest what height they might have been and so on. We show her lots of photos of Q people. Because of A's travels in X, we have a huge, you know, he went 5,000 miles to find her foster mother, we have a huge fund of photos now of people who just look dramatically like her and again it's a real opportunity to enter the fantasy life of an adopted child because we find ourselves just pouring over these photos and over the video tape and thinking, 'Is that her aunt? Is that her mother?' So, you know, there are people that are very like her so we show her those pictures and try to fill the gaps in that way.

Because Y was adopted from another country, no photographs or other records exist of her birth parents. However, after some exhaustive work by A, the family does have some photographs of people from what they estimate to be the same ethnic group as Y. Together, the adoptive parents and child make inferences about what Y might have looked like, based on these photographs. What is interesting here, though, is the way that B reflects on this as 'a real opportunity to enter the fantasy life of an adopted child' and describes how she and her partner have become immersed in the imaginative work of 'gap filling', wondering if any of the people in the images are actually related to Y. We might take this as evidence of the dangers of allowing technically false details into the process of reconstructing the past. Indeed, as Johanna Motzkau observes in her review of the field of suggestibility research, even

130   Managing the memories of others

when knowingly offered, false details tend to contaminate joint efforts at recollecting events.[29] Even those who supposedly know 'what really happened' can become confused. Once let loose, the genie of suggestibility is not easily bottled.

And yet, despite her reflections, what B describes here is a very considered practice, where she and her partner are cautious in the kinds of inference and 'extrapolation' they encourage Y to make, going so far as to admit, 'well we don't know', when faced with a lack of evidence. They have also taken guidance on their 'stratagems' from fellow adopters. What B then does is very different to the kinds of situation and practice that concern psychologists who research false memory. The classic scenario there is the therapist who suggests to clients the possibility of CSA as a means of gap filling and explaining current distress.[30] However, the relationship between therapist and client is comparatively short term (and often directly or indirectly monetised). Adoptive parents are, instead, building what is hoped to be a lifelong relationship with their adopted child. The gap filling that they do is intended to allow the child to construct a version of the past that will increase their present and future powers to act. It is a way of assisting the child in acquiring an otherwise absent past as a means of securing their future well-being, which is done in the context of a long-term commitment. We can see this clearly in the final extract:

Extract 5.14

F: OK for us the foster mother made up the life story books (. . .) when they went to the foster mother they came with nothing so there's no photographs prior um, R was about 2 and a half and S was about 1 and a half and the earliest pictures are with the foster mother and she's put together an absolutely brilliant life story book and it was made for them at their age when they were adopted by us, 2 and 3. So where there's no pictures, no photographs, she's still got that in their history but she's like got a page which is cut out of catalogues, 'these are the sort of toys you would have been playing with', 'the sort of equipment you would have been using' so they've still got something to latch onto. (inaudible) And she's, she's just built up this huge photo album, with this, photographs from (inaudible) photographs from pictures of the things she's drawn herself. She's sort of made it up and she's got a family tree at the beginning and found out a bit more about them (. . .) Lots of detail on absolutely nothing, that's what just so impressed me.

Here, a former foster parent has anticipated the problems that R and S will face as they grow up without adequate material links to their past. The solution that she has adopted is to create a life-story book that mixes existing photographs with specially created images, such as 'picture of things she's drawn herself'. The book mixes together the veridical with the fictive. And yet, F clearly sees the book for what it is: a gift that offers the children a carefully imagined and reconstructed past that will help them to secure the kind of future they deserve.

It is quite right for psychologists to be concerned with issues of truth around memory and how these are shaped in interactions between adults and children. However, in the case of adoption, we see a practice that has evolved among foster and adoptive parents where a subtly different relationship to 'truth' is being very carefully worked out. Where there are past events that are either difficult to remember or will create difficulties when they do eventually become known, or in cases where there is a relative absence of knowledge of the child's early years, strategies of gap filling, inference, extrapolation and even fictional representation may allow children to develop a manageable relationship to their past. Vicariously experienced vital memories can be every bit as important as those grounded in direct experience. For example, in his account of supporting his young son during their period of grieving, following the accidental death of his partner, Desreen, Benjamin Brooks-Dutton describes how he attempted to create vicarious memories of Desreen for his son, so that he might grow up believing that he actually remembered her.[31] This is a practice recommended by the charity for bereaved children, Winston's Wish, that they refer to as 'acquired memories'.[32] Here, the question to ask appears to be, not 'What is exactly true of the past?', but 'How can I present it in such a way so that the child is affectively touched by it in a positive way?'. To give children the possibility of having a past in their present life-space, rather than no connection, seems, under these circumstances, an act that is supportive, rather than detrimental to current and future agency.

Notes

1 Diary of a separation: 'Where have all the trousers gone?', *The Guardian*, Saturday 11 June 2011. Extract reproduced with permission.
2 See Brookfield *et al.* (2008) and Brown *et al.* (2013) for further details.
3 For more details on the practice, consult the very rich resource at www.lifestory works.org/Life_Story_Works/LIFE_STORY_BOOK.html.
4 Hirsch, 1997.
5 Hirsch and Spitzer, 2003: 93.
6 This kind of problem is famously dramatised in *Maus*, Art Spiegelman's graphic novel about his father's memories of Auschwitz (2003). At one point, father and

son dispute the existence of a band of musicians, made up of inmates, playing at the camp. Spiegelman depicts these divergent accounts by drawing the same scene twice, with and without the musicians playing. See the discussion in Young (2000).

7 Sloterdijk, 2011.
8 Hirsch, 1997; Kuhn, 2002; Langford, 2008.
9 See Edwards and Middleton, 1988; Middleton and Brown, 2005.
10 Fivush, 2011.
11 See Middleton and Edwards (1990, chapter 2) on photographs as 'inferential devices' for remembering.
12 See Sontag, 1979; Barthes, 1984.
13 Barthes famously referred to this detail as 'punctum'. This is a detail of the image that interrupts or disturbs the 'educated' cultural interpretation of the photograph, bringing about a sense of a direct relationship to an apparently chance element of the scene or person depicted – 'for *punctum* is also: sting, speck, cut, little hole – and also a case of the dice. A photograph's punctum is that accident which pricks me (but also bruises me, is poignant to me)' (Barthes, 1984: 27).
14 In other words, they felt that they had inherited characteristics from their biological parents that determined the subsequent course of their life, irrespective of their experiences of adoption.
15 Radley, 1990: 51.
16 Said, 1989.
17 Marcoux, 2001.
18 See, for example, edited collections by Miller, 1998; Henare *et al.*, 2007; Candlin and Guins, 2009; Harvey *et al.*, 2013.
19 Schachter, 1996.
20 Proust, 1996.
21 Connor, 2011: 2.
22 Halbwachs, 1950/1980: 128–57.
23 See Bollas, 2008.
24 See Middleton and Brown, 2005: 140.
25 Actual name replaced with pseudonym.
26 Derrida, 1987; Poe, 2003; Lacan, 2007.
27 Loftus, 1994, 2003; Loftus and Ketcham, 1996.
28 Lindsay *et al.*, 2004; Wade *et al.*, 2002.
29 Motzkau, 2009, 2010.
30 Loftus and Ketcham, 1996.
31 Brooks-Dutton, 2014.
32 See www.winstonswish.org.uk.

Chapter 6

Remembering with, through and for others

Surviving the 2005 London bombings

Remembering 7/7

On 7 July 2005, four explosive devices exploded in central London, killing fifty-two people and injuring hundreds of others. The devices were carried in rucksacks on to the London Underground train network by four young British men (Mohammad Sidique Khan, Shehzad Tanweer, Germaine Lindsay and Hasib Hussain). All four were also killed during the blasts. Three of the devices were detonated within a minute of each other, on trains in tunnels between underground stations, at around 8.50 a.m. The fourth was set off an hour later, on a bus in Tavistock Square, by Hussain, who had apparently been forced to change his plans owing to train delays. The bombings had an immediate impact, with rolling 24-hour news images of the scenes being immediately relayed, as the nature of the events gradually emerged over the course of the day.[1] In the following weeks of heightened security and anxiety, there was a second round of bombings on 21 July and the shooting dead of Jean Charles de Menezes by plain-clothes police at Stockwell undergound station, who was misidentified as one of the 21/7 bombers.

The 7/7 bombings were among the worst terrorist incidents in post-war UK. The bombings took place the day after the announcement of the awarding of the Olympic Games to London.[2] They followed the 2004 Madrid train bombings and were widely seen as part of a long-expected 'backlash' for the UK's involvement in the invasion of Iraq in 2003. In the months following the bombings, public debate was centred on the significance of 'home-grown terror', as the bombers were UK citizens (and, with the exception of Lindsay, British born), and the 'radicalisation' of young Muslims. This debate intensified with a government-led push to extend the pre-charge detention period for

134 Remembering with, through and for others

'terror suspects' to 90 days under revised anti-terrorism laws[3] and an increase in the use of 'control orders' restricting the rights and liberties of those suspected of involvement in planning terrorist acts. The 7/7 bombings also came to be key moment in how the international policies of Tony Blair's government were publicly viewed during the period of the so-called 'war on terror' between 2001 and 2008.

The place of the bombings in contemporary British history is now well established, particularly following the public inquest that reported in 2011. It was also clear in the immediate aftermath that 7/7 was an event that required public commemoration. The national flag was flown at half-mast on public buildings on 8 July, a 2-minute silence was observed across Europe on 14 July (repeated on 7 July 2006),[4] and a memorial service was held at St Paul's Cathedral in London on 1 November. In successive years, there have been public events marking the anniversary of the bombings, and a permanent memorial has been installed in Hyde Park.[5] The process of constituting 7/7 into an object of collective memory began very rapidly and continues to this day with the approach of the tenth anniversary.

Commemorations of events that are within 'living memory' (that is to say, the span of three generations that Jan and Aleida Assmann refer to as 'communicative memory'[6]) typically take a different form to those of events that are more remote to contemporary participants. The testimony and experiences of those who witnessed the events commemorated (or of their relatives who pass on the story[7]) are crucial elements in the shaping of the commemorative object. With 7/7, there were numerous survivors of all four bombings who were able to offer accounts of their direct experiences, along with a large number of photographic images, some taken at the scene by survivors using camera phones, others from broadcast media coverage.[8] These accounts and images have been recruited into the narratives of 7/7 and underpin the way it has been commemorated over the past 10 years.

The evolving 'official' narrative of 7/7 framed the bombings as an ideologically motivated attack on the nation, with many newspaper reports explicitly attributing the incident to Al-Qa'eda. This created a narrative coherence with the 9/11 attacks on the US World Trade Centre in 2001 and with the then-recent 2004 Madrid bombings (referred to as 11-M in Spain). Images of injured survivors, most notably John Tulloch and Davinia Douglass, were extensively used to represent the indiscriminate violence of the bombings. In the following days and months, survivors and relatives of the deceased were encouraged to 'tell their stories', which were typically framed as courage in the face of political terror. The most notorious example of this was when an image of a bloodied John Tulloch was placed on the front cover of the tabloid newspaper *The Sun* in November, in an article supporting the call for the 90-day terror suspect detention law, using the strapline 'Tell Tony he's right'. However, as has become clear in the intervening years, the stories that survivors and relatives want to tell about 7/7 do not necessarily support the commemorative narrative of national resilience in the face of political terror. Indeed, in some cases, the stories diverge completely, with John Tulloch taking precisely the opposite stance on anti-terrorism laws to the one his image was used by *The Sun* to support.

For a survivor or relative, to even speak of what they experienced is to find themselves positioned in a field of shifting and sometimes conflicting discourses that accord meaning and significance to the bombings. Even using the term '7/7' may be interpreted as adopting a particular orientation, because of its metonymic connection to 9/11 and 11-M and the overarching theme of the 'war on terror' to which these terms relate. In this sense, those affected do not entirely 'own' their personal recollections of 7/7, as their memories have been recruited, to some degree, by ongoing social and political commemorative work around the events. Take, for example, Esther Hyman, who lost her sister, Miriam Hyman, in the Tavistock Square blast. Esther was extensively involved in the media coverage of the bombings in their immediate aftermath and attended the public memorial services. She subsequently gave evidence at the 2011 public inquest. Along with her family, she established the Miriam Hyman Memorial Fund, which supports a children's eye-care centre in India. Esther participated in the documentary *Love Hate Love*, which sought to narrate her story, along with those of the parents of a victim of 9/11 and a survivor of the 2002 Bali bombings.[9] More recently, she has been involved in developing citizenship education for school children. She has also been forced to engage with the online speculation of 7/7 conspiracy theorists (and so-called '9/11 truthers') who have questioned the established version of events. Small wonder that Esther has described her life as divided into 'before' and 'after' 7/7.[10]

Relatives such as Esther typically feel that they have compelling ethical responsibilities to ensure that the stories and lives of the victims are commemorated and kept alive.[11] In Esther's case, this has involved both tremendous effort and multilevelled sets of public engagement. 'Doing justice' to Miriam's memory, in the sense that Blustein describes it, has required Esther to embed her own recollections of her sister and the bombings in many different media and material forms. Survivors can often feel a similar moral obligation to tell their own story, because it is a part of the narrative mosaic that constitutes the collective memory of 7/7. However, they are also aware of the responsibilities that emerge from the way in which their own personal recollections may intersect with, support and sometimes come into conflict with those of others. As we will see later on, this becomes heightened when survivors feel that their account of the events potentially 'fills the gaps' around what happened for bereaved relatives.

Recollections of the bombings are irreversible vital memories for those who were most closely affected: 7/7 is a bell that cannot be unrung. It divides up the flow of life experiences into two distinct periods, serving as the point that connects the contingent tributaries of experience (who I was, how I came to be there on that day) with subsequent distributaries (what I have become, the direction my life has taken since). As with all the vital memories we have discussed so far, there is interdependency between memories. Survivors and relatives are effectively custodians of one another's recollections. This was seen most clearly at the 2011 public inquest, where an attempt was made to sew together a huge number of individual testimonies into an 'official account' of the events on the day. However, it can argued that, almost from the very first moments when the survivors left the underground tunnels and bus wreckage, their accounts of what had happened were subjected to the force of media and public exposure. We might think of this as a kind of 'torque', where individual recollections are immediately pushed and pulled into the movement of the unfolding story.

The relationship between personal experience and public discourse appears to work in a very particular way here. The life-space of survivors and relatives is shaped by multiple intersecting practices and agendas (e.g. media, law, national security, international relations) that solicit and recruit their testimonies, but over which they have limited control. To conceptualise what this potentially does to the relationship between the personal and public, it is helpful to return to the topological description of life-space. In their discussion of what they term 'psychotopologies', Blum and Secor point to the importance of processes of deforming space:

> Topologically speaking, a space is not defined by the distances between points that characterize it when it is in a fixed state but rather by the characteristics that it maintains in the process of distortion and trans-formation (bending, stretching, squeezing, but not breaking). Topology deals with surfaces and their properties, their boundedness, orientability,

decomposition, and connectivity – that is, sets of properties that retain their relationships under processes of transformation.[12]

The 'bending, stretching and squeezing' that Blum and Secor describe can be equated here with the 'torque' applied to survivors' and relatives' recollections, as they were publicised, framed and remediated in the national (and international) accounts of 7/7. In this way, personal memories of the event become folded together with other elements – John Tulloch's recollections include the way his image was used by *The Sun*; Esther Hyman's efforts to preserve her sister's memory have had to be engaged with the way others have contested the official version.

Rather than thinking of individual memories and public debates as distinct domains, it is helpful instead to think of a continuity in experience that traces an unbroken movement from the personal to the public. The topological figure of a Möbius strip is a helpful device. This can be demonstrated by taking a strip of paper that is twisted and its two ends glued together, to form a continuous surface that can be navigated without the need to distinguish between an 'inside' and an 'outside'. The psychoanalyst Jacques Lacan famously used the Möbius strip as means of disrupting the idea of a fixed interiority to the subject and of theorising how psychic life folds together fantasy and reality.[13] Here, we can think instead of the deformation of life-space so that personal experience becomes folded together with public discourse and mediatisation. The survivor's account of what happened to them in the tunnel becomes 'stretched and squeezed' together with how the bombings were framed and contested in public debates.

In the following sections, we will explore three specific processes through which this deformation occurred: First was the interactional shaping of individual recollections, as survivors and relatives told their stories in the weeks and months after 7/7. The torque that arose through the efforts to place personal accounts in a broader collective understanding of the events resulted in a reconstruction of the significance and meaning of what happened. Second was the use of external mnemonic devices (e.g. photographs, diagrams, personal belongings) that survivors and relatives drew upon to support their recollections. These devices enabled a kind of distributed or extended cognition, through providing the means to co-ordinate accounts, but they also created tensions and possible contradictions. Finally, there were affective connections between bodies and space, where feelings and sensations rooted in the event became the means of folding together spatial and temporal remoteness.

The material that forms the basis for this chapter arises from the study 'Conflicts of memory: Commemorating and mediating the 2005 London Bombings'. The study attempted to explore the link between memories of 7/7 itself and the media framings of the event that unfolded in its aftermath.[14] As part of the study, a series of interviews were conducted with persons who were directly affected by the bombings.[15] Here, we discuss material that comes from three of those interviews, all of which were with survivors of the blasts. Rachel North and Susan Harrison were both travelling on the Piccadilly line train on which Germaine Lindsey detonated his bomb. Rachel became well known for running a blog about her experiences on the BBC website; she also set up the support group Kings Cross United and wrote a book, *Out of the Tunnel*, which described her recovery.[16] Susan overcame losing a leg in the blast to do promotional work for a number of charities. John Tulloch is an academic known for his work on media and politics. On 7/7, he was travelling through London and was seated next to Mohammad Sidique Khan on the Circle line train when the latter triggered his bomb. John has made many media appearances and published a book reflecting on his experiences, *One Day in July*.[17]

Telling your story

The events of 7/7 dominated news coverage in the UK for many of the successive weeks. Survivors were immediately placed in the situation of having to tell 'their story'. Journalists from national newspapers 'doorstepped' the private homes of survivors and relatives, particularly those whose images had been prominently featured in the media, such as Davinia Douglass. Survivors who had suffered lesser physical injuries were very rapidly recruited into the unfolding media coverage of the events. Rachel North, for example, was asked to write a blog for the BBC news website after a journalist saw her posts on a London-based message board (Urban75):

> I did feel incredibly responsible. I was writing the BBC blog in a way that I knew was kind of, erm . . . I was writing stuff that I thought would help people. I was writing the sort of stuff that I wanted to read that would have helped me if I hadn't been me, so I was doing that, I was very much writing for a kind of audience and trying to put out messages about, you know, keep calm, carry on.
>
> (RN)

Here, Rachel describes her blog as an attempt to 'put out messages' that sought to 'help people' by calming the general anxiety, fear and anger that were present across London in the wake of the bombings. She imagined her audience to be fellow Londoners who might themselves have been caught up in the blasts, or who could easily have been. She was, in effect, telling her story for an 'imagined self' – 'I was writing the sort of stuff that I wanted to read that would have helped me if I hadn't been me'. From the very beginning, Rachel's story was not entirely her own. It was a narrative of her experiences that was deliberately and consciously fitted to the task of 'normalising' the extraordinary events of 7/7 and providing a framework that emphasised resilience and a measured response.

The treatment that Susan Harrison received for her severe injuries, and subsequent rehabilitation, kept her away from the media for several weeks following 7/7. She decided, however, to keep a commitment to participate in a charity event – the Oxfam 'Big Run' – that was made before she lost her leg in the bombings. This resulted in an ongoing relationship with several charities, where she made media appearances as a survivor in order to promote the work of the charities. She sought to use her story as a means of supporting charitable work:

> I've always done it for the right reasons, you know, I've always done it, I'm quite tough really and I've always done it for the right reasons and, you know, I don't do sensationalistic stuff, I don't do it for the fame, I don't do it to get my face on the front of a newspaper, I do it so that the charity that I'm getting there gets their website on that bit of paper.
>
> (SH)

The distinction here between telling the story for 'right' and 'wrong' reasons implies that no personal narrative of 7/7 is ever entirely neutral. Susan here rejects motives such as seeking fame or financial reward for her media work (although note that the self-description of 'I'm quite tough really' suggests that she can understand the obvious temptation of such rewards). As she frames it, the 'right reasons' are ones where her telling her experiences is instrumental to the charities she works with 'getting their website on that bit of paper'. Placing her story in the service of charity work in this way does come with some cost. Susan was aware that having a media presence as a survivor would also likely result in her personal life being investigated by tabloid newspapers, in search of a story demonstrating some contradiction between her past life

140 Remembering with, through and for others

and her current charity work: 'So before I did anything I was thinking, have I got any skeletons in my closet, is there anything that I shouldn't, no, OK, I'm fine' (SH).

For survivors, recollecting what happened to them on 7/7 meant becoming part of the media frames that broadcast and print media placed around the event. Within these frames, they were required to offer a story that emphasised their victimhood. Susan's momentary anxiety about possible 'skeletons in my closet' was well founded, as the media logic of 'victimhood' is grounded in a one-dimensional representation of the survivor as being entirely faultless in all their attributes. Any personal details that cannot be subsumed within this simplistic image are taken to undermine the credibility of the victim. In this way, not only did their direct experience of the bombings become part of the story, but their entire life experience was also recruited, in part. Susan describes this, in similar terms to Esther Hyman's, as effectively dividing her past into 'life 1' and 'life 2', with 7/7 acting as the boundary crossing separating one from the other, but stories from 'life 1' were called upon to make sense of 'life 2'.

Accounts of surviving 7/7 also have to be formulated to acknowledge the fifty-two people who did not survive. John Tulloch, for example, tells of a media appearance he made on the BBC prime-time television programme *The One Show*. At this point in his recovery, John had resumed work as a professor in media studies and had begun to write a book about his experiences that was subsequently published as *One Day in July*. When he was initially contacted to appear on *The One Show*, the theme that was proposed for the segment in which an interview with John would feature was 'moving on'. John agreed, on the condition that he would speak about how, for him, developing an argument around the political use of the bombing by the UK media and government was enabling him to 'move on'. However, the television interviewer chose to focus on other issues, and none of the 'political' material was featured in the heavily edited interview that was eventually broadcast. Despite his dissatisfaction with this process, John describes his realisation, upon viewing the programme, of how inappropriate that narrative of his recovery would have been:

> Cos the other two people in that *One Show*, er, interview, their stories, both of them, tragic loss, one his wife, one of, er soul mate sister, were so, so moving, there's no way I would have wanted to be giving a kind of confident move forward into the politics of the world's images, no way . . . I still think, still thought at the time I saw it, still think that, that the

quality of what they did in that thing was so powerful in a way it was a privilege for me to be even in it.

(JT)

John's academic work afforded him a familiarity with media practices of editing and producing broadcast work. In this way, any media coverage of 7/7 is likely to be shaped by the format of the programming in which it appears (in this case, a popular, 'magazine'-type, prime-time show). However, the juxtaposition of the politicised version of events John intended to tell with the stories from bereaved relatives would have disrupted the emotional tone established in the other interviews and, ultimately, undermined the overall 'power' of the segment. Many of the survivors have spoken of the difficulty of engaging in commemorative activities alongside bereaved relatives.[18] Survivors tend to focus on how they have found a variety of meanings in their experiences, as they come to terms with 7/7 as part of their personal biography. For the bereaved relatives, absence and sudden loss remain the dominant themes of their recollections. Hence, many survivors consider formal commemorative activities, such as the Hyde Park memorial, to be 'for the relatives' rather than for themselves.[19]

In *The One Show* example, John's story was depoliticised to accommodate the stories of others. However, the converse may also be the case. Media reporting has sometimes sought to recruit survivors into a discourse around national and international politics. Susan Harrison speaks of this as part of the 'angle' that journalists seek to bring to their reporting:

> They're trying to, there's always, you know, initially obviously they're reporting and because it's an interesting story and people are interested in . . . and there does seem to be a sympathy thing, but they always want an angle and it's usually are you moaning about compensation, or do you want a public enquiry, did you feel you got the best out of the government, you know, there's always something . . . let's get a juicy story on this and actually there is no juicy story for me, there is nothing.
>
> (SH)

The 'juicy story' here is one where Susan's recollections and experiences are fitted into a narrative of the government failing in its duty of care towards those affected by 7/7. Here, Susan is represented as someone who is 'doubly victimised', first, by the actions of the terrorists and, second, by an uncaring

142 Remembering with, through and for others

public administration. However, other 'angles' are possible in these kinds of media story:

> I absolutely would hate to, for a view of mine to be put in a paper and like that, and I would hate to . . . I absolutely would hate to, for a view of mine to be put in a paper and misconstrued and actually suddenly I'm a racist, you know, or suddenly I hate all Muslims, or suddenly I hate, you know, Tony Blair or . . . it's just not me and I do have views, but they're personal.
>
> (SH)

Susan here draws equivalence between these very different perspectives on 7/7. To be represented as 'hating Muslims' is, for her, no different in kind from 'hating Tony Blair'. Both are media frames that attempt to subsume survivors' stories into the crudest form of political discourse in a sensationalist manner. John Tulloch describes the well-known case of his image being used in tabloid newspapers as a series of appropriations:

> I began to notice during the first few months, I was being used like a political football and you would know *The Sun* issue in November 2005 when, you know, I was my . . . supersaturated colour, in supersaturated colour there I was on the full front page of *The Sun*, supporting legislation, anti-terrorism legislation, which I didn't support, and where words were put next to my mouth as though it came from me. And then you'll get the *Daily Mail* a few months later having an attack on Blair after some so-called independent inquiry and there was a cross-party inquiry, and this time I'm used against Blair, so, erm, the whole ethics of that, erm, the whole experience of living with that.
>
> (JT)

The fact that John's image and story could be used on different occasions by different tabloid newspapers to support entirely different positions, pro- and anti-Blair, indicates that his experiences can be reassembled into collectivised narratives of 7/7 that are remote from his own personal perspectives on the bombings. And yet this appropriation of what John went through became itself part of his story. John engaged with the media reframing of his experience at the same time that he was attempting to come to terms with the physical and psychological effects of the blast: 'I'm faced with Rupert Murdoch's mob and others, er, just using me, constructing me, reconstructing me, at the very same time I'm trying to reconstruct myself' (JT).

We can view the 'construction' and 'reconstruction' that John speaks of here as a folding together of very different kinds of relation in his life-space. John's experiences now flow through national and international politics. The debates there (notably around terror suspect detention laws) have become an inextricable part of how his life has unfolded since 7/7.

For all of the survivors we have discussed here, 'telling their story' involved shaping their experiences in relation to those of others and through engaging with the broader collective frames that emerged around the bombing. This produced a kind of torque, where Rachel found herself attempting to speak to and on behalf of Londoners, Susan had to manage the extent to which her 'life 1' was recruited to gild a 'juicy story' around 'life 2', and John found his experiences reconstructed in ways with which he profoundly disagreed. In all three cases, there is no sharp distinction to be made between individual experience and the collective efforts at framing and understanding the bombings. Rather, we can see a movement from what happened on that day that expands their life-space to include relationships across many different kinds of practice. And, conversely, we can see a reverse movement where Rachel, Susan and John came to understand their individual experiences through the way their story had been publicly recruited and reassembled. However, rather like tracing the surface of the Möbius strip, at no point is it ever really clear where the crossing point, the break, between the personal and the public, the inside and the outside, actually occurs.

Mediating memory

The personal memories of survivors of the bombings are, of course, 'individual' in the sense that they are bounded by their own unique spatial and temporal perspective on the events. However, what is striking is the extent to which the participants discussed using tools and external resources to reframe their experience. Take, for example, Rachel North's description of using the Urban75 message board, once she had returned home following the bombings:

> I posted to my account and it was just one of loads, of about 900 people advising and contributing to one thread that day, erm, and as soon as I wrote it I felt a bit better, cos I . . . I'd managed to get the memories out of my head and onto . . . onto a screen and which kind of calmed me

down, I was, as you can imagine, very adrenalized by what had gone on that day.

(RN)

The key phrase here is, 'I'd managed to get the memories out of my head and onto a screen'. Rachel offers this description of the activity of telling her story to the other users of the service. She did this by making a series of posts, responding to other posts and answering queries. The activity generated a narrative organisation for her recent, distressing experiences. This framework was collaboratively developed, insofar as it emerged from the interaction between the users of Urban75. However, we might also note that the ordering of the recent past in the contributions to the message board differed in kind from the memories 'in her head'. John Sutton and colleagues emphasise that distributed cognition involves the combination of different, but complementary, sets of resources, some 'intra-cranial', others external.[20] Here, we can see Rachel elaborating and expanding on her experience, which becomes translated through the interaction around the Urban75 messages. This 'augmented' set of recollections then becomes the basis for what subsequently becomes 'her memory' of the events.

Susan Harrison engaged with the media coverage of 7/7 later, following her immediate recovery. One image in particular attracted her:

They released a picture of inside my train and that, I was actually fascinated with that picture, I've a copy of it, because I was trying to work out where I was in that train, er, and trying to . . . to figure out, you know, memories, trying to install some memories and were the things I was thinking real and . . . clearly it didn't come from the picture.

(SH)

Following the blast, Susan had been trapped in the wreckage of the Jubilee line underground train. During this time, she had assessed her own injuries and, using her medical training, had made a tourniquet for her severely injured leg. During the 2010 inquest into the bombings, Susan described reassuring a fellow passenger, Shelly Mather, who was trapped beneath her and, unfortunately, later died from her injuries. Such intense and distressing experiences in the dark of the tunnel would be clearly disorienting. Susan used the picture as a way of organising her experiences. She comments on looking at the photograph in order to place her experiences spatially – 'work out where I was on the train'. The layout of the wrecked train in the image serves as a device to establish the chronology of what happened: here is where she sat; there is where the bomber must have been; that piece of floor is where she was thrown and then trapped; over there is where the paramedics entered the train and ultimately found her.

The image does a particular kind of mnemonic work for Susan. On the one hand, it works as a piece of evidence against which she can 'test' what she remembers – 'were the things I was thinking real'. This was a particular concern of Susan's, because, in her initial interviews with police officers investigating the bombings, Susan had provided a description of the bomber as an 'Asian chap carrying a rucksack' (SH), who was actually a fellow passenger (Germaine Lindsey was Afro-Caribbean). On the other hand, the image provides a way for Susan to rehearse and reorganise what she recalls, using the train layout as a 'map' in which she can 'install some memories'. As with Rachel North, the process of 'augmenting' memory, of placing experience in a framework that expands her own life-space (the Urban75 message board, an image published by news media), appears important in making sense of what happened. Other kinds of relation – to fellow Londoners, to the activities that occurred in the dark train compartment – become folded together through the mediation of devices such as the message board and the photograph.

This process of folding together relations was also performed collectively by groups of survivors. Rachel North co-founded a support group, Kings Cross United, that brought together survivors of the Piccadilly line bombing.[21] During their meetings, they used a drawn image of the train as a tool to support their exchange of stories:

> We had a book, which I drew a kind of crap diagram of the train, layout in it, so people wrote their names where they remembered themselves as having been, which, and we kept taking the book back to every meeting so people would kind of plot themselves and then that way they would be able to work out clusters of where they are, so there were, sometimes people would come in and you'd get these incredibly emotional, oh my God, you're the woman who da, da, da, you know, you're the one who said you were going to a job interview and we all said, oh you should go, you'll get the sympathy vote.
>
> (RN)

The diagram of the train served as a tool to co-ordinate the different experiences told by each survivor. By writing themselves into the diagram, the group members were able to connect together their various life-spaces to constitute

146   Remembering with, through and for others

collective narratives around the bombings, such as the one Rachel tells above of the woman who was travelling to a job interview. The tool provided a means for the otherwise disconnected individual experiences to be woven together in an expanded space that was jointly produced through their interactions.

In both of the previous examples, the spatial layout of the train provided a framework around which recollections could coalesce and be stabilised. For John Tulloch, a similar mnemonic work was performed by three pieces of luggage. John was travelling on the westbound Circle line train towards Paddington when Mohammad Sidique Khan, who was sitting nearby to him, detonated his device as the train pulled out of Edgware Road station. The three large cases that John was carrying absorbed the blast sufficiently to protect him from major injury. These cases have become central to his narrative of the event, acting almost as talismans of his good fortune in surviving, despite being so close to the bomb. However, he describes an episode that occurred at a memorial event at Edgware Road on the 1-year anniversary. A fellow survivor approached him, having recognised John from his media appearances. The survivor told him that he had attempted to help some of the injured in the carriage, in particular a seriously injured man who lost his lower limbs in the blast. However, he was unable to reach the man, because John's cases blocked his way – 'He said, erm, I didn't see you and he said I know I saw what I now know to have been your bloody cases' (JT). This comment turned around the significance of the cases:

> OK, so my bags had always been part of a really positive narrative, a part of my good luck story, in my book, everywhere. OK, now what this guy said was I now know to have been your bloody bags, and it was worse than that, because, and he wasn't being unpleasant, er . . . what had happened, he'd found a man, grievously injured, he'd had the bottom half of his body blown off, erm . . . he couldn't get at him properly because of my bags, that's how he said it, and a bit of that story that I really remembered and really got to me emotionally was this man had . . . like I said to you before, the legs were part of something I kind of empathised with and I got really emotional about people who had lost their legs, it's happened a number of times and this was one of them, and the detail that got to me was that the attempt of dignity of this dying man, who . . . he somehow got his coat or jacket off and he'd just covered up the lower part of himself, and . . . so now my bags were in this horror story, because the people who were trying to help him couldn't help him as much.
>
> (JT)

The passenger who told this story had seen John on television giving his 'really positive narrative' about his bags. He had then realised that these same 'bloody bags' had formed an obstacle in the carriage that had prevented him from assisting a grievously injured man. John had vivid memories of the man concerned. The sight of the severe injuries to his legs and of the dignity with which the man had conducted himself has had a lasting emotional effect upon John. In his 'really positive narrative', told in his book and elsewhere, John had concluded that, were it not for the protection afforded by his cases, he might well have suffered similar injuries to his legs (or worse). During the period of his recovery, the bags offered up a conceptual affordance, a distinct proposition, to John – 'you are lucky to be alive'. However, in the conversation with the fellow survivor, John is made aware that this proposition is ambiguous, as it can be embedded in a very different account. In this 'horror story', they become implicated as a problem in the very scene that had such a lasting effect on John. His experiences now pass in two very different ways from the bags to the events in the wrecked carriage.

The three mnemonic devices that we have discussed – the photograph, the diagram and the cases – play significant mediational roles in the recollections of the survivors. They act initially as forms of evidence, material features of the event that assist in the effort to recall what happened. They also provide a means to augment experience, to fold together other kinds of relation into life-space. This may help develop narrative coherence around confusing and distressing experiences, accompanied by recollections of intense and disorienting sensations in the near darkness of the tunnels. Finally, they act as material and conceptual affordances that hold together different experiences – sometimes neatly, and sometimes, as with the story of John's cases, in tension – and make it possible to build expanded, collectively shared accounts of surviving the bombs.

Embodied connections

Clearly, all experience, and therefore recollected experience, is in some sense embodied, meaning that it is imbued with complex sensory and affective components. However, these embodied aspects of memory can be minimised or fall out of narratives of past events, particularly when these stories are tied to broader historical accounts. For the 7/7 survivors, the opposite appears to be the case. Bodies are central to their recollections. For Susan Harrison, the loss of her leg serves as a permanent marker of the bombings, but even for those who have not been left with life-changing physical injuries, the body acts as a particular locus of remembering. Here, John Tulloch recalls an episode that occurred several months after 7/7:

> I came out of the first few days of that, doing that, into my garden about, in Australia, about 5 in the evening, and it was drought, it was hot and I'd bought a little native tree and I was going to put it in the ground and the spade wouldn't even get into the soil and I thought what am I doing, what am I doing? I mean, this is ridiculous. But then I looked down at the foot and it's on the blade of the spade, and I say, hey, I've got legs.
>
> (JT)

As we have seen, legs and feet have a particular significance for John because of his memories of seeing the severely injured passenger who lost his lower limbs on the Circle line train carriage. Here, the sudden realisation that his injuries could have been far worse interrupts a moment in the garden. The futility of his efforts to plant the tree in the hard, water-starved soil is overtaken by the overwhelming sensation of having a whole body.

In this recollection, the body acts as a kind of affordance for memory. The physical organisation of limbs and torso provides a synecdochal link to the bombings. John moves, in his recollection, from the presence of his foot to the broken bodies of some his fellow passengers and the carnage of the blast itself. The body is, here, a living conduit of memory; 7/7 marks the bodies of survivors, literally (in Susan's case), symbolically (in the presence/absence of feet in John's recollection) and affectively. We can see the latter in a passage from Rachel North's book *Out of the Tunnel*, where she describes the moments after the explosion in the following way:

> Sharp grit in my mouth. Choking, lung-filling dust. It was no longer air that I breathed but tiny shards of glass, and thick heavy dust and smoke. Like changing a vacuum cleaner bag and pushing your face into the open dust bag and taking deep breaths. It made my tongue swell and crack and dry out like leather. I never covered my mouth because I had nothing to cover it with, and there didn't seem any point . . . There was an acrid smell of chemicals and burning rubber and burning hair. It filled my nose. It took over the memory of every smell I remembered and wiped it out.[22]

The smell and taste of the explosion left many survivors with an indelible sensory impression of the immediate damage caused by the bomb. It also left a strong, legitimate suspicion that breathing the toxic fumes could have resulted in further 'hidden' effects on their health. These concerns were shared in exchanges of electronic messages between survivors:

> Somebody would write how's everybody doing today, I'm feeling a bit freaked out, I don't like Thursdays, anybody else having this, and someone goes yeah I feel weirder on Thursdays too, and someone else I've got a cough, anyone else got a cough . . . yes, I'm smoking loads at the moment but I wonder if it's related to the smoke that we breathed in the tunnel, Oh God, that's really worried me.
>
> (RN)

In this description, the survivors appear to be in a state of hyper-vigilance, monitoring feelings and sensations. Each 'weird' feeling is referenced directly to the bombing, taken as a sign that links back to 7/7. For example, physical sensations such as developing a cough or feeling the need to smoke more are seized upon as possible symptoms of an undiagnosed illness caused by inhaling smoke in the tunnel. The body here is marked both visibly and invisibly by the bombings. Survivors carry forward an embodied connection to 7/7 in the affective work they do with one another, such as discussing their anxieties about particular sensations. The body is the means through which they collectively constitute their ongoing, shared relationship to the bombings. This is apparent in the discussion of the effects of noisy celebrations:

> Lots of people noticed that fireworks, and in London, you get fireworks like a whole week, because you get, you know, Diwali and Hindu festivals, then you get the kids who'll buy the fireworks and then let them off in the parks for a laugh, there is a constant bang, bang, bang, erm . . . and that really got people psyched up, as did the Buncefield disaster,[23] the people, some people lived in Hemel Hempstead and they really didn't like that at all, when there was a big bang and the cloud of smoke went up . . . and everybody . . . the great charm of it was everybody went aha, I know exactly what you mean.
>
> (RN)

We may view sensation here, not as a private, subjective experience, but rather as a set of feelings that are afforded by the very particular circumstances of the blasts in the underground tunnels. These feelings provide an ongoing affective link to the past that can result in temporal and spatial remoteness being suddenly collapsed, as the past is folded into the present. This can occur through the mediation of certain sounds, such as the noise of fireworks. Survivors physically respond to the noise in a way that places them back in the moments following the explosion, which leaves them distressed or 'psyched up'. However, this affective link also serves as a point of mutual recognition. As Rachel describes it, the 'great charm' of the exchange of messages was in allowing survivors to immediately recognise and accredit the physical sensations reported by others – 'I know exactly what you mean'. Relationships between survivors are built here through a felt sense of shared ongoing experience – a 'common notion' – along with a running commentary on feelings and sensations. This is a web of collectively shared and embodied common notions that connects survivors to one another.

There is a further, ethical dimension to these embodied connections. As noted earlier, a division between the survivors and the relatives of the fifty-two deceased victims emerged in the course of commemorative activities in the months and years after 2005. In the same way that John Tulloch described an accommodation between his story and those of relatives, so Susan Harrison comments on feeling the need to not speak publicly of some details of what happened in the tunnel:

> If someone asks me to describe something in particular about the tube and I would say that, you know, it was messy and it was nasty, but I wouldn't say oh, and this person's arm was hanging off as they were hanging half out of the tube, it's just not necessary and that person's got a family, you know, whoever they are, or potentially whatever, do you know what I mean? So . . . and I don't think we need to necessarily . . . people need to know it was horrific and people need to know, but unless you were there I don't think you can experience and I think that's . . .
>
> (SH)

Susan has given public accounts of what happened on the Jubilee line train. She also gave testimony to the 2010 inquest, where she spoke of her conversations with Shelly Mather while both were trapped, and was commended the presiding judge, Lady Justice Hallett, for offering 'great comfort' to the relatives by telling of how she sought to reassure Shelly and how neither was in any pain. However, Susan here reflects on the potential negative effects of speaking about the horrors inside the carriage. She prefers to use the somewhat abstract language of 'messiness' and 'nastiness', rather than provide graphic details, on the grounds that relatives would then be forced to dwell on these images in their commemorative efforts at reconstructing what happened – 'that person's got a family, you know, whoever they are'. There is then a tension between providing a veridical account of the results of the bombers' actions (which is what Susan feels is often demanded of her by the media) and giving relatives access to details that will be extremely distressing and difficult to manage. Susan is placed in the situation of managing the vicarious memories that relatives are desperate to gain of their absent loved ones.

Bodies and affects connect together survivors in ways that can be productive. They afford a mutual recognition of experience ('I know exactly what you mean') or common notions that expands the capacity to act individually and jointly. In this sense, this sharing of affective links to the past could be considered, in this particular instance, to have ethical value, from a Spinozist perspective. However, these same embodied and affective links may also connect together relatives and the dead. This connection is no less productive, but it would, as a consequence, thrust relatives into the position of becoming helpless witnesses to the suffering of their loved ones. To draw again on the Spinozist ethical scheme, this would appear to diminish rather than expand the capacity to act. It would reduce rather than expand the range of possibilities for relating to the past. As such, it is ethically undesirable.

The embodied and affective aspects of memory work at numerous different levels. They give survivors an intense personal connection to the event that is effectively 'written' across their body. This 'writing' is partly legible and partly illegible, as with the signs such as the coughing that provoke such anxiety. It also provides a basis for common recognition and for the sharing of experience in relation to what is afforded by the past event. This makes for highly contingent ethical judgements about the value of 'feeling' a relation to the past.

Time to forget 7/7?

Through the extracts we have discussed here, we have tried to show how the personal and the public are inextricably linked in the ongoing life experiences of survivors of 7/7. Like the Möbius strip, there is an indivisible folding together of experiences, without a clear break between the unique perspective of the individual and its augmentation in subsequent mnemonic work. Survivors' recollections accommodate and respond to both the memories of others and broader narrative frameworks. The vital memories also become populated and engraved with the affordances of things (i.e. images, diagrams, objects). They are woven around intense embodied connections, where survivors connect with one another and the event itself through sensations and feelings. This does not, of course, make these stories any less credible. On the contrary, the shaping of the stories and the blurring of the personal/collective distinction are precisely what make these stories such valuable testimonies to the ongoing commemorative work around the London bombings.

But does such work ever come to an end? Is it really possible for any of the survivors to escape the long shadow that 7/7 casts on their life after they exited the tunnels? Will any of them be allowed to fully disconnect themselves from the formal, national narratives that have attempted to recruit their experiences? Is it time, or will there ever come a time, for survivors to forget 7/7? As we approach the tenth anniversary, it is still, perhaps, too soon to say. But all three survivors discussed here have reflected on and envisaged what form that 'end' to some aspects of their relationship to 7/7 might take. Susan Harrison offers the following:

> I think you get to the point, like I said, where you're quite bored by your own story (laughs) and erm, maybe there comes a time in that point when you think, do you know what, actually this is getting boring.
>
> (SH)

Susan highlights here the element of repetition that has crept into telling her story: there are only so many times you can tell your story before you become 'bored' by it. She projects forward to a time where, despite the 'good reasons' she has for recounting her experiences in her charity work, she may simply have grown tired of doing so. For John Tulloch, the way out has been to refuse a straightforward story of victimhood:

> I've tried to draw Mohammad Sidique Khan into my story and I actually say in one of the better interviews that in terms of representation, there's not so much difference between the way the newspapers, certain newspapers, er, represent me and him, even though one's a good guy and one's a bad guy, there were both locked into this kind of, one dimensional, he is a victim, he is, er . . . crazed killer.
>
> (JT)

The dominant media frame for 7/7 is one where misguided young men become radicalised by extremist ideology and commit a horrific act of

Remembering with, through and for others 153

indiscriminate terror. However, John has attempted to tell a different story. If he is more than just a simple victim, if 7/7 does not define him as a person, then so too there must be more to Mohammad Sidique Khan than being a 'crazed killer'. John conducted a televised interview with young people in Beeston, Leeds, where Khan had worked as a school classroom assistant. He discovered what, for him, was a different story of Khan, one that was more complex and nuanced than the dominant narrative. However, he also notes that it was Khan who created a 'one-dimensional' story for himself through his actions on 7/7. Drawing Khan into his own story is, then, a means for John to escape his own limited definition by the media, and to begin to escape the commemorative pull of the bombings. Rachel North similarly has found a way out in rejecting the narrative of extremism and victimhood:

> You know, 9/11 became a carte blanche for the Republican administration to go where the hell they liked, just by waving themselves, you know, wrapping them round flags, you know, I think that's really quite distasteful and I would be happier if . . . if 7/7 became like the Kings Cross fire disaster, you know, it was, you know, a tragic event that people who were directly involved feel sad and sorry about and, erm . . . that becomes part of the fabric of the city. You know, people don't remember the IRA bombings, or . . . I just missed the, erm . . . the bombings at the, erm, Admiral Duncan by about 3 minutes, erm . . . so when I know it's the anniversary I always feel that, you know erm . . . I spare a thought for everybody, but then I just go about my day . . . and I think, I hope that eventually 7/7 will become like that as well, I hope so.
>
> (RN)

Rachel lists here a series of tragedies that have occurred in recent times in London (a fire at Kings Cross underground station; the bombing of the bar, the Admiral Duncan, at the centre of London's gay community by a neo-Nazi militant; and the bombing campaigns by the Provisional Irish Republican Army in the 1970s and 1990s, which together injured and killed more people than 7/7). For her, the way to disconnect 7/7 from the 'war on terror' is to place it alongside these other events, to remove its 'special significance'. She talks of wanting 7/7 to 'become part of the fabric of the city'. It ought to become part of the rich, and at times tragic, history of London, an object of memory for 'people who were directly involved', but no more than one piece in the social and historical landscape. By extension, we have to imagine that Rachel

154 Remembering with, through and for others

envisages a similar future for herself, that her life-space could be folded back into the broader sweep of the city, rather than tightly focused on this one particular event that has changed her life so irrevocably.

Notes

1 See Lorenzo-Dus and Bryan, 2011.
2 There is evidence to suggest that the bombings were, in fact, planned for 6 July, when they would have co-incided directly with the planned announcement.
3 This government-led proposal was defeated, with an increase to 28 days introduced, although this was reduced back down to 14 days in 2011.
4 That 2 minutes of silence was called for is significant. This number of minutes (rather than 1 or 3) is associated with the annual 11 November Remembrance Day commemoration of the First and Second World Wars. A 2-minute silence is, therefore, usually a 'war silence' (see Brown, 2012b).
5 See Allen and Brown (forthcoming) for an extended discussion of the Hyde Park installation and its memorial affordances.
6 See Assmann, A., 2011; Assmann, J., 2011.
7 See Hirsch, 1997.
8 Reading, 2011.
9 *Love Hate Love* (2011), directed by Dana Nachman and Don Hardy, KTF Films.
10 Hyman, 2011.
11 See Allen and Brown, 2011.
12 Blum and Secor, 2011: 1034.
13 Blum and Secor (2011) discuss a number of such examples in relation to the later 'topological turn' in Lacan's work, most notably the 'cross-cap' transformation of the R Schema that Lacan uses to reanimate the Freudian ego–id structure. See also Elizabeth Grosz's (1994) use of the Möbius strip to think outside body–mind dualism.
14 See Allen and Brown, 2011; Hoskins, 2011; Lorenzo-Dus and Bryan, 2011.
15 See Allen (2014) for a full-length discussion of all the material.
16 North, 2007.
17 Tulloch, 2006.
18 See Allen, 2014.
19 Allen and Brown, forthcoming.
20 Sutton *et al.*, 2010; Michaelian and Sutton, 2013.
21 The use of Kings Cross rather than Russell Square – the two underground stations that the southbound Piccadilly line train was travelling between when the blast happened – is important. Owing to the position of the bomb in the lead carriage of the train and the subsequent wreckage, many of the less severely injured exited the train at Kings Cross, whereas those with major injuries (including Susan Harrison) were taken through the tunnels to Russell Square. The two stations therefore have very different memorial significance for these two groups of survivors.
22 North, 2007: 38.
23 This was a major fire at an oil storage facility just north of Greater London that occurred in December 2005.

Chapter 7

Forgetting who you were
The forensic psychiatric unit

Entering the medium secure forensic ward feels something like crossing a threshold linking two related but disparate worlds. Like other hospitals spaces, there is a TV lounge, single ward bedrooms, a common area and a nurses' station (although this one is protected by shatter-proof glass). But this building is locked, shut off from the world, sat on the edge of the nearby suburban space, looking out towards a rural landscape. It is both familiar and utterly alien. Once the key turns in the lock, you feel a little nervousness. Not because of apprehension about meeting 'psychiatric patients'. No, it is something to do with the space itself. It feels like you have lost your freedom of movement and with it the 'normal' rules of social engagement. Of course, for visitors like us, this is a purely temporary state of affairs. In a few hours we will be able to leave the ward and the unit. Where are the patients? They seem to have gravitated towards the television. It looks fairly new, a large flat-screen mounted on the wall of the lounge. It is pumping out music, heavy bass sounds. A music video is playing. MTV Base. Partially dressed women are gyrating on the screen. Everyone is staring, silently watching, their attention captured by the sounds and images. Us too. Time seems to move sluggishly here, punctuated only by the call to eat, to receive an injection or to speak to a doctor about medication on the infrequent ward rounds. The next music video starts playing.

Institutional assemblages

What can this scene possibly tell us about processes of remembering? The account seems to show something of the way in which institutions operate around mental 'illness' and the medical production of docile bodies through medication and physical containment. More than 50 years ago now, the sociologist Erving Goffman brilliantly demonstrated how patients in asylums were disciplined via the systematic removal of their past identities (e.g. through symbolic gestures, such as the removal of personal items and clothing) to ensure maximum compliance with hospital procedures.[1] Many of those things do indeed seem to be happening on the ward. However, what we will argue in this chapter is that institutions such as the secure unit hold and stabilise persons in the present time, by displacing access to their past. These are indeed spaces for the displacement and erosion of memory.

The material we discuss comes from a study of a medium-secure forensic mental health ward in a part of Greater London.[2] This is a ward where forensic psychiatric patients are often detained or 'sectioned' for treatment under the Mental Health Act. These patients have committed an 'index offence', for which they have either been arrested or remanded, or they have been found guilty of.[3] Some patients have been transferred from prison; others have been referred directly to the unit. Detention on the ward typically lasts at least 2 years and, for about one in five patients, it can be for between 5 and 10 years, and, in some cases, for between 10 and 20 years or longer.

We did not set out to study memory in this project as such. Our concerns were, instead, with the role of personal relationships and sexuality for patients during their time on the ward.[4] Nevertheless, spending time on the ward led us to wonder about the way in which patients appeared inculcated with a state of perpetual *presenteeism* (being perpetually seen, monitored and treated in the moment). This made the issue of how patients relate to their past difficult to grasp. On speaking to patients and staff, it became clear that references to the past − to significant events, to recollections of the time before admission − were not deemed relevant to the smooth running of the ward, which was focused exclusively on the medical management of the patient. Staff were mindful of the patient's past only to the extent that their previous offences were central to the present need to contain and treat them (largely through medication alone), such that they were less likely to return to an 'unwell' state that might result in reoffending. Even the patients themselves commented on the effort they made to attempt to bury their past, until the time came when they could leave the hospital for good and resume their lives. In what follows, we will explore what we came to see as an example of 'institutional forgetting' that was enacted via the social topology of the ward, in terms of both its spatial and temporal complexity. Our analytical observations are based on interviews carried out with patients and a series of observations recorded in our research diaries.

Before proceeding, some words are in order about this phrase 'social topology'. The term comes from the joint work of Annemarie Mol and John Law.[5] Their longstanding project has been to seek alternative descriptions of how spatial and temporal relations are assembled in the domain that can be loosely termed 'the social'.[6] Drawing upon ideas from topology similar to those that we have described in earlier chapters, Mol and Law argue that, '"The social" doesn't exist as a single spatial type. Rather, it performs several kinds of space in which different "operations" take place.'[7] Social space does not come in one topological form, they claim, despite the traditional tendency of social scientists to think in terms of distinct regions and boundaries. Take Goffman's work, for instance, where the inside space of 'total institutions', such as psychiatric units or prisons, is closed off from the outside world in a way that allows for the control and management of relations between patients/ prisoners and staff. The social world one finds within the total institution is analytically treated as utterly different from that outside. However, Michel Foucault's highly influential study of the social architecture of power that emerges in what he calls the 'disciplinary societies' of the eighteenth and nineteenth centuries shows that the purpose of incarceration, whether it be in prisons, hospitals or factories, is not to exclude inmates from broader relations.[8] What these institutions do instead is create new patterns of circulation of people, knowledge and capital between institutions. Discipline is a distributed system of power for managing movement, rather than enclosing and holding still.[9]

Foucault's work led to a shift away from treating institutions as monolithic spaces of control towards a more nuanced account of assembling relations among heterogeneous sets of materials. This approach, broadly informed by the work of Foucault's contemporary, Gilles Deleuze, views institutions as *assemblages* (or '*agencements*') that perform a work of drawing together (i.e. 'assembling', 'connecting together') spatial and temporal relations. Jane Bennett offers a useful summary:

> Assemblages are ad hoc groupings of diverse elements, of vibrant materials of all sorts. Assemblages are living throbbing confederations that are able to function despite the persistent presence of energies that confound them from within. They have uneven topographies, because some of the points at which the various affects and bodies cross paths are more heavily trafficked than others, and so power is not distributed equally across its

surface. Assemblages are not governed by any central head: no one materiality or type of material has sufficient competence to determine consistently the trajectory or impact of the group. The effects generated by an assemblage are, rather, emergent properties, emergent in their ability to make something happen . . . as distinct from the sum of the vital force of each materiality considered alone. Each member and proto-member of the assemblage has a certain vital force, but there is also an effectivity proper to the grouping as such: an agency *of* the assemblage. And precisely because each member-actant maintains an energetic pulse slightly 'off' from that of the assemblage, an assemblage is never a solid block but an open-ended collective, a 'non-totalizable sum'. An assemblage thus not only has a distinctive history of formation but a finite life span.[10]

This passage is theoretically dense and speaks to a range of concerns around the adoption of the notion of 'assemblage' in social science.[11] Nevertheless, Bennett helps us to grasp some important features of secure forensic psychiatric institutions if we rewrite her words as follows:

The secure unit is a complex and changeable arrangement of medical, legal and governmental practices, mixing together nurses, former prisoners, airlock doors, depot injections, charts, televisions, plastic cutlery, cigarettes, staff rotas, sunlight, and bedrooms littered with belongings. The unit can be a lively place, especially during times when patients arrive on transfer from prison, where the contradictory demands of care and containment can rub up against one another uneasily, notably around issues such as personal relationships. The space of the unit is difficult to properly gauge, as patients may be allowed off the ward into the general hospital grounds and to make community visits; there is a distinctly different 'feel' to the common areas and the individual bedrooms, reflecting the various kinds of activity that are possible in each. Although there is a clear management structure, it is difficult to know where exactly the unit sits – are we in the prison system, the medical system or somewhere else entirely? This partial ambiguity allows for the emergence of practices and relationships that are particular to the unit, some of which would be difficult to understand if one approached the unit as either purely a space of containment or purely a space of treatment. Everyone and everything that enters the unit lends something specific, from East African nurses to long-term service users to middle-class psychiatrists mixed together in this space;

this unique confluence of identities and experiences seems integral to how the place seems to 'work' as a whole. Yet precisely because it is such a mixture, the unit seems to be rather porous – people, practices and objects seem to be displaced, to move through and across the extended space of the unit in unpredictable ways. The place has its own history, one that seems to be written and rewritten on an almost daily basis.

If Goffman found rituals and practices in 'total institutions' designed to divide and enclose social space, what one finds in institutional 'assemblages' is, instead, a complex arranging of spatial and temporal relations that connects together prisons, hospitals and local communities. Both staff and patients are put into patterns of circulation that reconfigure their life-space. Bodies are arranged in the shifting space of the unit (which can narrow to locked wards or dilate to include the general hospital, other units and community visits). This work of arranging serves to surface a diverse range of propositions, some of which are contradictory – 'she is doing better', 'he remains a danger to himself', 'right now things are more settled'. The stretching and compressing, or 'churn', of relations create a changeable affective atmosphere. And the hours pass by, marked only by occasional arguments about what channel should be on the television. Click.

Folding space and time on the ward

To understand how the reconfiguring of life-space occurs in the institutional assemblage, it is important to explore the affordances of the physical setting of the ward. The invariant qualities of the setting constitute very particular kinds of potential experience. In the unit where we conducted research, there are four wards that house patients at various stages of their treatment and rehabilitation. There are also a series of corridors, many leading to 'airlock' spaces, where one set of doors is required to be locked before the next may be opened. Each ward has its own specific category of patient, ranging from acute patients who were severely distressed (mostly deemed psychotic), through to patients on a rehabilitation ward who appeared calm and were mostly unsupervised. All patients are medicated, usually via depot injection.[12] On the rehabilitation ward, access to the community is gradually introduced, until some patients are permitted to leave the unit unaccompanied for several hours and even days at a time. Some of the patients we interviewed, therefore, had a less than clear delineation between hospital and community spaces.

On the whole, though, most patients are confined to a locked ward space, which has two or three communal spaces, including a television room, games room, bathrooms and communal dining space. In the centre of these communal spaces is a nurses' station, surrounded by glass and a locked door. To attract the attention of nurses outside times of regular, scheduled interaction, patients knock on the locked door or windows (this can be a source of routine conflict). For the majority of the time, nurses sit at computer stations, typing up notes on patient conduct and commenting on the presence or absence of 'symptoms' of mental illness. There is little physical interaction between nursing staff and patients, except at points of disruption/crisis. To escape the daily low-level irritations of communal living in this relatively restricted environment, patients often spend time in their bedrooms, where they have access to music systems and, occasionally, a television linked up to a DVD player. Despite such means of retreat, however, staff have continual access to patients and are able to 'look in' to bedrooms, even late at night, using window shutters controlled from the outside to enable regular observations.[13]

Together, these physical features of the setting help to constitute the social topology of the ward. They do this by shaping what actions are permitted and which become difficult or impossible to perform. For example, there is no place on the ward where a patient can be properly alone, without the poss- ibility of observation, even while sleeping. The design of the unit clearly communicates propositions of containment and observation through locks, observational windows, bolted-down chairs and tables (to prevent them being used as weapons). There is very little here that might offer a sense of 'homeliness' – no carpets or lamps or even toilet seats (which are removed, owing to risk of self-harm). Bedrooms are designed so that anything that might serve as a potential ligature point is removed. Windows open only the slightest amount. There are no sharp corners on any item of furniture. It is difficult to mount posters or photographs on a bedroom wall, because pins and Blu-Tack[14] are banned in case of swallowing. The environment clearly proposes to patients that the principal concern of the unit is the management of risk.[15]

The discourse of risk animates all relationships on the unit. A common experience is for patients to be kept waiting until appropriate numbers of staff are available to supervise activities such as being taken for an appointment with a GP.[16] Particular times on the unit, such as meal times, are anticipated as being potential 'flashpoints'. Staff tend to be especially vigilant at these times and are prepared to intervene in minor disputes over portion size or availability of particular meals, before they flare up into significant conflict. However, the concern with risk also results in the emergence of unexpected practices. Since 2008, smoking has been banned in all National Health Service (NHS) buildings in England, including forensic psychiatric units. However, the ban does not (yet) apply to prisons, from where many patients have been transferred.[17] This creates a dilemma for staff. The risks of having to manage the cravings of upset smokers are seen to outweigh those of organising informal, supervised 'smoking breaks' outside the ward. Yet, as this falls at the margins of common practice in the NHS, it falls to the on-duty nursing staff to unofficially timetable these escorted breaks. The calculation of risk affords novel interaction as well as constraining routine interaction.

Staff and patients alike experience the social topology of the unit as having a distinct affective atmosphere. For example, the acoustics of the ward means that sound is accentuated in the areas where bedrooms are located. The relative quiet of the bedroom space is regularly punctuated by the sound of the clinking keys that staff are obliged to have attached to their belts. Noise is also a key sign that staff monitor to gauge the collective mood of patients – if the ward is either too quiet or too noisy, trouble is likely to be brewing. The desired atmosphere of the ward is one that is 'settled'. This translates as stability among the patient population (i.e. few new transfers), a relative absence of conflict between patients and with staff, and minimal displays of distress by individual patients. A similar language is inculcated in patients to describe their own psychological states. Being 'well' is what one ought to aspire towards. Contrary to the usual sense of the term, 'wellness' here means the ability to self-manage distress, rather than the absence of 'symptoms'. Being able to display wellness is an important step towards being considered to be in recovery, and, hence, closer to a review of one's section.

What is striking about the way that wellness is performed on the unit is that it does not require reference to the patient's past experiences before they entered the unit. Although staff are certainly aware of the nature of the index offence that resulted in a patient being placed on their current section, alongside their 'history' with the psychiatric and legal system, this is not deemed to be relevant to establishing wellness. What matters is how the patient has managed himself or herself since the moment they entered the unit. Patients are not required to demonstrate a coming to terms with the index offence and the life circumstances that surrounded it, nor are they asked to reflect on the specific factors contributing to their formal psychiatric diagnosis. It is in this sense that the unit enacts a form of 'institutional forgetting'. Life-space is compressed to what happens on admission and what follows during the course of the patient's section. Anything prior to that is not a primary matter of concern in the institutional project of managing 'settled' wards of 'well' patients.

If life-space is compressed by the social topology of the unit, then it is also complexified in a range of ways. Lewin's insight holds: despite the clear physical barriers on wards, life-space does not map on to Euclidean or metric space; the relations through which patients feel and act cut across temporal and spatial remoteness. Take, for example, the relations between staff who administer psychotropic medication and patients. Medication is dispensed using two major techniques. The first is dispensing medication to be taken orally. Traditionally, this involved patients forming a queue on the ward to receive their specific batch of tablets, which they would then swallow under the watchful gaze of nursing staff. However, the development of depot injections has rendered the interaction around medication as both more and less personal at the same time. To receive medication via this method, patients must partially expose their buttocks to a staff member, who delivers a deep-muscle injection. Once this has been administered, there is no further need for staff to monitor the behaviour of the patient for compliance with their medication, as the medication remains active in the patient's body for a number of weeks. Although depot injections greatly reduce the need for the physical presence of staff, we might say that the relationship of compliance remains active, mediated through the patient's very veins. The relations between staff and patients are enacted through direct intervention at the biochemical level, as well as through ongoing physical interaction.

The spatial relations that are constituted by the ward seem to unfold in all manner of different directions. Despite the locked doors, various features of the world beyond, and the physical limits of wards are part of the relationships on the unit. One patient, for example, explained how his interactions with staff could be severely affected by what he perceived to be the member of staff's 'domestic troubles'. Whatever was occurring in the space of the staff member's home was felt to travel with them to the ward, shaping the relations that were enacted there. Another patient felt the inequalities between themselves and staff intensely. They described how staff were able to leave the ward at the close of each day, to return to 'a wife or husband, and find relief and support there', whereas patients had no such alternative space in which to retreat. To use Lewin's language, these other spaces, to which the social topology of the unit is connected, have quasi-physical effects on the daily interactions between staff and patients.

The boundaries of the unit are porous: the supposed 'outside' is continuously being folded into relations on the ward. When patients reach the point in their recovery where they are allowed to make community visits, their movements back and forth from the ward create perturbations. At a mundane level, staff are concerned with the possibility of contraband items, such as illicit drugs, pornography or mobile phones, being brought back into the unit. However, in terms of the affective atmosphere of the ward, patients also bring back stories of their experiences while back in the community – social occasions, sexual encounters, what it is to regain autonomy. These stories become threaded into relations between patients, who are able to vicariously place themselves outside the locked doors of the unit through the sharing of the experiences of community visits.

The examples so far suggest that the life-spaces of patients expand beyond the physical limits of the unit, but only in a relatively limited way, into local communities. However, if we consider the mixture of diverse elements that are brought together in the institutional assemblage, it begins to appear that the churn of relations has far greater reach. Many of the nursing staff working on these particular wards are migrants from East and West Africa, who have brought their skills and background to work in the NHS. The effects of migration, movements between societies, the conflicts and accommodations involved in working across different social and cultural settings can enter into relations on the ward. Conversely, many of the psychiatrists and other clinicians working on the unit come from a class and social background that are significantly removed from those of the patients. There are a variety of historical and cultural experiences that are all in play together here, acting to deform and reshape the social topology of the unit. These can come together in ways that have significant effects on the lives of patients. Black men, for example, especially those with larger body sizes, appear to be treated as presenting greater risks than other patients, which is reflected in calculations about medication levels. Female patients' relationships with male patients are viewed almost entirely, by staff, through the lens of possible predation and exploitation.[18]

The unit itself also has a history. One can see the changing patterns of practice around mental health care written into the very shape of the building. Older wards tend to be more cramped – 'rabbit runs' – with a focus on maximising the amount of bed space and keeping all non-essential facilities off the ward itself. Newer wards reflect the priorities of the 'care in the community' policy, where secure psychiatric care is seen as a short-term, last-resort option. Contemporary ward designs tend to place greater emphasis on communal spaces, including outdoor spaces, in order to foster the kind of social integration required during the transition back into living in the community. Moreover, secure psychiatric units tend to have a well-embedded reputation and historical character among the local communities in which they are sited. These are places that engender curiosity, humour and fear in equal measure. Patients may themselves have spoken of or joked about the site, long before being transferred to the unit on a section.

At the heart, then, of the secure unit is the paradox of an assemblage that has a distinctive historical formation and that draws together highly diverse spatial and temporal relations, but that is, nevertheless, focused on discounting and actively forgetting the past experiences of the patients around which it is constituted. The space of the ward operates somewhat outside conventional temporal systems. On the one hand, experiences on the ward are regimented by standard institutional time, such as meals, medical consultations and ward rounds, washing and perhaps the occasional group activity. On the other hand, time on the ward is indeterminate, to such an extent that patients feel as if time passes without any clear demarcation, where, literally, the ward is simply a time of containment, which they move through in a structureless fashion, without a clear sense of when this perpetual presenteeism will end.[19]

Categories of thought

In *How Institutions Think*, the anthropologist Mary Douglas offers an account of how the forms of social solidarity that we think of as 'institutions' emerge and develop.[20] She points in particular to the way in which institutions draw upon systems of classification, or ways of naming and ordering the world, over which they then claim ownership. Often, this is done, she claims, by using an overarching analogy with some aspect of the natural world, such that the classification system appears timeless and immutable. Ideas that fit this framework tend to be preserved; those that do not are rendered problematic and disruptive. Douglas goes on to assert that:

> Any institution . . . starts to control the memory of its members; it causes them to forget experiences incompatible with its righteous image, and it brings to their minds events which sustain the view of nature that is complementary to itself. It provides the categories of their thought, sets the terms for self-knowledge, and fixes identities.[21]

To become a member of an institution – either willingly or unwillingly – is to find oneself bound, to some degree, by the categories and ways of thinking that it enshrines. The identity that is subsequently conferred upon persons by virtue of their membership shapes their self-knowledge. One becomes the sort of person who is made over in the image of the institution. One starts to think as the institution thinks. Past experiences are then reconstructed and organised to fit with the patterns that are validated by the institutional framework, and one actively forgets those experiences that are 'incompatible with its righteous image'. In this way, institutions 'take charge' of memory,

Douglas's account puts us on the way to understanding both how and why the institutional assemblage requires patients to engage in active forgetting. One aspect of the assemblage is the set of codes and categories it deploys to make sense of what it does. These are the diagnostic categories of forensic mental health, such as personality disorder (PD) and schizophrenia. Critical scholars of mental health practices such as Richard Bentall and Mary Boyle have shown in painstaking detail exactly how these kinds of category are culturally and historically contingent, and the nature of the kind of work that goes into sustaining them, rather than exploring alternative accounts of mental health and distress.[22] However, in relation to the unit, it is important to recognise that, for practical purposes, these kinds of category are taken to have an independent, natural existence that serves to ground the work that goes on in the wards. As evidence of this, it is common to hear patients referred to purely in terms of diagnostic labels – a 'PD patient', 'psychosis patient', etc.

These categories form the basis for how the institution thinks and are the source of membership for patients. If one cannot be labelled by this classification system, then really one has no place on the unit (with the likely outcome of being transferred back into the prison system). It is a peculiar feature of how these diagnostic categories are defined that they require little reference to autobiographical memory. For example, a diagnosis of PD can be made based on current feelings (e.g. fear of being left alone), recent behaviour (e.g. personally damaging, impulsive activities) and general self-perception (e.g. disconnected from one's thoughts). Very little of this requires the person being assessed to offer an account of specific past experiences. In fact, when we interviewed patients, they often commented that this was one of the first occasions when they had been invited to discuss their life experiences. In the following, one of the researchers (R) asks the patient (P) their feelings about the interview they had just completed:

Extract 7.1

R: How do you think the interview went?

P: Yeah. Yeah, I think the first bit was the hardest thing

R: Yeah (laughs)

P: Like tell me about yourself, I've never really done that before (laughs) . . . I wasn't used to that, no-one's ever asked me.

It can seem extraordinary to people unfamiliar with mental health assessment that 'talking about yourself' is not central to the practice, but this is because the categories that structure how this particular institution thinks are concerned with patterns of thought, feeling and action that considered to have a clear, independent existence that transcends any particular occasion – That is to say, it is not necessary to hear about any life event in particular in order to make a diagnosis.[23] Moreover, in forensic psychiatric care, the recent behaviour of the person being assessed is already a matter of (criminal) record. The institution does not need to hear the life story of the prospective patient to make a decision on whether to admit and treat them or not.

If past life experiences are not particularly relevant during the process of initial assessment, then they become even less so once the person has been admitted as a patient to the unit. Many patients in forensic psychiatric care can recall very difficult histories, often involving experiences of extreme neglect, physical and sexual abuse. Addressing such issues is not part of the remit of the unit, rather, the primary concern is the stabilisation of symptoms of poor mental health. In part, this is because the working institutional assumption is that the kinds of mental health issues that are seen in forensic psychiatric care are lifelong conditions, which can be managed but are never 'curable' in the usual sense of that term. This can be a source of distress to patients, who do perceive their experiences as being directly relevant to their current mental well-being and self-esteem:

Extract 7.2

P: Sometimes you tell them things [the staff] and they don't give a shit about it [the patient here is referring to an alleged sexual assault by a staff member]. It's probably like being on trial. You have told one of the doctors, the junior doctors, and she just said to me, I can't really do nothing about it because it was in the past, in the past and we are here now.

In this extract, a patient reports a clear distinction being made between past experiences and the here and now. Medical intervention is limited to addressing her current feelings and thoughts. Nothing can be done to address anything that happened prior to the present admission. Getting 'well', therefore, appears to be a matter of ensuring adherence to medication and a suspension of deeper issues that might perhaps disrupt the process of becoming settled on the ward. As one patient remarks:

Extract 7.3

P: I find that they're generally not approachable you know if it comes – you talk about the medication, you talk about you know they've got a checklist of things that they want to talk about . . . And any deeper issues I find that I can't talk to them about it. Things that have happened before. No. No . . . The deeper issues no . . . You can talk about the medical side of things . . . and you know how you're feeling, whether you're experiencing symptoms, you know how – how are you coping on the medication with side effects and things like that. You know what's – you know in general terms how you are progressing, but deeper things, you can't talk to them about. I've tried and they just go back to their checklist . . . and just ticking boxes.

The patient describes discussions with clinicians as focussing solely on present thoughts and feelings. The past is thus treated as irrelevant, despite the clear sense this patient has of the significance of the 'deeper issues' for understanding his current situation. The sense of there being a 'checklist' of general clinical issues brings the patient's desire to discuss their personal history into direct conflict with the 'categories of thought' of the institutional assemblage. What clinicians seem to want from their interaction with patients are reports on 'wellness', covering matters such as current 'feelings', symptoms, responses to medication and so on. In Douglas's terms, this interaction establishes the matrix for the kinds of 'self-knowledge' and 'identity' that the institution will accredit. Only those personal experiences that can be made to fit with the terms of this matrix will be recognised. Being a well patient concerns purely what one thinks, feels and does in the present and the extent to which this maps on to the normative categories in play within the institution.

Here, we can see how the past becomes folded into the current system of monitoring behavioural and chemical indicators of 'well-being'. This was captured in our observations of nursing staff constructing patient notes that were solely directed towards the presence and absence of symptoms and signs of disruptive behaviour. In practical terms, this involved cutting and pasting the previous week's report on a patient into their current week's file, as there

168 Forgetting who you were

was 'no change in their symptoms', and thus no information on their experience outside of this. The physical space participates in this institutional process, as notes were produced literally behind the locked doors and glass surroundings of the nursing station, never in consultation with patients, but at a literal physical distance from them.

The major practices and 'categories of thought' operating within the unit aim at stabilisation of patients within the present, rather than facilitating access to the past or establishing its present relevance. What is, of course, absent from this current project of stabilisation is its continual mediation by the temporal and spatial complexities we have discussed so far. For example, the space of the ward, which serves as the environment for patients, folds within it relations from beyond its own physical boundaries, including the home spaces and intimate relations of the staff. Although considerations of what has happened outside the unit are not deemed relevant in understanding a patient's current 'wellness', patients claim that matters such as their confidence, behaviour and self-esteem are all affected by this folding-in of outside relations:

> Extract 7.4
> Um (. . .) I suppose looking at it maybe they've [i.e. staff members] had a fight at home, or they've had an argument with their wife, or whatever, they haven't paid the bill or whatever, they've had financial difficulty. They bring their emotions on to the ward, and they take it out on the patients, you know, you know they like they shout at you and talk to you like you're an animal, you're a third class person . . . it makes you, you feel like, it makes you feel like you're unworthy, you're not worth anything, you know. If you're trying to build up confidence because that's how you've felt before, you're trying to build your self-esteem and stay focused and try to make a life for yourself, you know, it's just makes you feel despondent.

Topologically speaking, even though the home spaces of staff are remote, they are still present and formative in the affective landscape of the patient (and staff). The project of 'wellness', which involves being able to display control over things such as self-esteem, is interrupted by relations on the ward, which are in turn shaped by relational vectors from the 'outside'. It seems that, although temporal and spatial relations beyond the ward are deemed irrelevant for assessing wellness, they are continuously entering into the life-space of patients via their interaction with staff. Or, put slightly differently, the institutional assemblage is porous and leaky with regard to its management of relations. However, this

Forgetting who you were   169

cannot be formally acknowledged, creating a paradox that is not lost upon patients: *you want me to be well by focusing only on the present, but you ignore how that present is being continuously pushed and pulled by forces from the outside.*

Corporeal transformations

If one aspect of the institutional assemblage is the deployment of categories of thought that constitute a 'regime of forgetting' focused on maintaining 'wellness', then the other is the organisation of bodies and corporeal relations on the unit. What we see here is the way that patient bodies become groupings within the institututional assemblage that are mediated by psychotropic medication. Patients on the unit are normally required to take a range of medication, ranging from 'typical' and 'atypical' antipsychotic treatment to drugs for depression and anxiety, along with other medication for managing side-effects and physical symptoms.[24] Medication can be experienced in a wide range of ways, depending on the individual concerned. Antipsychotics, for example, may sedate feelings of paranoia or hearing voices, but they can also bring about restlessness, sleepiness, felt slowness of thinking, sexual dysfunction, dizziness and excess saliva.

In this way, the body can act as a site of transformation, where new ways of relating to oneself are constituted. We call these novel self-relations *psychologically modified experiences* (PMEs). Using an analogy with genetically modified organisms, we have argued elsewhere that forensic psychiatric care reformulates experiences from the existing 'experience-ecology'.[25] For example, prior to entering care, patients may have had varied and diverse experiences around sexuality. On the unit itself, however, patients are encouraged to view sexuality as either something that must be entirely 'left behind' or as inherently risky and potentially compromising of 'wellness'. This reshaping of what sexuality is and what it can mean is further compounded by antipsychotic medication, which can leave patients feeling estranged from themselves as sexual beings – as one of the patients put it, 'this place has amputated my sexuality'.[26] Patients then come to experience a very different version of sexuality from that which they have known before. PMEs are constituted as novel experiences that combine elements that are both highly concrete (e.g. sexual feelings, bodily sensations) and highly abstract (e.g. discourses of risk and predation, the need to present oneself as 'well'). Having been adopted during the course of secure care, PMEs remain with patients as part of their efforts to demonstrate 'wellness' once they return to community-based care.

170   Forgetting who you were

As an institutional assemblage, the unit both organises bodies, placing them into particular temporal and spatial relations with one another, and organises *through* bodies, by acting directly on the feelings and experiences of patients, in part through direct intervention in their biological states. How the patient moves through the ward and hospital space is marked both by the invariant structures of the physical space and through the corporeal affordances created by the medication. The felt sense of detachment from the past that patients experience comes as much from this organising of bodies as it does from discursive practices of discounting prior experience. There can be, of course, direct cognitive impacts of medication that may impair memory. For instance, we have found in our work that 'settled' patients taking antipsychotics are rarely able to sustain a conversation in a research interview beyond 30–45 minutes. However, our particular interest here is in the experiential and felt sense of the past being literally *displaced* via the operations of medication upon the body and subsequent enactments in time and space. One of the major ways in which a separation between the past and present is created and sustained is through literal transformations in the shape and functioning of the body. Patients reported this with some regularity:

Extract 7.5
P: When I was on Clozapine, I put on a lot of weight. And the thing is I hate about Clozapine is that people really like just go on and on about it. But it's not all that you know. With me, it had such bad side effects . . . My heart beated really fast. It was like 130. You know, I was always drooling. I was tired a lot. You know, I slept a lot. I put on a lot of weight, you know. I went from size 12 to 22 and I'm still a 22 and I'm trying to lose weight.

Changes to the body were largely reported to be unpleasant and anxiety inducing, physiologically (rapid heartbeat) and psychologically (tiredness and weight gain). Female patients expressed particular concern about weight gain. Entry into the unit involved, not just a loss of liberty, but also a loss of control over one's body image. Gaining significant amounts of weight acted as a very visible marker of the transformation of one's identity brought about by being sectioned. The past is here directly indexed to one's physical appearance before being transferred and the lack of any subsequent significant development during time on the ward – 'I went from a size 12 to 22 and I'm still a 22'. Many patients commented on their 'past self' being lost to a newly modified self, brought about by changes to the body and, subsequently, mood. This was sometimes thought to be irreversible and, hence, problematic. However, it could also be recuperated by taking ownership of the discourse of 'wellness', such as in the following:

Extract 7.6
P: But I must admit the medication has helped me over the years, just calmed me down a lot . . . my moods stabilized as well with that. But I will say I am not the same person I was 22 years ago. I've changed completely. And the medication has helped me, you know, it has helped me really.

Here, ideas of being 'stable' and 'settled' are used to reformulate the loss of a former self. Being 'not the same person' is presented as a positive transformation.

Medication also heightens the stretching of temporal relations on the ward. Patients described a slowing down of time in general, due to fatigue. This can be clearly seen when one enters a ward on the unit. Patients tend to move slowly, often without clear purpose, and may at times simply lie on the floor or sofa. Many describe an alteration in their perception of time, feeling as though their 'body clock' no longer operated as it once did. As one patient remarked: 'I sleep during the day, and am awake during the night. My body doesn't know what it's doing. The way I was before doesn't resemble what I'm doing now at all. It's weird.'

If the invariant physical structure of the ward itself offers few opportunities to structure the day, beyond occasional routine appointments, then the effects of medication act to complexify further the sense of time passing. For the most part, patients are left to make their own choices about where they wish to spend the day in the relatively restricted space of the ward. Typically, this makes for an irregular pattern of sleeping, interacting with others, eating and watching television. Some patients describe this as retreating between their bedroom and communal areas, with no real comfort to be found in either space – you stay with others until it becomes too much, you be by yourself until you can handle it no longer. Time unfolds through this alternation without purpose.

The discourse of 'wellness' and 'settled' wards finds its counterpart in an ordering of patients as docile bodies, whose movements and patterns of activity are fairly stable. For patients, this means that control over their own bodies comes to be seen as emblematic of finding a way beyond the immediate boundaries of the unit. For example, in the following, one of the researchers asks a patient how she manages to deal with the interactional difficulties of life on the ward:

172   Forgetting who you were

Extract 7.7

R: You said . . . over here you found it quite difficult because you remember certain things that people said that were prejudiced. But it does sound quite difficult . . . how do you cope with that difficulty? . . . What sort of things do you focus on?

P: Well, getting out, losing weight, growing my hair, just having a future, like things I want to do in the future.

The 'future' the patient envisages here involves a return to a past physical state. For this woman, growing her hair back to its original state and losing the weight she had gained on medication signified a prior sense of self and a felt sense of agency. In this way, connecting with both the past and the future seems directly mediated by taking control of embodiment – if I can get back to how I used to look, I will become again the person I was before I came here. The way out of the regime of forgetting is through the self-relation to the body. However, it is not easy to find the means to be able to work on this self-relation, as the experiences that predate admission have been overlaid with PMEs.

In the next extract, a patient describes how his relationship to medication and his body has changed during his time on the unit:

Extract 7.8

P: [the medication means] I'm tired all the time

R: Mm

P: So, I don't know, if it's normal, but I guess it is normal but that's one thing like, that I don't really like it all really . . . Because I used to be much more active than I am now.

R: Hm, mm

P: And mm, I just haven't got the strength you need to like do exercise and stuff like that you know.

R: God and did you talk about these side effects with your Doctor?

P: Yeah, I mentioned it a few times . . . Now here's the funny thing about it, is that I, I, I could just laugh about it up until about 3 years ago, I said this about 4 years 'cos I've been away for a long time you know . . . I said to him, I used to go to the gym . . . then after that I'd go swimming, and skipping and he's like 'you've past your peak', and I'm like (young) . . . Do I don't know, I, I I I feel really frustrated if I couldn't get out and do stuff, so I just smoke instead.

Forgetting who you were 173

In this reporting of a doctor–patient interaction, the patient talks about his past active self being replaced by a tired and inactive version. For the patient, this is entirely attributable to the side-effects of medication, because, as he puts, 'I'm like young'. The comment he reports the doctor as making – 'you've past your peak' – is then double-edged. On the one hand, it could be interpreted as simple reference to the patient's age, because, as he himself acknowledges, 'I've been away for a long time'. But it seems more likely that this comment points to a shared knowledge between doctor and patient that ageing works differently in secure care. Long-term antipsychotic medication can accelerate the development of many physical markers usually associated with ageing, such as high blood pressure, stiffness and shaking, diabetes. Patients in secure care can also develop problems with teeth and gums, through lack of care and dietary issues. When this is taken together with weight gain and a general lack of exercise, patients can both look and feel 'past their prime' at a far earlier chronological age than would be expected. So, whereas patients are suspended in a present that allows little reference to past or future, their bodies may be marking out time at an excessive rate. Small wonder that, when confronted with this realisation that he will never be able to return to both the body and the self of the man he was before secure care, this patient decides to 'just smoke instead'.

Some patients make direct links between these kinds of transformation to the body through medication and being unable to remember what their body can do at a basic level, in terms of activities such as eating, moving and being sexual. This results in a changing relationship to self:

Extract 7.9

P: They want to . . . you've got . . . Yeah because I'm on medication, I can't sleep, yeah, you don't feel like eating, you don't feel like going to the gym, you don't feel like exercising, you know, but that's not what it should be like, you – you look after yourself, for the girls and you know that, but we don't have that do you can't that no more . . . we've got that – you don't have, you don't understand what sex is anymore.

R: Right . . . Could you tell me a bit more about that, that you don't understand what sex is. What you mean you sort of forget about it, or?

P: Yeah

R: Right, OK

P: It's like a (a drug) Yeah . . . making you work a lot of the time, work a lot of the time, you know . . . And they can't see, yeah. Obviously don't understand, but it changes, it does change the way you see contact, you know, it changes, your personality changes. So it changes after that – a long time off them and it changes . . . Because I don't really have thoughts (sexual), you know what I mean, you know, that, I can't appreciate it any more.

As this patient describes it, sexuality was previously integral to how he related to his own body, because 'you look after yourself, for the girls'. Once the possibility of sexual expression has been removed, following his transfer to secure care, he begins to neglect his body, a process that is intensified by the demotivating effects of medication. This leaves him in the situation of feeling displaced in relation to his own embodiment – 'you don't understand what sex is anymore'. Sexuality belongs with the person he was before. In his current state, he no longer experiences sexual thoughts: he has become estranged from that physical aspect of what he was. Another patient describes this process of corporeal displacement directly as 'forgetting':

Extract 7.10
R: Okay (. . .) So have you been able to continue feeling and being sexual while you've been here?
P: No . . . Well, I I don't plan, I don't really think of sex a lot, I don't even know if I remember how to do it, I've forgotten how to do it.

If sexuality belongs to a past that is neither relevant nor entirely thinkable in terms of the discursive practices and ordering of bodies on the unit, then it may, perhaps, be ceded to a future that lies after the ending of the section, on return to the community. However, as this patient describes it, the displacement or forgetting of that aspect of one's embodiment makes it difficult to imagine how one could resume life as a sexual being – 'I've forgotten how to do it'. The discounting of past experiences and feelings here seems to set up a future where, even if the patient does leave the ward, they will be, in a sense, stuck in the 'presentism' that it inculcates. It is this sense of the irreversible nature of the transformations that occur in terms of one's relation to oneself that seems most troubling to patients:

Extract 7.11
P: I would say this place has amputated my sexuality. Definitely, it's – it's not my home, it's not – it's not a free environment and (. . .) it's a – it's so anti-life. I just don't even think about sexuality in here and I grieve over that quite a lot. And (. . .) I try and cope with this place on its own

terms, you know and whatever it has to offer me I will engage with. So and try to make it a reality, its own reality but I still can't feel human enough to be a sexual being in this environment.

We read this extract as a description of what can happen to the life-space of the patient when it is absorbed into the ordering practices of the ward. This patient focuses in particular on the lack of private space and restricted movement. She uses the phrase 'anti-life' to sum up her feeling. Everything here seems corrosive of the vitality of living. She has become estranged from the feelings and experiences that made her the person she was. She is now a body without a past and, apparently, with little sense of the future.

The institutional forgetting performed by the unit, then, appears to reach its point of maximum intensity in this constitution of a thoroughgoing interactional and corporeal displacement of the personal pasts of patients. These are persons who most certainly have vital memories of the kind we have discussed throughout the book. In fact, many patients in secure forensic psychiatric care have past experiences of sexual abuse, physical neglect and distressing times that they take to be entirely relevant to understanding their current situation. Why should they not be allowed to speak of them, or to even feel the person they once were?

A straightforward counter-argument would be that these are people who have committed crimes and, even though they are not deemed to be responsible for their own actions, they ought to be punished to some extent for what they have done. However, we suspect that many patients would welcome being transferred back to the criminal justice system (where you can at least smoke . . .).[27] The issue here is that the unit is neither a space of punishment, nor a space of treatment. It is, instead, an assemblage that functions around notions of 'wellness' and 'being settled', and, in pursuit of these goals, it narrows the life-space of the patient to a concentrated existence in an ongoing present moment, while, at the same time, exposing patients to a churn of relations that causes the assemblage to continuously leak at many points.

In a sense, patients never really leave the unit. As an institutional assemblage, the unit extends into the community. Patients whose section comes to an end still remain within the discursive practices and medication regimes that are centred on the unit, which are then ceded to community psychiatric nurses and police authorities. An individual may cease to be technically a patient, but the need remains for them to be able to demonstrate 'wellness' continuously, under the potential threat of being sectioned again.

The issue then, as we see it, is as follows. If remembering is a means by which we can relationally expand life-space to make connections with others and with our lives together, then what kind of community is being fostered by disconnecting the users of forensic psychiatric services from their own pasts? Life-space expands when we work together to construct 'common notions'. It is on the basis of this commonness that we are able to make connections and to expand our joint capacities to feel and act, to build futures together. If we do not wish to simply incarcerate individuals in forensic psychiatric care, then it seems strangely self-defeating to rob them of the felt memorial capacity to participate in the building of the kind of 'non-carceral' societies that we value so greatly.

Notes

1 Goffman, 1991.
2 Forensic psychiatric units are graded from 'low' through 'medium' to 'secure'. Secure means that patients are not able to leave the unit without the agreement of clinicians. Although there are only three high-security units in England – Broadmoor, Ashworth and Rampton – medium- and low-security units are maintained by every NHS trust. Medium units are typically co-located with general hospitals. Around two-thirds of units use single-sex wards, but mixed-sexed wards are found in the remaining third (Fleming, 2007). The work we have conducted has been on single-sex wards.
3 Department of Health, 1983.
4 Although we are mindful of the problematic nature of the term *patient* to describe individuals who use mental health services in general, here we use the term to describe only persons registered as patients on the psychiatric hospital ward. Therefore, the term patient is used deliberately and specifically.
5 See Mol and Law, 1994; Law and Mol, 1998.
6 This can only be a loose term, because, as actor-network theory has demonstrated in some considerable detail, there are no firm distinctions to be drawn between domains such as 'society', 'science', 'technology', 'nature' etc. This argument is most closely associated with Bruno Latour's work (e.g. Latour, 1993, 2005, 2013).
7 Mol and Law, 1994: 643.
8 Foucault, 2003, 2007.
9 See Salter (2013) for an argument that relates Foucault's work to the current 'mobilities' paradigm in social science.
10 Bennett, 2010: 23–4.
11 See DeLanda, 2006; Phillips, 2006; Anderson and McFarlane, 2011.
12 A depot injection is a method of delivering antipsychotic medication that is administered directly into large-muscle tissue, such as the buttocks. It is slow releasing and typically lasts up to 6 weeks.
13 See Brown *et al.* (2014) for more details.
14 Blu-Tack is a trademarked name for low-adhesion putty.
15 These are, of course, very challenging environments for staff to work it, with physical violence towards staff being a continuous possibility.

16 A general practitioner (GP) is a non-specialist medical doctor. Patients have appointments with GPs for routine health issues, along with appointments with their consulting psychiatrists and clinical psychologists.

17 The ban on smoking on secure units is one major reason why some patients say they would actually prefer to be in prison. It is a practical and symbolic marker of the relative lack of autonomy on the unit compared with in the penal system.

18 Brown *et al.*, 2014.

19 In the UK, patients who enter an NHS facility through the criminal justice system can be detained indefinitely, through regular reviews of their section, if they are deemed to be a risk to society owing to their mental state.

20 Douglas, 1987.

21 Ibid.: 112.

22 See Boyle (2002) and Bentall (2004). For an overview of how one might systematically think alternative perspectives in mental health, including service-user perspectives, see Cromby *et al.* (2013).

23 See Cromby *et al.*, 2013.

24 Clozapine is the dominant form of antipsychotic medication used in secure care.

25 See Brown *et al.*, 2014.

26 Ibid.: 250.

27 Though a UK high court judge has recently ruled in favour of a nation-wide smoking ban in prisons, which could lead to a total ban in the near future.

Chapter 8

Recollection in later life
The reminiscence museum

When my grandmother was in the last few months of her life, she repeatedly told a brief story. She spoke of seeing a German zeppelin floating in the sky that had been struck by artillery fire. The zeppelin was consumed with flames. The crew, in a desperate bid to escape the fire, threw themselves from the airship. She described the sight of the falling bodies tumbling through the air to the earth.

I don't recall ever hearing this story as a child. This is very strange, considering just how dramatic and striking this image is. Perhaps it was not considered a story fit for children. Perhaps – and this is more likely – I simply hadn't paid enough attention. Why did she return to this story at the end? What was its importance? What was she seeking to communicate?

The more I think about this story, the more puzzled I am by it. The event she spoke of must have occurred around 1915–1917, during the First World War. At the time she would have been between 6 and 8 years old. Was this a story based on her direct experience? It seems strange that young child would catch sight of such a dramatic event in the middle of an air raid. Or was it a vicarious memory, someone else's experience as told to her at the time and subsequently recounted over the years? Or maybe, given how strongly the image seems to resemble the Hindenburg disaster, the story was a collage of sources that had gelled together over time through repeated telling.

So again – why that story then? What was that act of storytelling doing? And more importantly, why didn't I understand? What did I miss?

Remembering hard times

Throughout this book, we have been concerned to look at the memory practices of 'ordinary people managing difficult pasts'. Psychologists all too readily place the remembering of difficult and painful experiences within a framework of 'deficit' or 'extremity'. This is especially so when the persons concerned are deemed to be vulnerable – children, adults with mental health issues, survivors of sexual violence, survivors of indiscriminate terrorism, the elderly. In this penultimate chapter, we turn towards this last group. Ageing is, of course, marked by progressive physical changes, such as relating to mobility, which require adaptation. It also brings about cognitive and neurological changes, which have a progressive impact on capacities to remember. It is these latter changes that have become more prominent in public discourses around ageing. There is now, for example, a significant popular literature on changing family relationships around elderly persons experiencing dementia. Sally Magnusson's *Where Memories Go: Why dementia changes everything*, for example, describes her attempts to enable her mother, Mamie Baird Magnusson, to hold on to her capacity to relate to the past through storytelling in the face of cognitive decline.[1] Likewise, the memoir of Iris Murdoch, written by her partner John Bayley, focuses on the dissolution of her memory and sense of identity during the progress of Alzheimer's disease.[2]

In texts such as these, dementia is treated primarily as a *disease of memory*. An increasing inability to situate themselves in relation to past and present is seen to gradually pull apart the self of the sufferer, creating distress to those around them. In the cases of Mamie Bird Magnusson and Iris Murdoch, this is seen as a particularly cruel condition, as both were wordsmiths, skilled at the art of memory and storytelling. Dementia is seen here as robbing individuals of the most fundamental aspects of their character, as leaving them helpless in the care of those they love, but whom they no longer even recognise.

This way of approaching the memorial challenges of ageing speaks to an increasing number of people, given the demographic rise of an 'ageing population' in the Global North and the failure of many social welfare systems to adequately address the complex care needs of the elderly and their families. However, we should not allow these facts to persuade us that ageing needs to be solely placed in a framework of inevitable decline and associated familial and social problems. There is now a strong literature on 'critical social gerontology' that looks instead to the capacities and life experiences of older people.[3] Mike Hepworth's work focused on the tension between the cultural construction of 'ageing' and the lived, personal experience of later life.[4] Joanna Latimer has been concerned with how older persons perform identity and participation in care settings, and the ways these are responded to by care staff.[5] Michael Schillmeier discusses the affective and embodied dynamics that accompany the move to long-term nursing care.[6] The message that strongly comes through this work is that adaptation to the changes and challenges of ageing is co-constituted by persons within the socio-material settings through which they pass.

There is strong resonance here with the view of remembering as a distributed, setting-level accomplishment that we have been working with. The ways in which older persons make use of the past are interdependent with relational features of the settings in which they participate. For example, in Middleton and Brown's analysis of elderly people remembering together in 'reminiscence therapy' sessions, a shared 'habitable world' is co-constructed by participants through pointing to the embodied and material aspects of the past events they jointly remember.[7] What is remembered is the outcome of a collaborative activity, which, moreover, depends upon the affordances of particular objects (in the examples given by Middleton and Brown, these involve clothes, bottles, washing tubs, etc.). This is not to say that individual matters, such as neurological deterioration, are irrelevant. It is indisputably the case that being in possession of an 'ageing brain' has an effect on what one can remember. However, if remembering is performed at a setting level, then these 'intra-cranial' resources are not the sole determinants of what is recalled (in the same way that, as Manier notes, a wing is not a sufficient condition to enable flying).[8] As we will show in this chapter, external resources – other people, objects, the contours of the material environment – are involved in the interactional performance of memory.

The material we will discuss in this chapter comes from a study of a 'reminiscence museum' (*Herinneringsmuseum*) based in a care home for the elderly on the outskirts of Rotterdam in the Netherlands.[9] The reminiscence museum consists of a series of specially constructed rooms built in the basement of the care home. Most of the rooms have been arranged to resemble a Dutch domestic space from the first half of the twentieth century. For instance, 'the nursery' comprises a bed, cabinets and a large collection of toys that are arranged to create the effect of a child's bedroom. All of the objects in the space can be picked up and inspected (visitors are, in fact, encouraged to do so by staff in the museum). The museum has amassed a huge range of artefacts, ranging from period furniture, decorations and clothing to kitchen equipment and toys.

The items are, for the most part, donated or specially acquired by the curator, Inez van den Dobelsteen-Becker. Some rooms house large collections of key items (e.g. cameras), which are kept in glass cabinets. Others – such as the space known as 'the workshop' – are almost overwhelmed with objects that are heaped on top of one another. One room – 'the grocery shop' – stands out as it has been arranged to resemble a neighbourhood shop, filled with boxes of period grocery items, jars of sweets and a working cash register. This room was one of the earliest to be completed when work on the museum began in 2006.

The reminiscence museum draws upon techniques that have been developed in the now well-established practice of 'reminiscence therapy' with older people.[10] This is a therapeutic intervention that is designed to facilitate recollection by inviting participants to interact with objects, photographs or music. The immediate goal is to provoke spontaneous recollection of autobiographical memories, which are then scaffolded by the facilitator of the session. The longer-term benefit to the participant is the enabling of a process of 'life review' – a reflection on one's personal past and accomplishments.[11] Reminiscence therapy is typically conducted with groups, where it may have the additional outcome of generating interaction and common identification across the participants.[12]

Despite drawing upon the tools of the practice, the reminiscence museum was not explicitly designed as a therapeutic space. Hans Becker, the former director of the care provider – Humanitas – that runs the care home, has stated that the purpose of the museum is simply to facilitate 'happiness'. Humanitas is a care-provider organisation, based in the Netherlands, that specialises in care for the elderly (it also provides some care for marginal persons – drug users, sex workers and the homeless – whom it refers to as the 'young old').[13] The organisation has run care facilities for almost 50 years, principally in the Rotterdam area. It currently maintains over forty care homes. A pivotal moment in the history of Humanitas was the appointment of Hans Becker as director in 1992. Becker initiated a change process that sought entirely to reshape how Humanitas went about delivering care. As Letiche describes it, this new vision of care was based on a simple premise:

> The director of Humanitas began the change process by posing the following question: 'Assume that you are in the last two or three years of your life. You are alone and often very lonely. What would give you enough pleasure to get you voluntarily out of bed in the morning?' The

answer did not come as a grand flash of revelation, but as lots of small ideas. These ideas included: an appointment to set coffee for the neighbor, a primary school child who is coming for lunch, a plan to drink tea in the atrium. The answers all had to do with the social surroundings, in which one lives. It helps if there is lots of color and sunshine in the building and art and *objets d'art* are all about. A giant aviary or a 375,000 liter aquarium would help.[14]

Humanitas built a series of experimental spaces to realise this vision. These spaces are mixed (in fact, so mixed that planning permission was initially difficult to obtain, as the applications did not fit into existing local-government categories). For example, the Akropolis building, in which the reminiscence museum is based, comprises two blocks of apartments facing towards one another across a huge, central, covered atrium. The atrium opens out on to a restaurant and bar complex, which is open to both visitors and residents. This complex is augmented with a small supermarket, a hairdressing salon and an internet café. Together, these are known as the 'village square'. Visitors to the home pass by way of a 'petting zoo' that keeps a range of small animals. Once inside, visitors are confronted with a range of antique wheelchairs (all of which are usable) and space in which seemingly every inch is either brightly painted in vibrant colours, or contains an artwork or decorative object (e.g. a huge sitting Buddha, masks, old musical instruments). The atrium is typically filled with activity, as visitors and clients move around the various facilities. On occasion, visitors may encounter less predictable events. We have observed indoor markets, the arrival of coachloads of visitors to the museum and, on one particularly memorable visit, the construction of a life-size nativity scene attended by an entourage of specially dressed Sinterklaas helpers. Sadly, we missed the fondly remembered occasion on which the director celebrated his birthday by riding a camel through the building.[15]

The aim of this space is to transform what could be a 'misery island' into a place of continuous activity, where elderly clients have opportunities to focus their attention on things beyond their own immediate health.[16] For example, wheelchairs are usually potent symbols of debilitation. At Akropolis, they are first of all aesthetic objects, there as 'conversational pieces' and sources of ironic humour. Although there are the full range of healthcare facilities based on site at Akropolis (including a nursing home for clients entering into stages of severe debilitation), these are arranged on the periphery of the space, rather than at the centre. By integrating the homes into the surrounding area and by making them fully accessible to the local community, as well as the families of resident clients, Humanitas aims to turn its care spaces inside out. Visitors are drawn to Akropolis for many reasons other than obligation. The reminiscence museum is, in this sense, an extension of previous practice, rather than an entirely new direction. It was initially conceived as another innovation that would involve residents in their own environment (the museum is maintained in part by clients) and would bring visitors to Akropolis.[17] Over time, it has, however, become a significant attraction in its own right, with elderly and younger persons from across the Netherlands coming to Rotterdam specifically to visit.

The reminiscence museum can be characterised as an experimental space of memory. Unlike reminiscence therapy, which aims to steer participants towards recall of positive autobiographical memories, the museum is designed as a lure to all kinds of remembering – both good and bad. As Elena Bendien describes:

> The museum appears to have the power to generate an entire range of emotional responses amongst its visitors. One of them remarked thoughtfully that 'the museum gives the warmth of remembering'. Another visitor just wandered around the place dumbfounded, muttering 'Oh boy, oh boy!' from time to time and wiping his tears away shyly. Yet another one stated assertively that the first time she came to the museum she 'felt happy and satisfied'.[18]

The museum provokes strong feelings among visitors. As it has no therapeutic agenda beyond creating an experience, this can result in the surfacing of a wide range of affects. Whereas some elderly visitors experience joy through the recognition of objects from their past, others pass through the museum sullenly, with very few words to say. It's not uncommon for a few elderly visitors to become angry and to question why the curators have seen fit to keep hold of all this useless 'rubbish'.[19] There is a risk of drawing out problematic memories, through the setting up of a confrontation between past and present that might have been hitherto settled for some visitors. The past that visitors are asked to engage with contains within it difficult experiences – war, hard times, poverty, starvation. As we will see, some of these challenging experiences are directly inscribed on a number of objects that are on display.

The majority of visitors come accompanied or in groups. These can be groups of older people together or, more often, older persons accompanied by their now adult children (and grandchildren). The Akropolis home, like many owned by Humanitas, has gone to some lengths to draw relatives and members of the local community to visit, from providing free Internet access to high-quality, subsidised food and drink. We might say that the space of the home, and more specifically of the museum, 'collects' together social relations by offering the means for different kinds of intergenerational communication. In the museum, for example, older relatives may appoint themselves as guides for the duration of the visit, explaining the character of individual objects. Equally, elderly visitors who are less mobile or who are increasingly withdrawn may be taken round the museum by their younger relatives, who question them on particular things they encounter.

The intergenerational use of the reminiscence museum makes for a contrast with the work around memory done in the adoptive families that we discussed in Chapter 5. There, it was parents who took responsibility for managing the past of their children. In the museum, the roles are reversed, with adult children now feeling the obligation to act as witnesses and custodians of the memories of their elderly parents. The memories that emerge in the course of this intergenerational interaction can be surprising, difficult to immediately grasp, and sometimes difficult to manage.

In this penultimate chapter, we offer a small, partial tour around the reminiscence museum and explore the challenges of inviting good and bad memories. We will illustrate the tour with photographs of the museum and with snippets of material taken from visits by elderly people. Our guiding concern will be with what it means to reopen past difficulties – vital memories – in later life. What might the sudden expansion in life-space do for those who tell their stories? And what obligations does it come to confer on those who hear them?

The sitting room

One the major spaces within the reminiscence museum comprises two consecutive sitting rooms, arranged in the styles of the 1940s and the 1960s, respectively. It is striking to enter a room that feels like a 'home' (see Figure 8.1). Chairs are placed near one another. A board game is set up on the table, as though the occupants of the home had briefly decamped to another room.[20] There are pictures hanging on the wall, and a range of ornaments surround the room. In one corner there is a large radio unit that, through a not-strictly-historically-accurate technical sleight of hand, can be made to play music of the time. It is difficult, on entering the room, to keep in mind that one is actually in the basement of the care home.

Figure 8.1 The 1940s sitting room
Source: Photo © Elena Bendien

Daniel Miller speaks of the traces left on domestic space by the aesthetic decisions of its previous and current occupants.[21] Objects and material relations both embody the social relations in which they have become embedded, while, at the same time, appearing to transcend these relations. Crudely put, the objects tend to outlive their owners. This creates a peculiar relationship to the domestic space of others that Miller labels with the punning phrase 'estate agency'.[22] The material space seems to prolong the actions of others into our present. In the reminiscence museum, this takes on a particular form. Many of the objects in the museum have been donated by older persons who have undergone house 'clearance' prior to a move into care-home accommodation.[23] Donating possessions to the museum is a way of projecting something of oneself into the future. On entering the sitting room, one feels a sense of that work of projecting self, without being able to properly articulate who or what is the source of that feeling.

In the following extract, we can see two elderly visitors experiencing something of the 'estate agency' constituted by the arrangement of the 1940s sitting room. Their focus is on a drying rack that has been placed around a fireplace (see Figure 8.2). The woman (W) and man (M) are accompanied

186 Recollection in later life

here by a female museum volunteer (MW), whose role is to provide additional guidance, if desired:

Extract 8.1

(They walk into the living-room) — (*Ze lopen de woonkamer binnen*)

W: Oh, look, a drying rack. — W: *O kijk, een droogrekje.*

MW: Yes. — MW: *Ja.*

M: That is . . . yes. — M: *Dat is . . . ja.*

MW: This is a living-room dating back to the 1940s. And this one is from 1960. — MW: *Dit is een huiskamer van de jaren 1940, ongeveer. En dit is 1960.*

W: (unclear) — W: *(onverstaanbaar)*

MW: I find it a very warm, a truly warm living-room. — MW: *Ik vind het een hele warme, een echt warme huiskamer*

W: Yes. — W: *Ja*

MW: And the rack around of the stove, see? — MW: *En het rekje om de kachel, he?*

W (laughs): Yes. — W *(met een lachje): Ja.*

M: Nice, isn't it? (nostalgic) — M: *Leuk, hoor (nostalgisch)*

W: A pity, isn't it? And the tea cosy. Yes, it looks very cosy. — W: *Jammer, he? En de theemuts. Ja, ziet er echt gemoedelijk uit.*

W: Slippers, the father's, all ready (pause), for when he came home. — W: *Slofjes, van vader, staan al klaar, (pauze) als die thuis kwam.*

MW: Yes, yes. — MW: *Ja, ja.*

The extract starts with the woman visitor drawing attention to the drying rack. The volunteer acknowledges the recognition of the object and tries to develop further interaction by offering some additional commentary on the room they have all just entered. But there is something about the drying rack that clearly draws the visitors to it. They stay fixed, looking at the object, and offer only minimal responses to the volunteer's attempt to initiate dialogue about the room as a whole. The volunteer turns the conversation back to the drying rack and this time solicits the near simultaneous responses of 'Nice, isn't it?' and 'A pity, isn't it?'.

Recollection in later life 187

Figure 8.2 Drying rack in the 1940s sitting room
Source: Photo © Elena Bendien

188 Recollection in later life

Although the two comments from the visitors appear to be contradictory, they can be seen to affirm what is striking about the drying rack. It is 'nice', as it is a token of a world they both know. This is a world of domestic order centred on the sitting room, where objects are placed to anticipate daily routines – the washing and drying of clothes, the return of 'the father' from work. Things are exactly where they should be, and by extension family relations are in the right place. But it is also 'a pity', because this is a world that no longer exists. It is not simply that the people themselves who populated the 1940s sitting room are gone; it is that the social relations that can be traced outward from the arrangement of objects no longer endure. The sitting room is a *disruptive space*. It offers the opportunity to fold life-space back from old age to childhood. The visitors can see and touch objects that afford the feeling of past social relations, but they can do so only by affirming, at the same time, the irrevocable loss of the world in which those social relations were constituted.

This joint affordance of closeness and loss can make it difficult for visitors to know exactly how they ought to respond to the space. One strategy is to begin to repopulate the arrangement of objects with people and stories from the past. In the next exchange, an elderly couple discuss a rug hung on the wall of a living room, visible in Figure 8.2. The conversation then moves towards the table in Figure 8.1:

Extract 8.2

W: And such a rug above that dish, you draped it, didn't you, yes, indeed . . . (M: Was beautiful) . . . And do you know that your granddad cut the cloth sometimes?

W: *En zo'n kleed boven die schaal, die drapeerde je, he, ja, ja . . . (M: Was mooi.) . . . En weet je dat je opa het kleed wel eens sneed?*

M & MW: Oh!

M en MW: *O!*

M: Yes.

M: *Ja.*

W: He was going to cut something off.

W: *Hij ging wat afsnijden.*

M (starts talking simultaneously): That was dramatic. That man, he always repaired shoes. Then he hammered the new, new soles under

M: *(door de vr heen): Dat was dramatisch. Die man, die repareerde altijd schoenen. Dan sloeg hij de nieuwe, nieuwe zolen onder*

MW (interrupts): He doesn't need to do that on the table, does he?	MW: (*onderbreekt*): *Dat hoeft hij toch niet op de tafel te doen?*
M: No, on the last, right.	M: *Nee, over de leest, he?*
MW: Yes, on the last.	MW: *Ja, over de leest.*
M: Because he had a steady hand and that was on the inside, the nail heads stood out, they were flattened afterwards of course but then you couldn't walk on them anymore . . . with cardboard he then cut soles and that he did that on the table sometimes, so he would be cutting, like this, like this and like this and that was in the shape of the soles he had cut right through the table-cloth. Of course my grandma had something to say . . .	M: *Want hij had een stevige hand en dat was aan de binnenkant, staken die spijker koppen uit, die werden daarna plat geslagen natuurlijk maar dan kon je er niet meer op lopen . . . van karton sneed hij dan zooltjes en dat deed hij wel op tafel, dus hij was wel aan het snijden, zo, zo en zo en dat was in de vorm van de zolen had hij zo het tafelkleed door gesneden. Nou mijn oma zei toen natuurlijk wel wat . . .*
(They laugh together)	(*Lachen allemaal*)

The woman visitor begins the exchange by pointing to the uses that would have been made in her childhood home of a rug such as the one hanging in the 1940s living-room space. She then turns to her husband and invokes a story about his grandfather. He responds enthusiastically and launches into what is no doubt a fairly well-rehearsed story that involves the grandfather overestimating his skills at shoe repair and accidentally cutting sole-shaped holes into the cloth covering the table. This concludes with the punchline about the grandmother's anger.

What is particularly interesting about this exchange is the way the story gets going. The woman takes the sight of the rug as an opportunity to retell an old family story. In some sense, this story 'belongs' to the man, as it relates to an event that he either witnessed or was told about as a child, before the couple met. As he begins to tell the story, the volunteer interrupts with a question about the proper techniques for repairing shoes. It appears that the visitors and the volunteer have slightly different agendas here. The volunteer seems concerned with the objects themselves – how they were used, the routines and activities around them. But the visitors see the objects as a means to tell their own stories. The man's story is not really about a rug like the one on the wall at all. His wife treats it as a way to give him the conversational floor for a moment, to recall that bit of the past, as he has probably done on many other occasions. As the story progresses, he goes further and moves towards the table in the sitting room to begin acting out the scene of the grandfather cutting away – 'so he would begin cutting, like this, like this and like this'. Each 'like this' is punctuated with a wild hand movement to demonstrate the blade moving fatefully through both the shoe material and the tablecloth, before the story comes to its climactic moment.

With regard to its content, this recollection is not really a vital memory in the same sense as most of the other memories we have discussed so far; there is little that is distressing about it. The story seems instead to be a longstanding source of amusement. However, there is something about the way it is enacted in the space of the reminiscence museum that does connect with this theme. The story is a response to the combination of closeness and loss afforded by the arrangement of the sitting room. The couple populate the space with characters from their early years, who have long since departed. We might say that, in the husband's energetic acting out of the cutting of the tablecloth, the grandfather is 'summoned up' as an actor in the here and now. In the process, the couple temporarily resolve the sense of a disappeared world by folding the past into the here and now. Yet, in some sense, they must be aware that this may be one of the last occasions they will be able to tell the story of the grandfather's mishaps. Most certainly it will never again be aired in this fashion, surrounded by the displaced objects of that past time. Hence, the woman's keenness to have the man tell (yet again) that familiar story, and his enthusiasm to perform it in just the right setting. The piquancy of this exchange is that, although the objects in the museum afford the opportunity to summon up the grandfather and grandmother, they will retain nothing of them once the story finishes. The rug stays. The grandparents fade.

There are some objects in the museum that do, on the contrary, have a story embedded in their form. There is a sideboard in the sitting room that draws the attention of many visitors (see Figure 8.3.). Many recognise it as being of a type they saw many years ago in a relative's home. This attention is somewhat surprising, as the sideboard, although old, is of relatively poor quality. The drawers fit badly, and the whole piece looks rather drab. Why would such an uninspiring object become so recognisable to visitors? As Bendien tells its, there is a good reason:

Recollection in later life 191

Figure 8.3 The sideboard
Source: Photo © Elena Bendien

Rotterdam was one of the few places in the Netherlands, which was severely bombed during the Second World War. Most of the population in Rotterdam lost literally all their possessions. Because the town authorities wanted to support as many people as possible, they ordered relatively cheap furniture to replace the things that were lost due to the bombing. So the exterior of the sideboard looked all right, but in actual fact the quality was not very good. Yet understandably enough everybody was thankful and satisfied. Afterwards many people kept those pieces of furniture for various reasons, one of which was the memory of the most trying years in their lives.[24]

This is a truly displaced object. It carries within it the memories of very hard times in post-war Rotterdam, but it also hides these traces of the past within its own design. Like the Snoopy Dog we encountered in Chapter 5, this is a 'spectral object' that carries a proposition in steganographic form. The unusable drawers and poor construction hold the cultural memory, for those who know how to decipher it, of hardship and recovery. Whether or not the visitors to the museum who are drawn to the sideboard know how to act on that proposition, they are all, intentionally or unintentionally, acting as custodians of a vicarious memory translated into material form. They are participating in the work of its preservation into the future.

The kitchen

Leaving the sitting room brings visitors towards 'the kitchen'. This is a large space that actually comprises a number of different kitchen arrangements – see Figure 8.4 – with cookers, sinks, work surfaces and cooking implements. This space has a particularly powerful effect on female visitors, who are familiar with many of the objects, either from their childhood or their early adult lives. It is common for elderly visitors to reminisce about daily domestic activities, usually in response to seeing a particular piece of kitchen equipment.

Figure 8.4 The kitchen
Source: Photo © Elena Bendien

In the following extract, an elderly woman visitor (W) is viewing the 'kitchen' space with a female member of staff (MW):

Extract 8.3

W: Once a week a big tub came into the kitchen . . . the hot water went in, and then the three of us went in . . . The first one who went in, it was the same water. And there was always a fight who was allowed to go in first (both laugh).

MW: Wasn't it that the youngest always . . .

W: No, no, no.

MW: How many children were you?

W: Seven children . . .

W: I mean, it was a large zinc tub and that it, well not full of course but a couple of . . . pans with hot water went in and you have to heat it on the gas stove. And that cooled off quickly, and now I must . . . can I have some more? (Laughs)

MW: Yes, yes, and that was just a bar of soap, wasn't it?

W: Or the shower gel, something like that.

MW: Yes, yes.

W: And the washing glove, you have to wash . . . as well.

MW: But that wasn't every day?

W (almost whispering): No, on Saturdays we went into the tub. Yes.

W: *Eens in de week kwam een grote teil in de keuken. . . , kwam het heet water daarin, en dan gingen we met z'n drieën in. . .De eerste die dan ging, het was hetzelfde water. En het was vechten wie de eerste mocht (lachen allebei).*

MW: *Was het niet zo dat de jongste altijd . . .*

W: *Nee, nee, nee.*

MW: *Met hoeveel kinderen waren jullie?*

W: *Zeven kinderen . . .*

W: *Ik bedoel, het was een grote zinken teil en dat die, nou vol niet natuurlijk maar een paar . . . pannen heet water gingen er maar in en je moet het op het gas warm maken. En dat was ook snel koud, en nou ik moet . . . kan er nog een beetje bij? (Lacht)*

MW: *Ja, ja, en dat was gewoon een zeepblokje, he?*

W: *Of de douche gel, zo iets.*

MW: *Ja, ja*

W: *En de waslap, moet je ook . . . wassen.*

MW: *Maar dat was niet iedere dag?*

W: *(bijna fluisterend): Nee, s'zaterdags gingen we de teil in. Ja.*

The sight of a large tub in the kitchen area provokes an act of recollection on W's part. She tells of how, as a child in a large family, the routine of 'bath day' would unfold. As the same bath water would be used for all seven children, there was some competition around the order of who could go first (and thereby bath in the cleanest and hottest water). What is significant about this episode is that W chooses to situate herself as a child within the recollection. Presumably, it might well have been possible to tell a story of her adult experiences with such a tub (perhaps bathing her own children). W builds up the scene from the perspective and concerns of a child (e.g. fighting over turns in the tub) and uses active voicing to dramatise events further ('can I have some more?'). She momentarily becomes a child in the kitchen space, someone who is not in control, who follows instructions rather than gives them.

In this extract, we can see an unfolding of life-space. The woman visitor is 'in' the museum, in the here and now, but she is also 'in' the past, having found a way back upstream to her childhood 'bath days'. It is the material affordances of the 'big tub' in the kitchen space that provide the means for unfolding life-space. The size of the tub, the way it can be placed in the kitchen near to a source of hot water, the small children climbing in and out, the 'fighting' around who got to go first: all of these recollections are gradually unpeeled as the woman engages with the object. Note also that the woman is relatively unresponsive to the questions of the staff member. MW offers a series of questions designed to assist W in expanding her reminiscence through teasing out more details, but W offers little in return. She appears to be absorbed in her own description of the 'bath day' scene, to the point where her small narrative tails off into a whisper.

This raises an interesting question about the obligations between these two women in this space of memory. The staff member – MW – is adopting the default practice of reminiscence therapy in trying to get W to talk more about what happened in the 'old days', using the objects currently to hand as cues. Talk is considered to be an unalloyed good here, because it serves as a marker of active remembering, which in turn demonstrates cognitive engagement. However, W's responses might be better characterised as a kind of disengagement, turning away from the interactional business being performed in the here and now and immersing herself in this scene from her childhood. What, then, does her apparent unwillingness to engage more with the present interaction actually mean? Is this a desirable practice of remembering or not?

We can begin to formulate an answer by looking at another episode taking place in the kitchen around the same object. This time, there are four elderly women visitors (N, N2, W3, W4), accompanied by a staff member (MW). Here, the women collectively build a narrative around the tub, for the most part between themselves:

Extract 8.4

N: Do you see that tub?

N: *Zie je die teil?*

W3: Yes.

W3: *Ja.*

N: We used to have a very large one in the garden.

N: *We hadden een heel grote in de tuin.*

N2: And we have to go into the tub in the evenings.

N2: *En we moeten 's avonds in de teil.*

N: Exactly.

N: *Precies.*

N2: Not every day.

N2: *Niet elke dag*

N: No.
(All together)

N: *Nee*
(*Door elkaar*)

MW: How many of you at the same time?

MW: *Met hoeveel tegelijk?*

N: One at a time but on the same day.

N: *Een tegelijk maar wel dezelfde dag.*

MW: Yes, of course.

MW: *Ja, natuurlijk.*

N: Fetch water at the water boiler.

N: *Water bij de waterstoker halen*

MW: And how many children then?

MW: *En hoeveel kinderen dan?*

N: We were with five children at home . . . We were divided. My sister was the last-born one, so she didn't need to, she went in one of those small tubs (MW: Yes, yes, yes). And I had to go with my three brothers on Friday afternoons and with my two sisters on Wednesday afternoons.

N: *We waren met vijf kinderen thuis . . . We waren gedeeld. Mijn zusje was het nakomertje, dus ze hoefde niet, zij ging in zo'n klein teiltje. (MW: Ja, ja, ja) En ik moest met mijn drie broers vrijdagmiddag en met twee zusjes op woensdagmiddag.*

MW: Yes, that was well arranged.

MW: *Ja, dat was goed geregeld.*

N: . . . fetch water first . . . carry buckets with boiling water.

N: *. . . eerst water gaan halen . . . met emmers heet water sjouwen.*

W4: At the water boiler's.	W4: *Bij de waterstoker.*
N: Yes, at the water boiler's. I lived in the staircase (W4: Yes). And I really walked up the stairs with the buckets with hot water. I was, I am talking about when I was 8–9 years old. (W4: Yes) With that boiling water . . .	N: *Ja, bij de waterstoker. Ik woonde in het trappenhuis.* (W4: *Ja*) *En ik liep echt met de emmers heet water de trap op. Ik was, ik heb het toch over dat ik 8–9 jaar was.* (W4: *Ja*) Met dat heet water . . .
MW: That is the way it was, everybody did it.	MW: *Het was niet anders, iedereen deed het.*
N: I never burned myself.	N: *Ik heb me nooit van verbrand.*
MW: No, no, indeed.	MW: *Nee, nee, precies.*

As with the previous extract, this description focuses on the practical arrangements around 'bath day', with a particular concern for the order in which large numbers of children bathed in the tub successively. The contribution by W4 ('At the water boiler's') is significant, as she offers the word *waterstoker*. This is local Rotterdam dialect for a water boiler. Hence the receipt '*ja, bij de waterstoker*' by N in the next turn does a form of membership work. The women are here demonstrating their entitlement to situate themselves relative to a common past. They are present with one another in the reminiscence museum, in modern Rotterdam, but also in the past, in a shared historical Rotterdam, where life was considerably more challenging for children of large, working-class families. There is here a mutual folding together of life-space, where the visitors are simultaneously 'here' and 'there'.

The small description offered towards the end of the extract by N is very interesting. She describes a routine episode that would be almost unimaginable in the context of modern Dutch family life, where a young child is charged with the duty of carrying buckets of scalding hot water from the communal water boiler in the apartment block upstairs to the family home. It is tempting to see N's story as a kind of complaint, as a critical reflection on the past (although note that the staff member, MW, does a work of normalising and potentially defusing the story with her interjection, 'That is the way it was, everybody did it'). Dilating the present life-space around the tub to include this aspect of the past may indeed throw 'hard times' into sharp relief, but the converse is also possible. The past makes potentially unremarkable aspects of the present visible. Note the conclusion to N's story – 'I never burned myself'.

As a child, N experienced bathtimes as dangerous and arduous, but she accomplished the challenging tasks she was obliged to do without ever coming to harm. The story is being told by an elderly woman who now, once again, confronts physical challenges in her daily life. The implication of this story is that the strength and autonomy of the child remain in the elderly woman she has become. She did things as a child that people nowadays would not imagine were possible: she will do so again as an older person. And, insofar as the story is woven into a collective, shared past, that attribute may be taken as representative of the group as a whole in their shared present moment: How we dealt with those hard times then shows how we will approach the hard times to come.

Expanding life-space to fold together past and present does work here of making visible and asserting autonomy at a time when it might be questioned. In a very similar extract to the previous one, we see this explicitly done by another visitor, also describing the *waterstoker*:

Extract 8.5

W: And then she (*granny*) was living on the third floor, and then she went to the . . . water boiler's, she went to fetch buckets . . . such buckets with hot water, she would climb up all those stairs with the boiling hot water. It went into that and then it started to . . . I have done all that too as a child, where you get the water, yes.

W: *En dan woonde zij (oma) driehoog, en dan ging ze bij de . . . waterstoker, ging ze emmers . . . zulke emmers met het hete water halen, liep ze al die trappen op met het gloeiend hete water. Dat ging daarin en dan ging het een beetje . . . ik heb het ook allemaal gedaan als kind, waar je het water haalt, ja.*

Here, the relevance of the past for the present is clear. An elderly woman describes her own grandmother ('granny') carrying the boiling hot water up the stairs from the water boiler and notes that she also performed this task as a child. Personal autonomy is emphasised twice over in the past and thereby securely made relevant in the present. What seems important in both Extracts 8.4 and 8.5 is not so much the extent of the reminiscence or the ability to talk at length about the past, but rather what it means to have drawn together the past and the present. Being both 'here' and 'there' shows up possibilities for personal autonomy and a capacity to act that might otherwise not be in the foreground. Being immersed in the past, as W appears to be at the end of

Extract 8.3, as her story tails off into near inaudibility, might actually increase rather than decrease her capacity to engage with the present.

From the ethical perspective, informed by Spinoza, that we have adopted throughout the book, we would argue that, on these occasions, using past 'hard times' to show the possibility of autonomy in the present is both of worth and desirable. The folding in of the past – although not without risk, as both 'good' and 'bad' memories are invited by museum space – here seems to expand rather than diminish the possibilities for action in the present. However, note that this is a contingent judgement that turns on the very particular conditions and experiences that are afforded by the experimental space of memory constituted in the museum.

The folding back and forth of life-space can occur very rapidly. The next extract occurs in the context of a visit by an elderly woman (W2) and her middle-aged daughter (W1), accompanied by a female staff member (MW). They have just entered a small area to the back of the kitchen space that is filled with devices for washing and ironing clothes (see Figure 8.5). This area is a little awkward to enter, being rather enclosed and packed with an odd

Figure 8.5 The washing machine
Source: Photo © Elena Bendien

assortment of domestic machinery. It does, however, tend to evoke quite powerful reactions from some visitors, as we see in the following:

Extract 8.6

(In the washing corner, looking at the irons)

(In het washokje, kijkt naar de strijkijzers)

W1: These are 50 years old, because then you had them with . . . when Nicolette was born, then I had the first electric one.

W1: *Deze zijn 50 jaar oud, want toen had je met . . . toen Nicolette geboren werd dan had ik de eerste elektrische.*

MW: You are saying school. Was it an ordinary school?

MW: *U zegt school. Was het een gewone school?*

W2: Housekeeping school . . . For girls it was a very good education in those days, you know.

W2: *Huishoudschool. . . . Toen voor de meisjes het was een heel goede opleiding, hoor.*

MW: Yes, yes.

MW: *Ja, ja.*

W2: And the difference between Ingrid and my education is like between day and night. We were already sewing a coat when after two years . . . laying the table and serving, very tidy all that.

W2: *En het verschil van Ingrid en mijn opleiding is dag en nacht verschil. We naaiden al een jas als we twee jaar . . . dekken en dienen, heel netjes alles.*

W2: Such a washing machine, had one as well . . . Yes, I used to have this one but I also have a wooden . . . And that one I had in the beginning of my married (MW: Yes). I am 75 years, my daughters are 51 and 50, eldest.

W2: *Zo'n wasmachine, ik ook nog een gehad. . . . Ja, deze heb ik gehad maar ik heb ook een houten . . . En dat had ik in het begin van mij trouw (MW: Ja). Ik ben 75 jaar, mijn dochters zijn 51 en 50, oudste.*

W2: Oh yes, a big washing pan like this I put on the stove with water . . . and the washing was boiled in that too.

W2: *O ja, zo'n grote wasbus ik heb met water op de kachel gezet . . . en daar werd de was ook in gekookt.*

MW: Yes, yes, exactly.

MW: *Ja, ja, precies.*

200 Recollection in later life

W2: And then my husband would throw it in and it would stand on the stove soaking during the night and then in the mornings before he left for his work I would fill a wooden washing machine, but the spinning went a little bit different from this one, that flywheel was underneath (she is speaking very fast now, almost without breathing) highly dangerous because . . . my boy, unfortunately he died when he was 40, 4 years ago, but he was (very) as quick as anything and before you knew it he was fiddling at that flywheel.

W2: *En dan gooide mijn man het daarin en stond het op de kachel 's nachts te trekken en dan 's morgens voordat hij te werk ging eerst dan laadde ik een houten wasmachine, maar het snel draaien deed ietsje anders dan deze, dat vliegwiel zat daaronder (praat snel, soort van zonder ademhaling) levensgevaarlijk want . . . mijn jongen, die is helaas overleden toen hij 40 was, 4 jaar terug, maar die was watervlug en hij zat al gauw even aan dat vliegwiel.*

MW: O my God!

MW: *O God!*

W2: That's why, highly dangerous.

W2: *Dus levensgevaarlijk.*

W2: My son who was 40, he would be 44 now, till he was 4, only then did I get a spinner. (MW: Yes, yes). But my daughter recently said: I still remember that you only . . . they said then, fantasising: it is practically dry. (MW: Yes, yes.). It wasn't though. It wasn't that dry. (MW: No, no) But later on, my son is, my youngest son is 40, and then I says: I don't mind having a baby but the horrible thing was always to dry things in my house, I find it awf(ul), and then I got a dryer.

W2: *Mijn zoon die 40 was, die zou nu 44 zijn, tot zijn 4de jaar, toen pas kreeg ik een centrifuge. (MW: ja, ja) Maar mijn dochter zei laatst: ik weet nog dat jullie maar . . . ze zeiden dan, fantaseerden ze: het is praktisch droog. (MW: ja, ja) Dat was toch niet. Dat was niet zo droog. (MW: nee, nee) Maar later, mijn zoon is, mijn jongste zoon is 40, en toen zeg ik: dat ik een kind krijg dat vind ik niet erg maar dat ellendige was altijd in mijn huis te drogen, ik vind het verschrik(kelijk), en toen kreeg ik een droogtrommel.*

The extract starts with the elderly woman (W2) comparing her early years and education with those of her daughter (W1). She speaks with apparent pride of the challenges of those years, and in particular of the attention she paid to maintaining domestic order. This then gives way to an extended story about a particular wooden washing machine. At this point, the tone shifts. A hitherto unmentioned third child — her youngest, a son — is introduced in a dramatic way. His recent death is interleaved with a story about his childhood misadventures playing with the dangerous spinner on the washing machine. Her anxiety as a mother then ('before you knew it he was fiddling at that flywheel') is juxtaposed with the repeated details of his death. This is audible in MW's shocked uptake — 'Oh my God!'. The concluding turn by W2 continues this alternation between the recent past and the more distant past, arriving at a strange resolution. It was not the ever-present danger of the son injuring himself that was problematic about the old washing machine: it was in fact the 'awful' experience of having to dry clothes in the house. In arriving at this resolution, W2 in effect tames the potential vulnerability that is invoked by the recent death of her son. One does what one can, but life is dangerous. It is not the danger to which I object, it is instead the ongoing inconveniences that we must endure that are so tiresome.

A lot seems to be happening here very quickly. Life-space appears to be rapidly dilating and contracting. At one moment, W2 is deep in the past, in her school years. Within a breath, she is married, and keeping house while her husband works. Then there is a son, who switches back and forth between the recently deceased adult and the baby boy. The threatening movement of the flywheel of the machine, which all three women in the present are currently looking at, seems to draw all these threads together momentarily, until, as the story ends, the machine is replaced ('and then I got a dryer').

There are good and bad autobiographical memories here that come together around the object tucked into a side corner of the museum. It is difficult to gauge exactly what kind of affective experience it is for the elderly woman to spontaneously recollect all of these events together. Clearly, some of what she recollects is potentially distressing. Yet, there is little sense of her becoming particularly upset. Wanted and unwanted past experiences are woven together and then undone. As with the previous extracts, it seems that the outcome of this folding together of hard times in the past with the present is to articulate a sense of resilience. These are the things that have happened to me. My life moves on. As indeed do the visitors themselves, immediately after the extract finishes, when they leave the kitchen for a different part of the museum.

The bedroom

The nature of the material that we have been working with in this chapter might make it seem that talking is the main activity that occurs in the reminiscence museum. This is not entirely the case. Visitors are free to handle the majority of the items in the museum. There is a great deal of touching, stroking and holding of objects. Some visits may pass by with very few words, but with apparently intense concentration on the part of elderly visitors. On occasion, staff have cooked food in the museum, preparing dishes popular in the Netherlands between the 1930s and the 1950s. The aim here is to create a range of forms of engagement with the space of memory.

There are, however, some risks attached to inviting unstructured reminiscence within the museum. The bedroom space is composed of three separate bedroom layouts, from childhood to adulthood. At the end of the adult bedroom, there is a bathroom space and some cabinets containing toiletries (see Figure 8.6). Attentive visitors who stay long enough at this display may be able to pick out a product that has some rather problematic associations. This is a hair product manufactured by the German company Schwarzkopf. German products from the 1930s/1940s have a particular meaning for many Dutch people who lived through the wartime occupation and the subsequent 'Hunger Winter' of 1944–5, when a blockade of food supplies, coupled with the destruction of agricultural resources, resulted in a widespread famine across western Holland (where Rotterdam lies). To encounter such a symbolically rich item in the context of the reminiscence museum can act to draw out recollections of an especially difficult time.

Given that many of the elderly people who visit the reminiscence museum are likely to have memories from the war years, a strategy has been adopted to anticipate and manage the consequence of problematic spontaneous recollections. There is a display of wartime memorabilia placed in a display cabinet outside the museum itself, near the lifts that lead to its entrance. The items in the display have been carefully chosen to emphasise the liberation of the Netherlands in 1945 by including, for example, biscuit tins that were part of the air drops of food. The display acts as a kind of memorial 'innoculation' – by deliberately invoking the war in the space outside the museum, it reduces the chances of war memories arriving unexpectedly within the museum. Nevertheless, some visitors do experience distressing spontaneous recollections of wartime events. The museum staff tend to manage these incidents by calling upon the assistance of particular elderly clients living within the care home

Figure 8.6 Toiletries on display in the bathroom
Source: Photo © Elena Bendien

who are able to share their own experiences of the war years in a way that is reassuring to distressed visitors.

Spontaneous autobiographical memories that emerge from interacting with objects may also be characterised by the relative impermanence. These can be details of a life that have great significance for the elderly person, but yet, at the same time, are scarcely likely to have become embedded in the kinds of

204 Recollection in later life

well-rehearsed family story of the kind that we saw in Extract 8.2. In the following example, an elderly woman (W) is talking to a museum volunteer (MW). This is not the first visit the woman has made to the museum. In her words, she 'cannot get enough of it. I see all kinds of things again of which I think: Oh God, I used to have that as well'.[25] Here, they are looking at bottles used for feeding babies in the bedroom space:

Extract 8.7

W: Wonderful. It was very nice. And to make clothes. Always. I never . . . hardly ever had to buy anything. And knitting. And making new things from old ones. (MW: Ye-es, yes) That I had from my mother, she made new from old, so can I, well, so can I, to make new little things from old things. A bottle that would break a hundred times. (MW laughs). It was still made of glass then and it stood on the granite kitchen sink, and fell over and it was broken (laugh) (MW: O my God).

MW: Yes of course, the kitchen sink was made of stone (W: Yes, indeed), it went like that (W: Oh, dear) But could you still buy a new bottle, somewhere?

W: Yea, yes, yes. Well yes, I was still at home then, my mother had seven children, so there was a baby there, so there was also a bottle. You have to wash it and then I would rub it with a cloth . . . One broken again? Well, then I had to go to the chemists to buy a new one. (Laughs)

W: *Prachtig. Het was heel erg leuk. En kieertjes maken. Altijd. Ik heb het nooit . . . haast nooit wat hoeven te kopen. En breien. En uit oud nieuw maken.*(MW: *Ja, ja*) *Dat had ik weer van mijn moeder, die maakte uit oud nieuw, kan ik ook, nou ja, kan ik ook, dus ook uit oud nieuwe dingentjes maken. Een flesje wat honderd keer brak. (*MW lacht*). Het was nog van glas en dat stond op een granieten aanrecht, en omviel en het was kapot (lachen)* (MW: *O God*).

MW: *Ja natuurlijk, het aanrecht was van de steen* (W: *Ja, ja*)*, het ging gewoon zo* (W: *O jee*) *Maar was het nog een nieuw flesje te kopen, te vinden?*

W: *Ja, ja,ja. Nou ja, ik was toen nog thuis, mijn moeder had zeven kinderen, dus daar was ook een baby, dus er was ook dan een flesje. Je moet het afwassen en dan ging ik met een doekje langs afwas . . . Alweer één kapot? Nou, toen ik naar een drogist moest om een nieuwe halen. (Lacht)*

MW: Nowadays there are plastic things. Just drop it. Just drop it. (W simult. unclear) And the microwave?	MW: *Nu zijn er plastic dingentjes. Laat maar vallen. Laat maar vallen. (W tegelijk onverstaanbaar) En de magnetron?*
W: Well, yees. In the pan with hot water, and I would wait for a moment to feel . . .	W: *Nou, ja-a. In het pannetje met heet water, en wacht ik even met voelen . . .*
MW: And then still taste for yourself first . . . (Laugh)	MW: *En dan nog zelf proeven eerst . . . (Lachen)*
W: Awful, wasn't it?	W: *Ontzettend, he?*
MW: But time was short. You couldn't do any more than that.	MW: *Maar de tijd was vol. Meer konden de mensen niet doen.*
W: That is what we are complaining about all the time.	W: *Dat klagen we steeds daarover.*
MW: Yes, absolutely.	MW: *Ja, zeker.*

One of the significant features of this extract is the way the elderly woman switches positions within a generational structure. She alternates between being a young mother feeding her own children, and then being a child herself and assisting her own mother with a large family. The extract opens with a discussion of the glass feeding bottle. This has the characteristic of being an object that can be easily cleaned and, hence, reused and potentially passed on between mothers. But it is also, as a glass object, fragile if carelessly handled. The phrase 'One broken again?' is a piece of active voicing, where the woman speaks as her mother, reprimanding her for just such an act of carelessness. However, as the subsequent laughter indicates, the reprimand is remembered fondly, because it speaks to the intergenerational bond between the women around raising children. The glass bottle of the story may have been physically broken, but the one in the museum affords the proposition of an unbroken chain of motherhood. Hence, W's enthusiasm for seeing again all the objects she used to have is based on feeling once more that intergenerational bond through the affordance of the bottle.

Towards the end of the extract, another reason for the desire to feel that bond becomes clear. The chain was not completely unbreakable, it seems. As the museum worker (MW) reminds W, nowadays it has all changed. Bottles are made of plastic; they can be dropped as many times as you like. There is no need for complex domestic arrangements around these feeding devices – simply place them in the microwave. Moreover, who would think to see, in these disposable objects, any particular intergenerational bond between mothers? The world that W recollects has passed. The details that she remembers – her mother's voice calling out at the sound of the breakage, tasting the milk from the bottle dunked in boiling water – are unlikely to be passed on, because changes in feeding practices and domestic arrangements have denied her the opportunity for their repetition. The bottle that the two women look at together connects W to her own past, but it does not connect her own children or grandchildren to her. It no longer 'collects' intergenerational social relations.

For older persons, a great deal of their life cannot be fitted into discrete autobiographical memories. Much of the texture of the past – daily routines, familiar objects and clothes, ways of interacting – simply becomes unspeakable because it lacks any clear narrative 'hook' for others. However, in the reminiscence museum, there do appear to be ways in which this memorial activity can be supported. In the bedroom space, there is a display where a baby doll is placed near a chest of drawers filled with infant clothes and related child-care paraphernalia (see Figure 8.7). Some elderly visitors choose to sit in this space and handle the baby doll, often stroking its hair with a brush or rocking the doll as though it were a slumbering infant. Visitors with less mobility – such as clients in the nursing-home section of Akropolis, who may be in quite advanced stages of dementia – are sometimes brought into the space in wheelchairs or on moveable beds at times when there are no external visitors. These older people are not necessarily able to physically interact with the objects in the space, but appear cognisant of the space itself, which is both unusual and strangely familiar to them.[26]

There are a number of wardrobes in the bedroom space. Some contain adult clothes, such as dresses and suits, and more intimate items, such as lingerie. Some elderly visitors spend considerable time taking the clothes out of the wardrobe and exploring their textures through touch. What does it mean to be absorbed in this activity? To feel a piece of clothing, such as a dress, is to imagine the body on which it might be draped, how the fabric might lie against the skin, how the cut and fit of the garment might feel as one stood, walked, sat, danced. Clothes in general invoke bodies, and specific items of clothing afford particular kinds of person, activity and mood. Here is the sort of dress I wore when we had enough money to go out on the town. Those look like the shoes he shined everyday and had reheeled until they wore out. Those stockings – I can see my mother darning them as she sat by the fireplace.

Figure 8.7 Doll and infant clothes in the bedroom
Source: Photo © Elena Bendien

We feel other people and our relations to them through the objects with which they were so closely associated.[27]

And, ultimately, we also feel ourselves, both 'there' and 'here'. The main ethical objection to what the experimental space of the reminiscence museum seems to afford is that allowing older persons to become absorbed in the past encourages them to disconnect from the present, making both their cognitive engagement with the here and now and social integration more difficult.[28] However, that objection is premised on a clear separation between past and present. It demarcates a world that is, for practical purposes, absent, from the one in which we must, in the end, get on with our lives. Our argument throughout this book has been to the contrary. We are never really in any one place. Our life-space, defined as the possibilities for action that are relationally afforded to us, folds together spatial and temporal relations that do not map on to simple metrics of physical distance or chronological remoteness. An older person who strokes the fabric of the dress is not transported miraculously back in time. The dress affords a dilation of life-space, a way of swimming upstream in the flow of experience that might not otherwise be possible, but it does not abolish the present.

We want to conclude our journey around the reminiscence museum with two reflections on what it might mean for older persons to experience this kind of space of memory, perhaps at a time when their 'intra-cranial' resources for remembering are in severe decline. At such a point, would we not see it as ethically highly desirable to supplement the attrition of 'internal' resources with as many 'external' resources as possible? What could be better than a space packed with affordances, where past agency can be tangibly felt through the arrangement of objects? And do we really need to insist on stories and narratives, a commentary on the past, as being the best indicators of cognitive and social engagement? Stroking dresses, smelling fabrics, combing a doll's hair – these are all subtle, yet powerful, ways in which past agency is being channelled and expressed in the present, without the need for words. One way, perhaps, of fulfilling our memorial obligations to our elders is to allow them the space to *not* speak, if they choose to do so, to not have to repeat the narratives that tame and manage the past, but instead to have the means of feeling the ongoing presence of their past and what it offers up to them at that moment.

Epilogue

I am not sure that I did right by my grandmother. She had been living with my mother and father before eventually moving to the nursing home. I should have visited more. I should have taken my son. Now he has no real memories of her. So I got that bit wrong too.

Recently I watched some old cine-films shot by my grandfather. They show a world that I don't know. A world where it seems that wearing hats on the beach was expected, and everyone smoked continuously. The films don't really speak to me.

But I noticed that my mother has kept hold of a small wooden souvenir that I gave my grandmother when I came back from travelling when I was young. She has placed it with a similar object that I gave to her. I picked it up and opened the lid, felt how smooth the surface feels. And I thought: one day both of these will come back to me.

Notes

1 Magnusson, 2014.
2 Bayley, 2012.
3 See Bond *et al.*, 1993; Jamieson *et al.*, 1997; Victor, 2004; Biggs, 2008.
4 Hepworth, 2000.
5 Latimer, 1999.
6 Schillmeier and Heinlein, 2009.
7 Middleton and Brown, 2005: 118–32.
8 Manier, 2004.
9 The study was carried out by Elena Bendien (2010).
10 See Gibson (2011) for an overview.
11 Schweitzer and Bruce, 2008.
12 See Buchanan and Middleton, 1995.
13 The best summaries in English of Humanitas's work are Becker (2003) and Letiche (2008). The description in this section draws heavily on the latter.
14 Letiche, 2008: 187.
15 Although a partial record of this event remains, for the moment, at www.youtube.com/watch?v=bOfOiEZHxRE. Towards the end of the clip, there is video footage of a visit to the reminiscence museum.
16 Becker, 2003.
17 The idea of the museum emerged when Becker, inspired by reminiscence work practised by some staff members, had an old Singer sewing machine and a bean cutter belonging to his mother brought into his office. As his office has an open-door policy, the objects quickly became of interest to a wide number of people throughout Akropolis and appeared to elicit the sharing of memories and telling stories. The museum was envisaged as an extension of this process.
18 Bendien, 2010: 27.
19 Bendien, 2010.
20 Dutch visitors know the board game by the rather wonderful title 'Don't be angry, man', rather than the more prosaic British name, 'Frustration'.
21 Miller, 2001.
22 An estate agent is the British term for a salesperson of house properties – what North Americans call a 'real-estate professional'.
23 See Marcoux (2001) on the memorial dynamics of house clearance.
24 Bendien, 2010: 72.
25 Bendien, 2010: 213.
26 See Bendien *et al.* (2010) for further examples.
27 See Middleton and Brown (2005, chapter 8) for an extended argument on this point.
28 See Bendien, 2012.

Chapter 9

Ordinary people living with a difficult past

Over the course of the book, we have heard from a range of ordinary people who are recollecting events that are either distressing or difficult to manage in the present. For the most part, they are doing so incredibly well. Rather than emphasise what people cannot do, or the overwhelming nature of irreversible past events, we have chosen instead to focus on the practices and techniques that people who recollect vital memories have evolved and adopted for themselves. We have tried to show how life-space can be expanded through folding the past into the present, despite the many significant challenges to be confronted. For example, the porous nature of the boundaries in secure forensic psychiatric care means that patients can maintain some kind of stake in the past, despite the institutional drive towards forgetting. What we have called the 'restricted' view of memory is primarily concerned with questions of the accuracy or otherwise of what people remember. We have, instead, explored the difficult affective and ethical issues that arise from efforts to tame and settle the significance of past difficulties, especially when our experiences have relevance for others or when we find ourselves having to manage memories vicariously for the people we care for.

Our approach to vital memories is not meant to be a step towards a general theory of memory. We see our work as being in dialogue with a variety of very different bodies of work, from the fascinating developments in distributed cognition and sociocultural approaches to autobiographical memory, through to discursive work and research on the material cultures of remembering. However, for us, the most important aspect of recollecting vital memories is setting specificity. Remembering is an accomplishment of specific arrangements of persons and materials that together constitute very particular spatial and temporal relations. This goes beyond saying that remembering occurs in

Ordinary people living with a difficult past   211

context.[1] What we can do in mnemonic terms depends upon how we are placed with respect to a given setting. As we have seen, what elderly visitors to the reminiscence museum can remember, and the manner in which they do so, is shaped by the affordances of this particular arrangement of relations. Likewise, the settings in which abuse occurred in childhood persist for survivors in the form of invariances when they recall their extremely difficult pasts.

The issue, as we see it, is to develop concepts and analytic descriptions that make visible the specific features of these different settings. We need to be able to offer highly grounded accounts of the contingencies that are involved in each particular setting where vital memories are being recalled and managed. For instance, in relation to memories of the 2005 London bombings, we sought to show the specific affective connections that were in play between the bodies of survivors and the affordances of objects and devices. With adoptive parents, our analysis was drawn towards the role played by images (e.g. both actual and 'invented' photographs, drawings, cut-out and found images) and toys (e.g. Snoopy Dog, Pooh Bear, the firefighter costume) in managing the vicarious memories of children.

However, this does create a problem – one that you, as a reader who has made it all the way through to this last chapter, probably feel just as acutely, if not more, than we do! What is one to do with all this detail? How can it be applied to other material? If there is no general model – just accounts of specific settings – is there not at least some sense of how all of this might be generalised? Luckily, we are scarcely the first authors to have run up against this dilemma. Deleuze and Guattari's collaborative work, for example, is framed around very narrow sets of problems, such as how spaces of desire are worked out in Kafka's writing,[2] or the role of the stirrup in the assembling of relations in a nomadic 'war machine'.[3] Nevertheless, the ideas that they develop in relation to these diverse materials are meant to make connections beyond the particular cases. Each of their analyses constitutes a kind of experiment. The concepts that emerge when one thinks through their particular historical and textual materials are specific to that particular case, but they can also have a life of their own if they are themselves treated as sites for further experimentation. Think, for example, of how remixing and sampling take melodies or rhythms from one piece to create what is both an entirely different piece and yet still rooted in the original.

One of the strategies that Deleuze and Guattari adopt to afford this experimentation is to draw diagrams of their analyses. These are often crudely realised, sometimes resembling flow charts or movement patterns,[4] whereas others are more figurative and striking.[5] These diagrams are not meant to be literal representations in any sense. They are, instead, translations of the analysis that have more in common with artistic experimentation. The point is to allow the reader to have an experience, to be affected by the analysis and the materials in which it is grounded, in ways that differ from the text alone.[6] The diagrams open up the analysis – they are conceptual affordances that allow for new kinds of thought to emerge.

John Mullarkey has expanded on this practice, to develop what he calls 'thinking in diagrams'.[7] Mullarkey is elaborating upon a tradition in contemporary continental philosophy of rejecting external or 'transcendent' theorising.[8] Philosophy is rather *of* and *in* this world, instead of occupying some privileged position of knowledge outside or above it. As such, philosophical writing expands or transforms life, rather than reducing it to a bare set of explanatory principles. It is as much a part of the 'ecology' of thinking and acting as the people and things it seeks to analytically engage with. However, this does bring with it the difficulty of knowing how to evaluate the contribution made by analysis that seeks to stand alongside, rather than explain away, its objects of research. The answer, following Deleuze and Whitehead, is to connect with the transformative potential of analysis (What affects and possibilities for actions are afforded? What does it do to the subject matter? What does it do to me? What ideas are made thinkable?). The role of diagrams, then, is to offer a means for the analysis to be experienced by others, to be directly related to life, such that potential common notions can be surfaced.

To place this in relation to our work in this book, take the contrast between the 'restricted' and the 'expanded' views of memory that we have been working with. For the former, there is a clearly defined domain of human activity called 'memory', which is firmly located in a specific space (i.e. the head) that is defined in terms of overarching mechanisms and processes. Analysis here consists in relating any given act of memory to the general model. However, for the latter, 'memory' encompasses a vast array of persons and materials that are spread across a wide number of settings, all of which have their own specific practices and modes of remembering. Analysis here is akin to a sort of ecological exploration that involves a careful comparison of similarities and difference and that aims at elaborating on possible points of connection between these diverse memorial arrangements and affordances. If the first approach is to be judged in terms of its fit with the 'standard model' of cognition, then what we have tried to do in our approach is unlock the potential for an 'expanded'

Ordinary people living with a difficult past 213

model of memory to find common notions across diverse, interlocking transcranial programmes of activity.

So, in that spirit, we want to conclude by offering up a series of diagrams that seek to elaborate and open up the analyses we have done throughout the book.[9] What we hope is that, by engaging with these diagrams, you might experiment with how the ideas we have developed might connect with (or perhaps contradict) the experiences of memory that interest you. As Whitehead says, no proposition is ever true or false in principle; everything turns on how it is taken up in the feelings of she or he who attempts to think it. But, in another sense, what we are doing with the diagrams is putting into practice what we have learned from our participants. The adoptive parents in Chapter 5 showed us that, to make sense of the past, in order to realise a future, it was necessary to engage in a creative work of imagination by inventing images that would augment and translate the gaps in the past or the turbulence downstream. In their different ways, all of the participants we have met have engaged in related kinds of resourceful and vicarious restructuring of their life-space. This is our attempt to respectfully do something similar.

The first diagram is of the 'flow of experience' (Figure 9.1). This can be depicted like a river system that runs from upstream to downstream. Thinking of experience in this way suggests that the past is never over, nor finished in any straightforward sense. We may choose not to face 'upstream', through practices of active forgetting or displacement, but the flow continues to connect us to what has gone before. Looking at the course of the river, the way it twists and turns through the landscape, captures something of the contingency of how our lives unfold. We may feel a sense of inevitability around how some things have turned out for us, and, indeed, the topographic features of the landscape through which the river turns do facilitate certain directions of flow, but there is little by way of determinism here. We might think of this topographical landscape as akin to the contribution of social and historical forces, of perhaps as a genetic–biological matrix. Over time, past contingencies accumulate to push us in a particular direction, such that many tributaries start to collect in the river basin, or chreod. But even here it is possible for unexpected events to impact upon that direction, such as when an obstacle breaks the flow into distributaries, creating a river delta. These irreversible events have considerable impact on the flow of experience. Yet, despite this irreversibility, it remains possible, in principle, to find a way of travelling upstream, to follow the course of the flow back through its contingent progress,

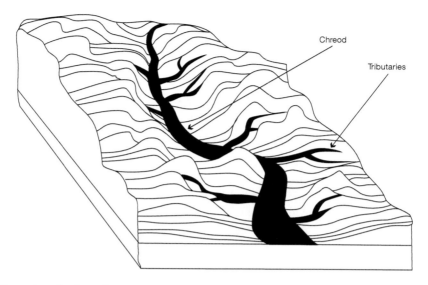

Figure 9.1 The flow of experience

although this requires great effort, inventiveness and, ultimately, the realisation that, as experience flows, what we will find upstream will always be different to what we imagined it to have been.

The second diagram is a Möbius strip (Figure 9.2). You might prefer to make one yourself, by twisting a strip of paper and gluing the ends together. Hold the strip in front of you and place your finger at the point where the ends are joined. Now run your finger in one direction. The path you trace soon moves behind the strip, so that you can no longer see your finger directly, before eventually returning and passing from one side to the other (this bit may require some skilful manipulation) and ending up back at the start. There is no real 'inside' and 'outside' here, just a movement where things are closer and further. Now, try and recall an autobiographical memory that has some meaning for you. Which bits of that experience are definitely yours alone, completely personal to you, and which parts come from the participation of others? Think of the event in as much detail as you can. Can you separate out the parts that are definitely based on your direct experience at the time and those that have become entangled in how that memory has been shared, retold and reconstructed over time? Consider further the significance and meaning of the memory. Which aspects are meaningful to you because of your unique personal characteristics and life experiences, and which because of the cultural values and socio-historical

Ordinary people living with a difficult past 215

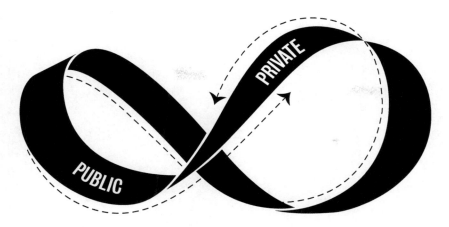

Figure 9.2 Möbius strip connecting the public and the private

moments by and through which you have lived? Finally, try this experiment. See if you can remove all of these supposedly 'external' elements – other people, broader cultural meanings, the times the memory has been recollected and shared. What is left? Is it the 'same' memory? The point here is not that there is no such thing as the 'personal' as distinct from the 'public'. It is instead that, through the twisting, stretching and deforming of our experiences, we cannot really tell where one begins and the other ends.

If the division of the personal and the public, the individual and the environment, is not really workable in relation to memory, then we need to think differently. Figure 9.3 is an attempt to capture some of the most significant aspects of 'life-space'. We engage with the world primarily in terms of the possibilities for action that are offered up to us as embodied beings. Our life-space is defined by the engagement we maintain with others and with the material surfaces of the world around us. Temporal and spatial relations – closeness and distance, now and then – are constituted by patterns of interaction in life-space. We make the space what it is through how we feel, think and act upon it. This is, in turn, reciprocally shaped by the way the space is 'marked out' through invariant features or affordances that offer up these possibilities for action. Although we may be held responsible for our actions and may take ownership of the things we think and feel, we are not, in a strict sense, the originators of these things. We are, instead, the realisers or actualisers of the cognitive, affective and behavioural possibilities of our unfolding life-space. And life-space itself is not static, but continuously expanding and dilating in

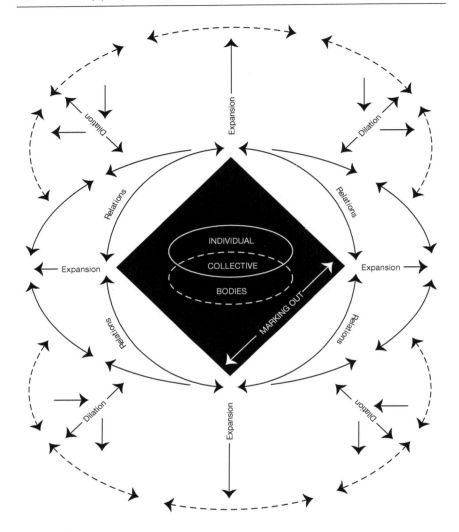

Figure 9.3 Life-space

a rhythm tied to our capacity to act. It is the deformations and transformations of life-space that make up the contours of our ongoing experience.

To grasp how remembering operates in relation to life-space, consider Figure 9.4.[10] It is made of three planes that are superimposed in relation to one another. The uppermost plane depicts a field of action, with the person (P) at the centre. You can think of this as a simplified version of the previous diagram – this is a life-space at a particular given moment, constituted relationally. Remembering

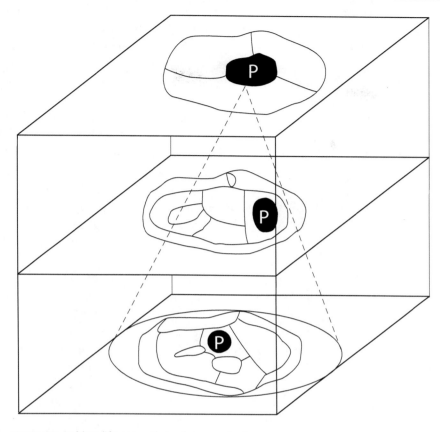

Figure 9.4 Folding life-space through remembering

then serves to expand life-space. The second plane of action is a deformation of the first. The boundaries and connections of what is possible become relaxed and expanded through recollection. Remembering folds aspects of the past into the present, which together afford different possibilities for feeling, thinking and acting. In this way, the second plane incorporates and transforms the first. The process is repeated in the third plane, which is a further deformation of the second, accomplished through a successive act of recollection. The common features that link the planes of action together are the invariances – the assemblies of relations – that are common to each. The inverted cone shape then marks the range of possible expansions of life-space corresponding to different efforts at remembering. The more concerted these efforts become, the further the cone expands, realising new possibilities. However, expanding life-space through remembering also increases the range of ways in which the person is relationally affected and acted upon. Remembering then involves a work that unsettles or destabilises the present. We then have to think of a corresponding movement whereby the planes of action opened up by remembering become compressed or concentrated back in the present through our efforts to settle or resolve matters. This would be akin to a movement back up through the cone, as life-space becomes dilated and focused on particular thoughts and actions.[11]

The 'marking out' of life-space in Figure 9.3 occurs through the material and conceptual affordances of invariant assemblies of relations. Figure 9.5 depicts these as they appear in Bella's story from Chapter 4. The wall offered a variety of material affordances for Bella and her friend as they climbed upon it, which they experienced in terms of pleasure, choice and companionship. However, it also afforded vulnerability, owing to the height, which was seized as an opportunity for abuse by the friend's father. Through recollection, these invariant features remain part of Bella's life-space, where she continues to feel the various material affordances of the girls/wall/adult arrangement. Bella also picks up on a conceptual affordance, a proposition that the arrangement offers up to her. This is of the adult as a 'good father', one who demonstrates care and attention to his daughter and her friend. However, in engaging with the proposition, Bella also finds the means of falsifying it. The moment the father looks around, presumably to check he is not being watched, the arrangement shifts to a different proposition – 'even here, in public, in front of his daughter, he will take the opportunity to abuse me'. Arrangements of relations in life-space then offer up intertwined material and conceptual affordances that we are lured into feeling and thinking through our engagement. These arrangements form invariant features of life-space when they are folded into the present through remembering. Managing the way these invariances continue to act upon us is a major aspect of living with vital memories.

Objects are not simply cues to cognitive processes: they are one of the relational means by which the past can be folded into the present. In Figure 9.6, we contrast the idea of direct access to the past (B) from the present (A) with the idea of objects as mediators that translate properties of persons and events. Think of the water tub in the reminiscence museum discussed in Chapter 8. Through this object in the kitchen area, elderly visitors were collaboratively able to unpack an absent past that involved family relationships, domestic routines, gendered and economic relations and more. The material surfaces of the object offered a means to trace out how that object was embedded

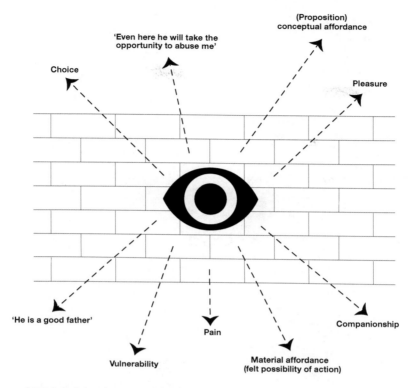

Figure 9.5 Material and conceptual affordances

in the home life of Rotterdam families from the 1930s and 1940s. From the shape and volume of the tub, the women move to it being filled with water, the children who were bathed in it (including themselves as infants), the bringing of hot water and the ordering of domestic life. When we engage with objects that have been displaced from the past, we pass through them to a web of relationships that they appear to bring along with them. And, as we saw in Chapter 5, this is precisely what can make certain kinds of object so threatening, as they appear to be gilded with traces of past agency and subjectivity that they can lure us into thinking.

We do not just think the past: we are touched by it affectively. The material and cognitive affordances of invariant assemblies of relations lure us into feelings about past persons and events that can be both ambiguous and challenging. Throughout the book, we have defined affect as the 'feeling of affordance', the felt sense of the possible (what we can do and what can be done to us)

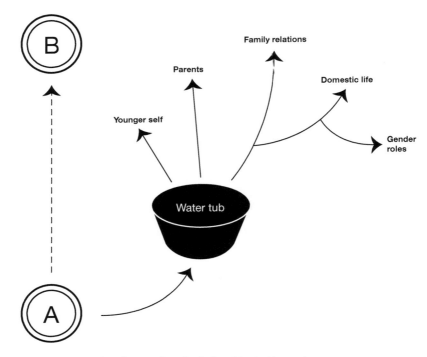

Figure 9.6 Mediated and unmediated relationships to the past

that arises from our engagement with assemblies of relations. Defining affect in this way helps to clarify why our feelings tend towards the indeterminate. Affordance does not determine action. The tub does not 'make' the elderly visitors remember domestic life, any more than a wall necessarily 'makes' children feel companionable or adults behave abusively. The feeling of affordance has an anticipatory character; it stretches out and expands our sense of what we can do. Think perhaps of the experience of dancing, as depicted in Figure 9.7. This involves a range of feelings and sensations that are bound in the collective movement of dancers. So long as the dance continues, these feelings oscillate in tone, without perhaps settling on any particular emotion. However, once the dance stops, the possibilities for movement cease, and we have to take ownership of our feelings. As we saw with the unfortunate Morris in Chapter 3, affect seems to work a little like the child's game of musical chairs or pass the parcel. While everything is in movement, our feelings are unsettled, ambiguous. It is once the music stops, and we have again taken up a clear relation to the affordance, that we have to confront clearly defined sets

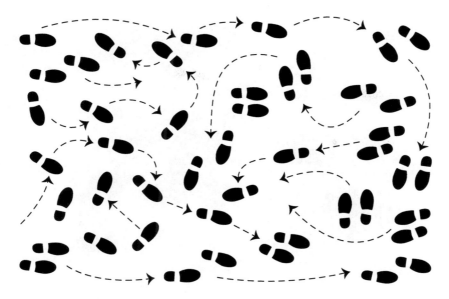

Figure 9.7 Affect as movement and settlement

of feelings – we are 'it', the winner or loser, the survivor or the victim. The question we should ask ourselves of vital memories concerns, then, the extent to which we want to create a sense of movement in relation to our past through feeling the affordances of invariant relations, or whether we instead want to use this affordance to attempt to put a full stop to the possibilities the past continues to offer up to us. It is on this basis that we have suggested that exploring how to 'feel' the past in different ways, through invariant assemblies of relations, may be more important than the search for narrative closure.

One of the most important arguments for us in this book has been for the setting specificity of remembering. Figure 9.8 draws out some threads of this argument. In a restricted view of memory, our capacities to remember are psychological properties that are more or less fixed across the contexts where we recollect the past. On this basis, when we engage with formal practices where we are required to offer testimony about our past experiences – such as in courts of law or in therapy – then these 'external' settings may either facilitate or distort what we remember. The problem then becomes that of establishing how this external influence manifests itself and separating it out, to clarify the degree of falsity or accuracy in recollection, such that a 'definitive account' can be established. We think this entire approach needs to be inverted.

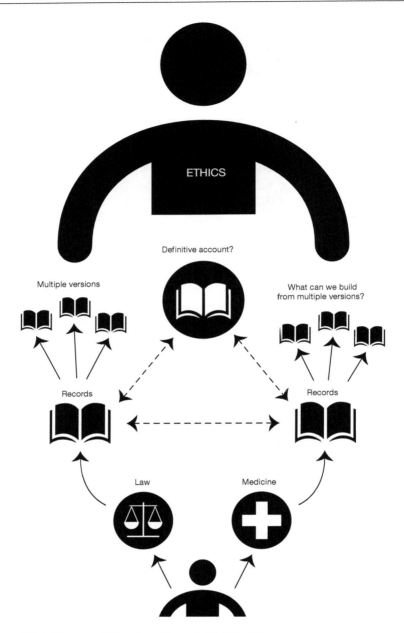

Figure 9.8 Setting specificity of practices of remembering

It is settings themselves that are collective agents of recollection. As individuals, we contribute our own cognitive, interactional and embodied resources, but these are one part of a distributed mnemonic system.[12] So, a finished record, such as a witness statement or an account of a therapy, is a hybrid product of the interpersonal, embodied, material and technical relations of the setting. This assertion does not lead us into the wilder reaches of relativism, where nothing can ever be true or false, that some scholars of memory fear.[13] No – it means instead that we must look at the particular standards and procedures of the practices involved to make situated judgements about our confidence in the end product, or lack of it. Having worked for a long time now with clinicians and legal professionals, we have a clear sense of what the differences and similarities are in legal and therapeutic mnemonic practices. The other side of this issue is to understand how the formal recollections of practices then become attached to individuals. At the end of a court case, or at the conclusion of a therapeutic programme, the person who has participated as witness or client is, in effect, invited to take ownership of the collectively produced version of events. Where the person has simultaneously participated in two or more practices (e.g. being in therapy while pursuing a court case), this may result in their being offered two very different versions of events, where matters of agency, responsibility and future prospects are worked out in ways that do not immediately appear compatible. The most pressing question, as we see it, is how people engage with multiple intersecting versions of their past as a function of their participation in distinct settings and practices, with divergent standards and techniques for establishing matters of accuracy, truth and morality. This seems to us to be at the heart of many of the problems around vital memories, and why we need to begin from an idea of the dynamics of life-space rather than clearly demarcated 'inside' and 'outside'.

It is rather ironic that, in order to understand a very modern problem around memory, we should be drawn back to a pre-modern approach to ethics.[14] Figure 9.9 offers a rough depiction of the Spinozist idea of 'common notions'. Our lives are constituted through the relations we have to other people and to the material surfaces of the world that frame our life-space. These relations expand our joint capacities to act. Much of what we are, in psychological terms, is the emergent outcome of the relations with which we become engaged, which supervene upon whatever specific cognitive or embodied qualities we might have initially contributed. We see this clearly in all the areas we have been concerned with in this book. Survivors of childhood abuse, adoptive families, victims of terrorism, mental health services users, elderly

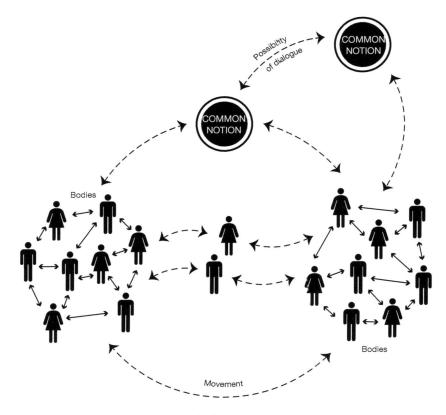

Figure 9.9 Common notions in remembering

visitors and clients: the vital memories of all are shaped by the collective settings in which they have participated, and it is this participation that is the proper object of ethical reflection. What is it that we share with the people with whom we jointly build our past? What are the qualities that become translated in our engagement with objects? What possibilities for being and acting are afforded to us when we are drawn into assemblies of relations? A common notion is a sense of an emergent property of a relationship that expands our life-space. Reflecting on these common notions is a basis for further expanding our capacity to connect with and experience relationships with diverse others and materials. If a given act of remembering affords the ability to surface common notions, then, in ethical terms, it has moral value. This is not to say that our lives ought to be seen as a project of ceaseless expansion. Sometimes, not least for our own well-being, we need to dilate and focus attention.

Ordinary people living with a difficult past 225

However, the ethical horizon, the basis on which we ought to make very contingent judgements about what to remember and what to forget, needs to be based on what, collectively, can transform and unfold our lives, in whichever directions that may lead. We remember such that we might live better, together, taking care of one another's pasts.

Notes

1 A good framing of 'context'-based arguments is made by Bietti *et al.* (2014).
2 Deleuze and Guattari, 1986.
3 See Chapter 12 of Deleuze and Guattari (1988).
4 For instance, the line diagrams in Chapter 5 (ibid.).
5 Such as the strange, crab-like creatures in Chapter 7 (ibid.).
6 The relationship between 'experiment' and 'experience' is neatly captured in French, where the phrase *'faire une expérience'* has the dual meaning of 'to have an experience' and 'to conduct an experiment'. See Lapoujade (2000) and Brown and Stenner (2009, chapter 9).
7 Mullarkey, 2006.
8 This counter-tradition is sometimes referred to as 'philosophies of immanence'. Deleuze is the key figure here, along with thinkers such as Alain Badiou (2005) and François Laruelle (2010). In the social sciences, themes from these philosophical sources are often referred to as constituting 'non-representational' (Thrift, 2008) or 'performative' approaches to research (Law, 2004). For an account of the relevance of this kind of thinking to psychology, see Brown and Stenner (2009).
9 Our thanks to Alex John for his beautiful renditions of our amateurish scribbles.
10 This diagram is drawn from Brown (2012a), where its derivation from a combination of Lewin and Bergson is described.
11 This is a shorthand and somewhat modified version of the account of remembering made by Bergson in *Matter and Memory*. See Bergson (1908/1991) and Middleton and Brown (2005).
12 Hence, the importance of the work that John Sutton and colleagues are doing to conceptualise the 'distributed' and 'transactional' processes that are involved – see Harris *et al.* (2011, 2014) and Sutton (2008).
13 Loftus, 1994, 2003.
14 Although, as Latour (1993, 2013) has pointed out, the problem perhaps is understanding how the divisions of knowledge associated with modernity (such as subject/object dualism) have made it all but impossible to grasp the actual nature of our contingent and situated procedures of judging both psychological and sociological matters, such as memory.

References

Abbas, N. (ed.) (2005). *Mapping Michel Serres*. Minneapolis, MN: Minnesota University Press.

Adams, F. and K. Aizawa (2010). *The Bounds of Cognition*. Oxford: Wiley-Blackwell.

Allen, M. (2014). *The Labour of Memory: Memorial culture and 7/7*. Basingstoke, UK: Palgrave Macmillan.

Allen, M. and S.D. Brown (2011). Embodiment and living memorial: The affective labour of remembering the 2005 London Bombings. *Memory Studies* 4(3): 312–27.

Allen, M. and S.D. Brown (forthcoming). Memorial meshwork: The making up of the commemorative space of the Hyde Park 7/7 memorial. *Organization*.

Anderson, B. and C. McFarlane (2011). Assemblage and geography. *Area* 43(2): 124–7.

Andrews, M., C. Squire and M. Tamboukou (eds) (2013). *Doing Narrative Research* (2nd edn). London: Sage.

Angelides, S. (2004). Feminism, child sexual abuse, and the erasure of child sexuality. *GLQ* 10(2): 141–77.

Ashmore, M. (1989). *The Reflexive Thesis: Wrighting sociology of scientific knowledge*. Chicago, IL: University of Chicago Press.

Assmann, A. (2011). *Cultural Memory and Western Civilization: Functions, media, archives*. Cambridge: Cambridge University Press.

Assmann, J. (2011). *Cultural Memory and Early Civilization: Writing, remembrance and political imagination*. Cambridge: Cambridge University Press.

Baddeley, A.D. and G. Hitch (1974). Working memory. In G.H. Bower (ed.) *The Psychology of Learning and Motivation: Advances in research and theory*. New York: Academic Press, pp. 47–89.

Badiou, A. (2005). *Being and Event*. London: Continuum.

Baker, C. (2002). *Female Survivors of Child Sexual Abuse*. London: Routledge.

Ballard, P.B. (1913). *Oblivescence & Reminiscence*. Cambridge: Cambridge University Press.

Balzac, H. (2002). *The Unknown Masterpiece and Other Stories*. New York: Dover.

Barthes, R. (1984). *Camera Lucida*. London: Flamingo.

Bartlett, F.C. (1932). *Remembering: A study in experimental social psychology*. Cambridge: Cambridge University Press.

Bass, E. and L. Davis (1988). *The Courage to Heal: Women's guide to survival*. Bolton, UK: Cedar Press.

References 227

Bayley, J. (2012). *Iris: A memoir of Iris Murdoch*. London: Duckworth Overlook.

Becker, H. (2003). *The Art of Living in Old Age: Happiness-promoting care in an ageing world*. Delft, Netherlands: Eburon.

Bendien, E.M. (2010). *From the Art of Remembering to the Craft of Ageing: A study of the reminiscence museum at Humanitas, Rotterdam*. Rotterdam, Netherlands: Humanitas.

Bendien E.M. (2012). Remembering (in) the past perfect: Ethical shifts in times. *Memory Studies* 5(4): 445–61.

Bendien, E.M., S.D. Brown and P. Reavey (2010). Social remembering as an art of living: Analysis of a 'reminiscence museum'. In M. Domenech and M. Schillmeier (eds) *New Technologies and Emerging Spaces of Care*. Farnham, UK: Ashgate, pp. 149–67.

Bennett, J. (2010). *Vibrant Matter: A political ecology of things*. Durham, NC: Duke University Press.

Bentall, R. (2004). *Madness Explained: Psychosis and human nature*. London: Penguin.

Bergson, H. ([1908] 1991). *Matter and Memory*. New York: Zone.

Bergson, H. ([1933] 1992). *The Creative Mind: An introduction to metaphysics*. New York: Citadel.

Bergson, H. ([1913] 2001). *Time and Free Will: An essay on the immediate data of consciousness* (trans. F.L. Pogson). Mineola, NY: Dover.

Bietti, L.M., C.B. Stone and W. Hirst (2014). Contextualising human memory. *Memory Studies* 7(3): 267–71.

Biggs, S. (2008). Ageing in a critical world: The search for generational intelligence. *Journal of Aging Studies* 22(2): 115–19.

Blackman, L. (2012). *Immaterial Bodies: Affect, embodiment, mediation*. London: Sage.

Blum, V. and A. Secor (2011). Psychotopologies: Closing the circuit between psychic and material space. *Environment and Planning D: Society and Space* 29: 1030–47.

Blustein, J. (2008). *The Moral Demands of Memory*. Cambridge: Cambridge University Press.

Bollas, C. (2008). *The Evocative Object World*. London: Routledge.

Bond, J., P.G. Coleman and S. Peace (eds) (1993). *Ageing in Society: An introduction to social gerontology*. Buckingham, UK: Open University Press.

Boyle, M. (2002). *Schizophrenia: A scientific delusion?* London: Routledge.

Braidotti, R. (2006). *Transpositions: On nomadic ethics*. Cambridge: Polity.

Brennan, T. (2004). *The Transmission of Affect*. Ithaca, NY: Cornell University Press.

Brookfield, H., S.D. Brown and P. Reavey (2008). Vicarious and postmemory practices in adopting families: The construction of the past in photography and narrative. *Journal of Community and Applied Social Psychology* 18(5): 474–91.

Brooks-Dutton, B. (2014). *It's Not Raining, Daddy, it's Happy: Surviving grief, a father and a son start again*. London: Hodder & Stoughton.

Brown, G.W. and T. Harris (1978). *Social Origins of Depression*. London: Routledge.

Brown, S.D. (2002). Michel Serres: Science, translation and the logic of the parasite. *Theory, Culture & Society* 19: 1–27.

Brown, S.D. (2008). The quotation marks have a certain importance: Prospects for a 'memory studies'. *Memory Studies* 1(3): 261–71.

Brown, S.D. (2012a). Memory and mathesis: For a topological approach to psychology. *Theory, Culture & Society* 29(4/5): 137–64.

Brown, S.D. (2012b). Two minutes of silence: Social technologies of commemoration. *Theory & Psychology* 22(2): 234–52.

Brown, S.D. and A. Locke (2008). Social psychology. In C. Willig and W. Stainton Rogers (eds) *Handbook of Qualitative Methods in Psychology*. London: Sage, pp. 373–89.

228 References

Brown, S.D. and P. Stenner (2009). *Psychology Without Foundations: History, philosophy and psychosocial theory*. London: Sage.

Brown, S.D., P. Reavey and H. Brookfield (2013). Spectral objects: Material links to difficult pasts for adoptive parents. In P. Harvey, E. Casella, G. Evans, H. Knox, C. McLean, E. Silva, N. Thoburn and K. Woodward (eds) *Objects and Materials: A Routledge companion*. London: Routledge, pp. 173–82.

Brown, S.D., P. Reavey, A. Kanyeredzi and R. Batty (2014). Transformations of self and sexuality: Psychiatric inpatients accounts of sexuality and relationships. *Health* 18: 240–60.

Bruner, J. (1986). *Actual Minds, Possible Worlds*. Cambridge, MA: Harvard University Press.

Bruner, J. (1992). *Acts of Meaning* (new edn). Cambridge, MA: Harvard University Press.

Buchanan, K. and D.J. Middleton (1995). Voices of experience: Talk, identity and membership in reminiscence groups for older people. *Ageing and Society* 15: 457–91.

Campbell, S. (2003). *Relational Remembering: Rethinking the memory wars*. Lanham, MD: Rowman & Littlefield.

Candlin, F. and R. Guins (eds) (2009). *The Object Reader*. London: Routledge.

Carruthers, M. (2008). *The Book of Memory: A study of memory in medieval culture*. Cambridge: Cambridge University Press.

Caruth, C. (ed.) (1995). *Trauma: Explorations in memory*. Baltimore, MD: Johns Hopkins.

Caruth, C. (1996). *Unclaimed Experience: Trauma, narrative and history*. Baltimore, MD: Johns Hopkins.

Clark, A. and D. Chalmers (1998). The extended mind. *Analysis* 58(1): 7–19.

Clough, P.T. (ed.) (2007). *The Affective Turn: Theorizing the social*. Durham, NC: Duke University Press.

Connerton, P. (2008). Seven types of forgetting. *Memory Studies* 1(1): 59–72.

Connerton, P. (2009). *How Modernity Forgets*. Cambridge: Cambridge University Press.

Connerton, P. (2011). *The Spirit of Mourning: Memory and the body*. Cambridge: Cambridge University Press.

Connor, S. (2011). *Paraphernalia: The curious lives of magical things*. London: Profile.

Conway, M.A. (1990). *Autobiographical Memory: An introduction*. Buckingham, UK: Open University Press.

Conway, M.A. (ed.) (1997). *Recovered Memories and False Memories*. London: Routledge.

Conway, M.A. (2005). Memory and the self. *Journal of Memory and Language* 53(4): 594–628.

Conway, M.A. and C.W. Pleydell-Pearce (2000). The construction of autobiographical memories in the self-memory system. *Psychological Review* 107: 261–88.

Conway, M.A. and L. Jobson (2012). On the nature of autobiographical memory. In D. Berntsen and D.C. Rubin (eds) *Understanding Autobiographical Memory: Theories and approaches*. Cambridge: Cambridge University Press, pp. 54–69.

Conway, M.A., J.A. Singer and A. Tagini (2004). The self and autobiographical memory: Coherence and correspondence. *Social Cognition* 22: 491–529.

Conway, M.A., Q. Wang and K. Hanyu (2005). A cross-cultural investigation of autobiographical memory. *Journal of Cross-Cultural Psychology* 36: 739–49.

Cooper, R. (1992). Formal organization as representation: Remote control, displacement and abbreviation. In M. Reed and M. Hughes (eds) *Rethinking Organization: New directions in organization theory and analysis*. London: Sage, pp. 254–72.

References 229

Cooper, R. (1993). Technologies of representation. In P. Ahonen (ed.) *Tracing the Semiotic Boundaries of Politics*. Berlin: Mouton de Gruyter, pp. 279–312.

Cooper, R. (1998). Assemblage notes. In R.C.H. Chia (ed.) *Organized Worlds: Explorations in technology and organization with Robert Cooper*. London: Routledge, pp. 108–30.

Coren Mitchell, V. (2014, 9 February). My Woody Allen conunudrum. *The Observer*, p. 40.

Coulter, J. (1979). *The Social Construction of Mind*. London: Sage.

Craik, F.M and L.S. Lockhart (1972). Levels of processing: A framework for memory research. *Journal of Verbal Learning & Verbal Behavior* 11: 671–84.

Cromby, J., D. Harper and P. Reavey (2013). *Psychology, Mental Health and Distress*. Basingstoke, UK: Palgrave.

Crook, C. and R. Dymott (2005). ICT and the literacy practices of student writing. In M. Monteith (ed.) *Teaching Secondary School Literacies with ICT*. Maidenhead, UK: Open University Press, pp. 96–113.

Danziger, K. (1990). *Constructing the Subject: Historical origins of psychological research*. Cambridge: Cambridge University Press.

Danziger, K. (1997). *Naming the Mind: How psychology found its language*. London: Sage.

Danziger, K. (2008). *Marking the Mind: A history of memory*. Cambridge: Cambridge University Press.

Davidson, T.K., O. Park and R. Shields (eds) (2011). *Ecologies of Affect: Placing nostalgia, desire, and hope*. Waterloo, ON: Wilfred Laurier University Press.

DeLanda, M. (2002). *Intensive Science and Virtual Philosophy*. London: Continuum.

DeLanda, M. (2006). *A New Philosophy of Society: Assemblage theory and social complexity*. London: Continuum.

Deleuze, G. (1988). *Spinoza: Practical philosophy*. San Francisco, CA: City Lights Books.

Deleuze, G. (1990). *The Logic of Sense*. New York: Columbia University Press.

Deleuze, G. (1992). *Expressionism in Philosophy: Spinoza*. New York: Zone.

Deleuze, G. (1993). *The Fold: Leibniz and the baroque*. London: Athlone Press.

Deleuze, G. (1998). To have done with judgment. In *Essays Critical and Clinical*. London: Verso, pp. 126–35.

Deleuze, G. and F. Guattari (1986). *Kafka: Towards a minor literature*. Minneapolis, MN: University of Minnesota Press.

Deleuze, G. and F. Guattari (1988). *A Thousand Plateaus: Capitalism and schizophrenia*. London: Athlone Press.

Department of Health (1983) *Mental Health Act*. London: Department of Health.

Derrida, J. (1978). Freud and the scene of writing. In *Writing and Difference*. London: Routledge, pp. 196–231.

Derrida, J. (1987). *Le facteur de la vérité*. In *The Post Card: From Socrates to Freud and beyond*. Chicago, IL: University of Chicago Press, pp. 413–96.

Derrida, J. (1995). *Archive Fever: A Freudian impression*. Paris: Éditions Galilée.

Draaisma, D. (2000). *Metaphors of Memory: A history of ideas about the mind*. Cambridge: Cambridge University Press.

Douglas, M. (1987). *How Institutions Think*. London: Routledge.

Duncan, N. (1996). Renegotiating gender and sexuality in public and private spaces. In N. Duncan (ed.) *Body Space: Destablising geographies of gender and sexuality*. London: Routledge, pp. 127–45.

230 References

Ebbinghaus, H. ([1885] 1913). *Memory: A contribution to experimental psychology*. New York: Dover.

Eco, U. (1988). An Ars Oblivionalis? Forget it! *Proceedings of the Modern Language Association* 103(3): 254–61.

Edwards, D. (1997). *Discourse and Cognition*. London: Sage.

Edwards, D. and R.Q. Goodwin (1985). The language of shared attention and visual experience: A functional study of early nomination. *Journal of Pragmatics* 9(4): 475–93.

Edwards, D. and D. Middleton (1986a). Joint remembering: Constructing an account of shared experience through conversational discourse. *Discourse Processes* 9: 423–59.

Edwards, D. and D. Middleton (1986b). Text for memory: Joint recall with a scribe. *Human Learning* 5: 125–38.

Edwards, D. and N.M. Mercer (1987). *Common Knowledge: The development of understanding in the classroom*. London: Methuen.

Edwards, D. and D. Middleton (1988). Conversational remembering and family relationships: How children learn to remember. *Journal of Social and Personal Relationships* 5: 3–25.

Edwards, D. and J. Potter (1992a). *Discursive Psychology*. London: Sage.

Edwards, D. and J. Potter (1992b). The Chancellor's memory: Rhetoric and truth in discursive remembering. *Applied Cognitive Psychology* 6: 187–215.

Edwards, D., D. Middleton and J. Potter (1992). Towards a discursive psychology of remembering. *The Psychologist* 5: 56–60.

Erll, A. (2011). *Memory in Culture*. Basingstoke, UK: Palgrave Macmillan.

Fivush, R. (2007). Maternal reminiscing style and children's developing understanding of self and emotion. *Clinical Social Work* 35: 37–46.

Fivush, R. (2008). Remembering and reminiscing: How individual lives are constructed in family narratives. *Memory Studies* 1(1): 45–54.

Fivush, R. (2011). The development of autobiographical memory. *Annual Review of Psychology* 62: 559–82.

Fivush, R., T. Habermas, T.E.A. Waters and W. Zaman (2011). The making of autobiographical memory: Intersections of culture, narratives and identity. *International Journal of Psychology* 46(5): 321–45.

Fleming, N. (2007, 10 May). One in six hospitals treat in mixed wards. *The Telegraph*.

Foucault, M. (2003). *Society Must Be Defended: Lectures at the Collège de France, 1975–1976*. London: Penguin.

Foucault, M. (2007). *Security, Territory, Population: Lectures at the Collège de France, 1977–1978*. New York: Picador.

Fraser, S. (1989). *My Father's House*. London: Virago Press.

Freud, S. (2001). A note upon the 'mystic writing pad'. In *The Ego and the Id and Other Works*. New York: Vintage, pp. 227–34.

Garry, M., C.G. Manning and E.F. Loftus (1996). Imagination inflation: Imagining a childhood event inflates confidence that it occurred. *Psychonomic Bulletin & Review* 3(2): 208–14.

Gatens, M. (1996). *Imaginary Bodies: Ethics, power and corporeality*. London: Routledge.

Gibson, F. (2011). *Reminiscence and Life Story Work: A practice guide* (4th edn). London: Jessica Kingsley.

Gibson, J.J. (1966). *The Senses Considered as Perceptual Systems*. Boston, MA: Houghton Mifflin.

References   231

Gibson, J.J. (1979). *The Ecological Approach to Visual Perception.* Boston, MA: Houghton Mifflin.

Gilbert, G.N. and M. Mulkay (1984). *Opening Pandora's Box: A sociological analysis of scientists' discourse.* Cambridge: Cambridge University Press.

Goffman, E. (1991). *Asylums: Essays on the social situation of mental patients and other inmates.* London: Penguin.

Greco, M. and P. Stenner (eds) (2008). *Emotions: A social science reader.* London: Routledge.

Gregg, M. and G.J. Seigworth (eds) (2010). *The Affect Theory Reader.* London: Routledge.

Grosz, E. (1994). *Volatile Bodies: Toward a corporeal feminism.* Bloomington, IN: Indiana University Press.

Haaken, J. (1998). *Pillars of Salt: Gender, memory and the perils of looking back.* London: Free Association Press.

Haaken, J. and P. Reavey (eds) (2010). *Memory Matters: Contexts for understanding recollections of child sexual abuse.* London: Routledge.

Hagen, T. and A.L. Tota (eds) (2015). *The Routledge International Handbook of Memory Studies.* London: Routledge.

Halbwachs, M. ([1950] 1980). *The Collective Memory.* New York: Harper & Row.

Halbwachs, M. ([1925] 1992). *On Collective Memory.* Chicago, IL: University of Chicago Press.

Hall, J. (1996). Geography of child sexual abuse: women's narratives of their childhood environments. *Advances in Nursing Science* 18(4): 29–47.

Harris, C.B., A.J. Barnier, J. Sutton and P.G. Keil (2014). Couples as socially distributed cognitive systems: Remembering in everyday social and material contexts. *Memory Studies* 7(3): 285–97.

Harris, C.B., P.G. Keil, J. Sutton, A.J. Barnier and D.G.F. McIlwain (2011). We remember, we forget: Collaborative remembering in older couple. *Discourse Processes* 48: 267–303.

Harvey, D. (1990). *The Condition of Postmodernity.* Oxford: Blackwell.

Harvey, P., E. Casella, G. Evans, H. Knox, C. McLean, E. Silva, N. Thoburn and K. Woodward (eds) (2013). *Objects and Materials: A Routledge companion.* London: Routledge.

Henare, A., M. Holbraad and S. Wastell (eds) (2007). *Thinking Through Things: Theorising artefacts ethnographically.* London: Routledge.

Hepworth, M. (2000). *Stories of Ageing.* Buckingham: Open University Press.

Herman, J.L. (1992). *Trauma and Recovery.* New York: Basic Books.

Hirsch, M. (1997). *Family Frames: Photography, narrative and postmemory.* Cambridge, MA: Harvard University Press.

Hirsch, M. and L. Spitzer (2003). 'We would never have come without you': Generations of nostalgia. In K. Hodgkin and S. Radstone (eds) *Contested Pasts: The politics of memory.* London: Routledge, pp. 79–96.

Hoskins, A. (2011). 7/7 and connective memory: Interactional trajectories of remembering in post-scarcity culture. *Memory Studies* 4(3): 269–80.

Hume, D. ([1739] 1985). *A Treatise of Human Nature.* London: Penguin.

Hutchins, E. (1995). *Cognition in the Wild.* Cambridge, MA: MIT Press.

Hyman, E. (2011, 12 January). 7/7 London bombings inquest: Tavistock Square bus bombing. *ITN News.*

232 References

James, W. ([1890] 1950). *The Principles of Psychology*. New York: Dover.

Jamieson, A., S. Harper and C. Victor (eds) (1997). *Critical Approaches to Ageing and Later Life*. Buckingham, UK: Open University Press.

Jänich, K. (1995). *Topology*. Berlin: Springer Verlag.

Kahn, C. (1981). *The Art and Thought of Heraclitus*. Cambridge: Cambridge University Press.

King, A. (1998). *Memorials of the Great War in Britain: The symbolism and politics of remembrance*. Oxford: Berg.

Kuhn, A. (2002). *Family Secrets: Acts of memory and imagination*. London: Verso.

Lewin, K. (1936). *Principles of Topological Psychology*. New York: McGraw Hill.

Lacan, J. (2007). Seminar on 'The Purloined Letter'. In *Ecrits: Complete edition*. New York: W.W. Norton, pp. 6–50.

Lamb, S. (1996). *The Trouble With Blame*. Cambridge, MA: Harvard University Press.

Langford, M. (2008). *Suspended Conversations: The afterlife of memory in photographic albums*. Montreal: McGill-Queen's University Press.

Lapoujade, D. (2000) From transcendental empiricism to worker nomadism: William James. *Pli* 9: 190–9.

Laruelle, F. (2010). *Philosophies of Difference: A critical introduction to non-philosophy*. London: Continuum.

Latimer, J. (1999). The dark at the bottom of the stair: Participation and performance of older people in hospital. *Medical Anthropology Quarterly* 13(2): 186–213.

Latour, B. (1988). The politics of explanation: An alternative. In S. Woolgar (ed.) *Knowledge and Reflexivity: New frontiers in the sociology of knowledge*. London: Sage, pp. 155–76.

Latour, B. (1993). *We Have Never Been Modern*. Cambridge, MA: Harvard University Press.

Latour, B. (2005). *Reassembling the Social: An introduction to actor-network theory*. Oxford: Oxford University Press.

Latour, B. (2013). *An Inquiry Into Modes of Existence: An anthropology of the moderns*. Cambridge, MA: Harvard University Press.

Lave, J. (1988). *Cognition in Practice: Mathematics and culture in everyday life*. Cambridge: Cambridge University Press.

Lave, J. and E. Wenger (1991). *Situated Learning: Legitimate peripheral participation*. Cambridge: Cambridge University Press.

Law, J. (2004). *After Method: Mess in social science research*. London: Routledge.

Law, J. and A. Mol (1998). On metrics and fluids: Notes on otherness. In R.C.H. Chia (ed.) *Organized Worlds: Explorations in technology and organization with Robert Cooper*. London: Routledge, pp. 20–38.

Lazarus, R.S. and S. Folkman (1984). *Stress, Appraisal and Coping*. New York: Springer.

Lee, N. and S.D. Brown (2002). The disposal of fear: Childhood, trauma and complexity. In J. Law and A. Mol (eds) *Complexities: Social studies of knowledge practices*. Durham, NC: Duke University Press, pp. 258–79.

Letiche, H. (2008). *Making Healthcare Care: Managing via simple guiding principles*. Charlotte, NC: Information Age.

Leys, R. (2011). The turn to affect: A critique. *Critical Inquiry* 37: 434–72.

Leys, R. (2013). *Trauma: A genealogy*. Chicago, IL: University of Chicago Press.

Lindsay, D.S., L. Hagen, J.D. Read, K.A. Wade and M. Garry (2004). True photographs and false memories. *Psychological Science* 15: 149–54.

References 233

Loftus, E.F. (1994). Tricked by memory. In J. Jeffrey and G. Edwall (eds) *Memory and History: Essays on recalling and interpreting experience*. Boston, MA: University Press of America, pp. 17–32.

Loftus, E.F. (2003). Make-believe memories. *American Psychologist* 58(11): 867–73.

Loftus, E.F. and K. Ketcham (1996). *The Myth of Repressed Memory: False memories and allegations of sexual abuse*. New York: St Martins.

Loftus, E.F. and J.E. Pickrell (1995). The formation of false memories. *Psychiatric Annals* 25: 720–5.

Lorenz, K. (2002). *King Soloman's Ring*. London: Routledge.

Lorenzo-Dus, N. and A. Bryan (2011). Dynamics of memory: Commemorating the 2005 London bombings in British television news. *Memory Studies* 4: 297.

Luhmann, N. (1996). *Social Systems*. Redwood, CA: Stanford University Press.

Luhmann, N. (2008). *Law as a Social System*. Oxford: Oxford University Press.

McCarthy, J. (2006). Rural geography: Alternative rural economies: The search for alterity in forests, fisheries, food, and fair trade. *Progress in Human Geography* 30(6): 803–11.

Magnusson, S. (2014). *Where Memories Go: Why dementia changes everything*. London: Two Roads.

Manier, D. (2004). Is memory in the brain? Remembering as social behaviour. *Mind, Culture & Activity* 11(4): 251–66.

Markus, H.R. and S. Kitayama (2010). Cultures and selves: A cycle of mutual constitution. *Perspectives on Psychological Sciences* 5: 420–30.

Martin, L. and A.J. Secor (2013). Towards a post-mathematical topology. *Progress in Human Geography* 1–19.

Massumi, B. (2002). *Parables for the Virtual: Movement, affect, sensation*. Durham, NC: Duke University Press.

Marcoux, J.S. (2001). The refurbishment of memory. In D. Miller (ed.) *Home possessions*. Oxford: Berg, pp. 69–86.

Margalit, A. (2002). *The Ethics of Memory*. Cambridge, MA: Harvard University Press.

Matsuda, M.K. (1996). *The Memory of the Modern*. Oxford: Oxford University Press.

Meyer, S. (2009). *New Moon*. New York: Atom.

Michaelian, K. and J. Sutton (2013). Distributed cognition and memory research: History and current directions. *Review of Philosophy & Psychology* 4(1): 1–24.

Middleton, D. and D. Edwards (eds) (1990). *Collective Remembering*. London: Sage.

Middleton, D. and S.D. Brown (2005). *The Social Psychology of Experience: Studies in remembering and forgetting*. London: Sage.

Miller, D. (ed.) (1998). *Material Cultures: Why some things matter*. London: UCL Press.

Miller, D. (2001). Possessions. In D. Miller (ed.) *Home Possessions*. Oxford, UK: Berg, pp. 107–22.

Miller, G.A. (1956). The magic number seven plus or minus two: Some limits on our capacity for processing information. *Psychological Review* 63: 81–97.

Mitchell, M. (2011). *Complexity: A guided tour*. New York: Oxford University Press.

Mol, A. and J. Law (1994). Regions, networks and fluids: Anaemia and social. *Social Studies of Science* 24(4): 641–71.

Motzkau, J.F. (2009). Exploring the transdisciplinary trajectory of suggestibility. *Subjectivity: International Journal of Critical Psychology* 27: 172–94.

References

Motzkau, J.F. (2010). Speaking up against justice: Credibility, suggestibility and children's memory on trial. In J. Haaken and P. Reavey (eds) *Memory Matters. Contexts for understanding sexual abuse recollections*. London: Psychology Press, pp. 103–18.

Mullarkey, J. (2006). *Post-Continental Philosophy*. London: Continuum.

Nachman, D. and D. Hardy (dirs) (2011). *Love Hate Love*. KTF Films.

Negri, A. (1991). *The Savage Anomaly: The power of Spinoza's metaphysics and politics*. Minneapolis, MN: University of Minnesota Press.

Negri, A. (2013). *Spinoza for Our Time: Politics and postmodernity*. New York: Columbia University Press.

Neisser, U. (1978). Memory: What are the important questions? In M.M. Gruneberg, E.E. Morris and R.N. Sykes (eds) *Practical Aspects of Memory*. San Diego, CA: Academic Press, pp. 3–24.

Neisser, U. (1981). John Dean's memory: A case study. *Cognition* 9: 1–22.

Neisser, U. (1982). *Memory Observed*. Oxford: WH Freeman.

Neisser, U. (1988). Five kinds of self-knowledge. *Philosophical Psychology* 1(1): 35–59.

Neisser, U. (ed.) (1993). *The Perceived Self: Ecological and interpersonal sources of self-knowledge*. Cambridge, UK: Cambridge University Press.

Neisser, U. (1994). Multiple systems: A new approach to cognitive theory. *European Journal of Cognitive Psychology* 6(3): 225–41.

Nelson, K. (2003). Self and social functions: Individual autobiographical memory and collective narrative. *Memory* 11(2): 125–36.

Nelson, K. (ed.) (2006). *Narratives From the Crib* (new edn). Cambridge, MA: Harvard University Press.

Nelson, K. (2009). *Young Minds in Social Worlds: Experience, meaning and memory*. Cambridge, MA: Harvard University Press.

Nelson, K. and R. Fivush (2004). The emergence of autobiographical memory: A social cultural developmental theory. *Psychological Review* 111: 486–511.

Nietzsche, F. (1997). On the uses and disadvantages of history for life. In *Untimely Meditations*. Cambridge, UK: Cambridge University Press, pp. 57–127.

Nora, P. (1996). General introduction: Between memory and history. In *Realms of Memory: Conflicts and divisions vol 1: The construction of the French past*. New York: Colombia University Press, pp.1–20.

North, R. (2007). *Out of the Tunnel*. London: The Friday Project.

O'Dell, L. (1997). Child sexual abuse and the academic construction of symptomatologies. *Feminism & Psychology* 7(3): 334–9.

Olick, J., V. Vinitzky-Seroussi and D. Levy (eds) (2011). *The Collective Memory Reader*. New York: Oxford University Press.

Oyama, S. (2000). *The Ontogeny of Information: Developmental systems and evolution* (2nd edn). Durham, NC: Duke University Press.

Pelzer, D. (2004). *My Story: A child called It, the lost boy, a man named Dave*. London: Orion.

Phillips, J. (2006). Agencement/Assemblage. *Theory Culture Society* 23: 108–9.

Phillips, J.W.P. (2013). On topology. *Theory, Culture & Society* 30(5): 122–52.

Pickering, M. and E. Keightley (2009). Trauma, discourse and communicative limits. *Critical Discourse Studies* 6(4): 237–49.

Plotnisky, A. (2002). *The Knowable and the Unknowable: Modern science, nonclassical thought and the two cultures*. Ann Arbor, MI: University of Michigan Press.

References   235

Poe, E.A. (2003). The purloined letter. In *The Fall of the House of Usher and Other Writings*. London: Penguin, pp. 281–300.

Polkinghorne, D.E. (1988). *Narrative Knowing and the Human Sciences*. New York: SUNY Press.

Potter, J. (1996). *Representing Reality: Discourse, rhetoric and social construction*. London: Sage.

Proust, M. (1996). *In Search of Lost Time, Vol 1: Swann's way*. London: Vintage.

Radley, A. (1990). Artefacts, memory and a sense of place. In D. Middleton and D. Edwards (eds) *Collective Remembering*. London: Sage, pp. 46–59.

Reading, A. (2011). The London bombings: Mobile witnessing, mortal bodies and globital time. *Memory Studies* 4(3): 298–311.

Reavey, P. (1998). *Child Sexual Abuse: Professional and everyday constructions of women and sexuality*. Unpublished PhD thesis, Sheffield Hallam University.

Reavey, P. (2010a). Spatial markings: Memory, narrative and survival. *Memory Studies* 3: 314–29.

Reavey, P. (2010b) The spaces of memory: Rethinking agency through materiality. In J. Haaken and P. Reavey (eds) *Memory Matters: Contexts for understanding recollections of child sexual abuse*. London: Routledge, pp. 131–42.

Reavey, P. and S. Warner (eds) (2003). *New Feminist Stories of Child Sexual Abuse: Sexual scripts and dangerous dialogues*. London: Routledge.

Reavey, P. and S.D. Brown (2006). Transforming past agency and action in the present: Time, social remembering and child sexual abuse. *Theory and Psychology* 16(2): 179–202.

Reavey, P. and S.D. Brown (2007). Rethinking agency in memory: Space and embodiment in memories of child sexual abuse. *Journal of Social Work Practice* 21(4): 5–21.

Reavey, P. and S.D. Brown (2009). The mediating role of objects in recollections of adult women survivors of child sexual abuse. *Culture & Psychology* 15(4): 463–84.

Reavey, P., R. Wilcock, S.D. Brown, R. Batty and S. Fuller (forthcoming). Policing the boundaries: Perception and knowledge of mental distress and professional dilemmas in collecting witness statements. *International Journal of Law and Psychiatry*.

Richards, G. (2009). *Putting Psychology in its Place: Critical historical perspectives* (3rd edn). London: Routledge.

Ricoeur, P. (2004). *Memory, History, Forgetting*. Chicago, IL: University of Chicago Press.

Riessman, C.K. (2008). *Narrative Methods for the Human Sciences*. London: Sage.

Ryden, K.C. (1993). *Mapping the Invisible Landscape: Folkore, writing and the sense of place*. Iowa City, IA: University of Iowa Press.

Said, E. (1989). *After the Last Sky: Palestinian lives*. London: Verso.

Salter, M.B. (2013). To make move and let stop: Mobility and the assemblage of circulation. *Mobilities* 8(1): 7–19.

Samuel, R. (2012). *Theatres of Memory: Past and present in contemporary culture*. London: Verso.

Schachter, D.L. (1996). *Searching for Memory: The brain, the mind and the past*. New York: Basic.

Schachter, D.L. (2003). *How the Mind Forgets and Remembers: The seven sins of memory*. New York: Souvenir.

236 References

Schillmeier, M. and M. Heinlein (2009). Moving homes: From house to nursing home and the (un-)canniness of being at home. *Space and Culture* 12(2): 218–31.

Schweitzer, P. and E. Bruce (2008). *Remembering Yesterday, Caring Today: Reminiscence in dementia care: A guide to good practice*. London: Jessica Kingsley.

Sedgwick, E.K. (2003). *Touching Feeling: Affect, pedagogy, performativity*. Durham, NC: Duke University Press.

Semon, R. (1923). *Mnemic Psychology*. London: George Allen & Unwin.

Serres, M. (1982). *Hermes: Literature, science and philosophy*. Baltimore, MD: Johns Hopkins.

Serres, M. (1995a). *Genesis*. Ann Arbor, MI: University of Michigan Press.

Serres, M. (1995b). *The Natural Contract*. Ann Arbor, MI: University of Michigan Press.

Serres, M. (1995c). *Angels: A modern myth*. Paris: Flammarion.

Serres, M. (2007). *The Parasite*. Minneapolis, MN: University of Minnesota Press.

Serres, M. (2008). *The Five Senses: A philosophy of mingled bodies*. London: Continuum.

Shaviro, S. (2012). *Without Criteria: Kant, Whitehead, Deleuze, and aesthetics*. Cambridge, MA: MIT Press.

Singer, J.A. and M.A. Conway (2008). Should we forget forgetting? *Memory Studies* 1(3): 279–85.

Sloterdijk, P. (2011). *Bubble: Spheres 1*. Cambridge, MA: MIT Press.

Sontag, S. (1979). *On Photography*. London: Penguin.

Spiegelman, A. (2003). *The Complete Maus*. London: Penguin.

Spinoza, B. ([1677] 1996). *Ethics*. London: Penguin.

Stengers, I. (2010). *Cosmopolitics 1*. Minneapolis, MN: University of Minnesota Press.

Stengers, I. (2011a). *Cosmopolitics 2*. Minneapolis, MN: University of Minnesota Press.

Stengers, I. (2011b). *Thinking With Whitehead: A free and wild creation of concepts*. Cambridge, MA: Harvard University Press.

Stenner, P. (2008). A.N. Whitehead and subjectivity. *Subjectivity* 22: 90–109.

Stone, C.B., A. Coman, A.D. Brown, J. Koppel and W. Hirst (2012) Toward a science of silence: The consequences of leaving a memory unsaid. *Perspectives on Psychological Science* 7: 39–53.

Sutton, J. (2008). Between individual and collective memory: Coordination, interaction, distribution. *Social Research* 75(1): 23–48.

Sutton, J., C.B. Harris, P.G. Keil and A.J. Barnier (2010). The psychology of memory, extended cognition and socially distributed remembering. *Phenomenology and the Cognitive Sciences* 9(4): 521–60.

Thrift, N. (2006). Space. *Theory Culture Society* 23: 139–46.

Thrift, N. (2008). *Non-Representational Theory: Space, politics, affect*. London: Routledge.

Tulloch, J. (2006). *One Day in July: Experiencing 7/7*. London: Little, Brown.

Tulving, E. (1983). *Elements of Episodic Memory*. Oxford: Clarendon.

Tulving, E. (1985a). How many memory systems are there? *American Psychologist* 40(4): 385–98.

Tulving, E. (1985b). Memory and consciousness. *Canadian Psychologist* 25: 1–12.

Valsiner, J. and A. Rosa (eds) (2007). *The Cambridge Handbook of Sociocultural Psychology*. Cambridge: Cambridge University Press.

Van der Kolk, B. (2014). *The Body Keeps the Score: Brain, mind, and body in the healing of trauma*. New York: Viking.

References 237

Victor, C. (2004). *The Social Context of Ageing: A textbook of gerontology.* London: Routledge.

Vygotsky, L. (1978). *Mind in Society.* Cambridge, MA. Harvard University Press.

Wade, K.A., M. Garry, J.D. Read and D.S. Lindsay (2002). A picture is worth a thousand lies: Using false photographs to create false childhood memories. *Psychonomic Bulletin & Review* 9: 597–603.

Waldrop, M.M. (1992). *Complexity: The emerging science at the edge of order and chaos.* New York: Simon & Schuster.

Walkerdine, V. (2010). Communal beingness and affect: An exploration of trauma in an ex-industrial community. *Body & Society* 16(1): 91–116.

Warner, S. (1996). Constructing femininity: Models of child sexual abuse and the production of 'woman'. In E. Burman, P. Alldred, C. Bewley, B. Goldberg, C. Heenan, D. Marks, J. Marshall, K. Taylor, R. Ullah and S. Warner (eds) *Challenging Women: Psychology's exclusions, feminist possibilities.* Buckingham, UK: Open University Press, pp. 36–53.

Weinrich, H. (2004). *Lethe: The art and critique of forgetting.* Ithaca, NY: Cornell University Press.

Wetherell, M. (2012). *Affect and Emotion: A new social science understanding.* Buckingham, UK: Open University Press.

White, M. and D. Epston (1990). *Narrative Means to Therapeutic Ends.* New York: W.W. Norton.

Whitehead, A.N. ([1925] 1967). *Science and Modern World.* New York: Free Press.

Whitehead, A.N. ([1929] 1978). *Process and Reality.* New York: Free Press.

Wood, D., J.S. Bruner and G. Ross (1976). The role of tutoring in problem solving. *Journal of Child Psychology and Psychiatry* 17: 89–100.

Wood, D. and D. Middleton (1975). A study of assisted problem solving. *British Journal of Psychology* 66(2): 181–91.

Worrell, M. (2003). Working at being survivors: Identity, gender and participation in self-help groups. In P. Reavey and S. Warner (eds) *New Feminist Stories of Child Sexual Abuse: Sexual scripts and dangerous dialogues.* London: Routledge, pp. 210–25.

Yates, F.A. (1966). *The Art of Memory.* London: Routledge.

Young, A. (1995). *The Harmony of Illusions: Inventing post-traumatic stress disorder.* Princeton, NJ: Princeton University Press.

Young, J.E. (2000). *At Memory's Edge: After-images of the Holocaust in contemporary art and architecture.* New Haven, CT: Yale University Press.

Index

7/7 attacks 133–54
9/11 attacks 134–5

abuse 65–6; *see also* child sexual abuse
acquired memories 131
'actions and passions' 63; *see also* affect
active forgetting 13–14, 68–75, 125
adequate ideas 79–80
adopted children 8, 10, 107–32; life-space 17–18, 74–5, 108, 110–18; ordinary people/difficult pasts 211; spectral objects 118–27; truth 127–31; 'Where have all the trousers gone?' 107–8
affect: 'affective universe' 52–3; child sexual abuse 89, 94–7, 102–6; definition 15–16; life-space 48, 54–5, 61–8, 79–80; ordinary people/difficult pasts 218–21
affordances: child sexual abuse 89, 94–7, 102–6; life-space 54–5, 61, 65, 68; ordinary people/difficult pasts 218, 219–20
agencements 155–9
agency: child sexual abuse 89–94, 98, 101, 105–6; definition 12–13
Akropolis buildings 182–4
Allen, W. 86–9
ambivalence: affordances 94–7, 102–6; agency 90–4; child sexual abuse 86–106; 'choice' 102–6; life-space 97–102; Woody Allen case 86–9
analogies *see* metaphors
anti-life 175
antipsychotic treatments 165, 169–73
anti-terrorism *see* London bombings

Archive Fever (Derrida) 70
ars oblivionis 72–3
art of forgetting 72
art of memory 72
assemblages 155–9
Assmann, J. and A. 134
atmosphere 16
atypical antipsychotic treatments 169
auditory metaphors 7–8
Auschwitz 71
autobiographical memory: definition 11–12; expanded view of memory 25–30; life-space 76–7; reminiscence museum 203–6, 207
autonoetic consciousness 25–6

Baby P. 65–6, 111
Balzac, H. 4
Barthes, R. 116
Bartlett, F.C. 12, 23, 64–5
BBC news 138–9
Becker, H. 181–2
'becoming' 79
bedrooms (reminiscence museum) 202–8
Bendien, E. 183, 190–1
Bennett, J. 157–9
Bergson, H. 5, 71–2
bias 88
'Big Run' 139
Blair, T. 134
Blum, V. 136–7
Blustein, J. 14–15, 75–8, 80–1, 104–5
bombings *see* London bombings
Brown, S.D. 66–8
Bruner, J. 24
Buchanan, K. 42–6

240 Index

Campbell, S. 77
Cartesian procedures 60, 62–3
cathedrals 134
CCTV 65–6
Chalmers, D. 39
children 8, 10, 107–32; life-space 17–18,
  74–5, 108, 110–18; neglect and abuse
  65–6; ordinary people/difficult pasts
  211; spectral objects 118–27; truth
  127–31; 'Where have all the trousers
  gone?' 107–8; *see also* child sexual
  abuse
child sexual abuse (CSA): affect 15–16;
  affordances 94–7, 102–6; agency
  89–94, 98, 101, 105–6; ambivalence
  86–106; 'choice' 102–6; ethics 14–15;
  expanded view of memory 29;
  forgetting 13–14; institutional practices
  18–19; life-space 58–61, 76–8, 81, 89,
  97–102; managing of past 8–10; truth
  86–9; Woody Allen case 86–9
'choice', affordance of 102–6
chreods: child sexual abuse 87–8; life-
  space 68; mixtures and flows 6–7
Clark, A. 39
clothing 107–8, 207
cognitive processing 23, 39–40, 49,
  53–4, 62–3, 218
collective memory 30–9, 121, 145–6,
  149, 223
common notions 82, 176, 223–5
communicative memory 134
complementarity of resources 40
conatus 79
concealed writing 73–4
conceptual affordances 218, 219
conceptual self 27
Connerton, P. 13, 69–70
Connor, S. 119–20
Conway, M. 11–12, 18–19, 24, 26–7, 29
corporeal transformations of mental
  health 169–76
creative forgetting 69
Czernowitz ghetto 109

'datum' for thought 63–4
deficit models 8–9, 10, 179
Deleuze, G. 52–3, 62, 66, 79, 157–8,
  211–12
democratising knowledge 62–3
dependent variables 31–2
Derrida, J. 70
'destining' of the child 121–2

diagrams: affect 219–21; affordances 218,
  219–20; conceptual affordances 218,
  219; 'flow of experience' 213–14;
  folding of life-space 216–17; life-space
  215–18; London bombings 145–6;
  material affordances 218, 219;
  mediated relationships to the past
  218–20; Möbius strips 214–15;
  ordinary people/difficult pasts 210–25;
  specificity of remembering 221–2;
  unmediated relationships to the past
  218–20
'Diary of a separation' (column) 107–8
difficult pasts 8–11, 210–25
direct perception, life-space 53–4
disciplinary societies 157
discursive psychology 30–9, 49
displacement 72, 190–2
disruptive space 188
doll and infant clothes 207
Douglas, M. 18, 164–5
Douglass, D. 134–5
drugs 162, 169–73
drying rack (reminiscence museum) 187
duration 5, 71–2

Ebbinghaus, H. 22–3
ecological self, life-space 54
Edwards, D. 30–9
elderly care 8, 119
embodied connections 147–51
endeavour to persist in being 79
'engrams' 68
episodic memory 11, 25–6
Essais (Montaigne) 69
ethics: definition 14–15; life-space 48,
  75–83; London bombings 150–1;
  ordinary people/difficult pasts 223–5;
  reminiscence museum 198
Ethics (Spinoza) 62
Euclidean view of life-space 60
exchange values 70
executive systems 23
expanded view of memory 22–47;
  autobiographical memory 25–30;
  collective remembering 30–9;
  discursive psychology 30–9; laboratory
  studies 22–5; settings 39–46
experience, flow of 213–14
extended cognition 39–40
external mnemonic devices 137, 145–7;
  see also mnemonic devices
extremity models 8–9, 179

'fallacy of misplaced concreteness' 7
false memories 128–9
Farrow, D. 86–9
feeling of affordance 66; *see also* affect
First World War memorials 56–7
Fivush, R. 27, 28–30, 75, 111
flow, life-space 71–2
'flow of experience' 213–14
flows 3–8
folding of life-space 216–17
folding of space and time 159–64
forensic psychiatric units 155–77;
    categories of thought 164–9; corporeal
    transformations 169–76; folding of
    space and time 159–64; institutional
    assemblages 155–9
forgetting: active 13–14, 68–75, 125; art
    of 72; definition 13–14; institutional
    156–7, 161–2; life-space 48, 68–75;
    London bombings 151–4; spaces of
    memory 53–61; textile factories 48–53
Foucault, M. 157–8
Fraser, S. 58–61
Freud, S. 3

Gatens, M. 81–2
generative grammar of relations 102–3
ghettos 109
Gibson, E. and J. 53–4, 63
Goffman, E. 157, 159
good victimhood 90–1, 102
'the grocery shop' (reminiscence
    museum) 181
The Guardian newspaper 107–8
Guattari, F. 211–12

Haaken, J. 29, 90–1
Halbwachs, M. 58, 70, 121
'hard times' recollections 179–84
Harrison, S. 138, 139–42, 144–5, 147–8,
    150–2
Hepworth, M. 179–80
Heraclitus 6
Herinneringsmuseum (reminiscence
    museum) 178–209; bedroom 202–8;
    'hard times' 179–84; kitchen 192–201;
    sitting room 184–92
higher-order invariants 54–5; *see also*
    affordances
Hirsch, M. 109
history of forgetting 69
history of memory 40–1
Holocaust 109

homeomorphic memory 60
homeostasis/homeorhesis 6–7, 79
How Institutions Think (Douglas) 18,
    164–5
Humanitas 181–2
Hyde Park memorials 55–7, 134
Hyman, E. 135, 137

implicit memory 11
impression/imprinting 2–4
incest 78
independent variables 31–2
infant clothes 207
institutional assemblages 155–9
institutional practices 18–20
intentional acts 73
'interaction' 49
intra-cranial cognitive processes 40
invariances 54–5, 218; *see also* affordances
irreversibility of memory 2–3

James, W. 4, 5
Jewish refugees 109
joyful affects, life-space 79–80
joyful encounters, life-space 82

Khan, M.S. 152–3
kitchens (reminiscence museum)
    192–201
knowledge, life-space 62–3, 79–80

laboratory studies, expanded view of
    memory 22–5
Lacan, J. 137
Lamb, S. 104
Latimer, J. 180
Law, J. 157
Lee, N. 66–8
Lewin, K. 17–18, 48–50, 59–61, 97, 162
'life reviews' 181
life-space 48–85, 213, 215–18; active
    forgetting 68–75; adopted children
    17–18, 74–5, 108, 110–18; affect 48,
    54–5, 61–8, 79–80; child sexual abuse
    58–61, 76–8, 81, 89, 97–102;
    definition 17–18; ethics 48, 75–83;
    forgetting 48, 68–75; London
    bombings 136–7, 145–6, 153–4;
    mental health 160–3, 168–9, 174–6;
    reminiscence museum 196–201,
    207–8; spaces of memory 53–61;
    textile factories 48–53
life-story books 108–9, 112, 131

242   Index

living memory 134
Loftus, E. 25, 88
London bombings 133–54; embodied
  connections 147–51; forgetting 151–4;
  life-space 55–7; mediating memory
  143–7; ordinary people/difficult pasts
  10–11, 211; recounting 138–43;
  remembering 133–8
long-term self 26–7, 29
Love Hate Love documentary 135
'lure for feeling' 63–4, 66–8, 94, 116

Magnusson, S. 179
managed accessibility of memories 14
'manifold' memory 60
Margalit, A. 14–15
'marking out' of life-space 58–9, 216,
  218
master narratives 29, 77
material affordances 218, 219
mathematics: life-space 59–60; *see also*
  topology
Matsuda, M. 41
mediated relationships to the past 218–20
mediating memory 143–7
medication 162, 169–73
memorials 55–7, 134
'memory palaces' 73
'memory traces' 68
mental health 8–10, 17; *see also* forensic
  psychiatric units
mental time travel 5, 26
metaphors 3–8, 68–9, 71–2
Middleton, D. 25, 30–5, 42–6
Miller, D. 185
'misplaced concreteness' 7
Mitchell, V.C. 86–9
mixtures 3–8
mnemonic devices: affect 219–21;
  affordances 218, 219–20; conceptual
  affordances 218, 219; 'flow of
  experience' 213–14; folding of life-
  space 216–17; life-space 215–18;
  London bombings 137, 145–7;
  material affordances 218, 219;
  mediated relationships to the past
  218–20; Möbius strips 214–15;
  ordinary people/difficult pasts 210–25;
  photographs 111–18; specificity of
  remembering 221–2; unmediated
  relationships to the past 218–20
Möbius strips 137, 214–15
Mol, A. 157

monster objects 98–9
Montaigne, M. de 69
The Moral Demands of Memory (Blustein)
  75–8, 80–1
moral imperatives 14–15
moral values 70
Motzkau, J. 129–30
Mullarkey, J. 212
Murdoch, R. *see The Sun* newspaper
museums 178–209; bedroom 202–8;
  'hard times' 179–84; kitchen 192–201;
  sitting room 184–92
Muslim radicalisation 133–4, 152–3
My Father's House (Fraser) 58–61

narratives: adopted children 112–14;
  child sexual abuse 90; London
  bombings 134–6, 145–7, 152–3;
  narrative thinking 24
Narratives from the Crib (Nelson) 22
National Health Service (NHS) 161–3
natural contexts 23–4
neglect and abuse 65–6
Neisser, U. 23–4, 53–5, 56–7
Nelson, K. 24–5, 27, 28–30
newspapers 107–8, 137, 142–3
NHS *see* National Health Service
Nietzsche, F. 13, 69
nonsense syllables 22–3
Nora, P. 70
North, R. 138–9, 143–6, 148, 150,
  153–4

objects and material relations 185–92
oblivescence 68–9
ordinary people and difficult pasts 8–11,
  210–25
otherness 6
Out of the Tunnel (Harrison) 138, 148
Oxfam 'Big Run' 139

paradigmatic thinking 24
parenthood: parentification processes
  100–1; *see also* adopted children
park memorials 55–7, 134
passivity 78, 90
Pelzer, D. 70–1
personality disorder (PD) 165–6
Peter Pan 66–8
photographs 111–18
PMEs *see* psychologically modified
  experiences
post-traumatic stress disorder (PTSD) 12

Potter, J. 35–9
power dynamics 93–4
presenteeism 156, 174–5
privacy boundaries, child sexual abuse 99–101
procedural memory 11
Process and Reality (Whitehead) 63
propositions 63–4, 66–8, 94, 116
psychiatric units *see* forensic psychiatric units
psychologically modified experiences (PMEs) 169, 172
psychosis 165
psychotopologies 136–7
PTSD *see* post-traumatic stress disorder

quasi-conceptual memory 51
quasi-physical memory 51
quasi-social memory 50

radicalisation of Muslims 133–4, 152–3
Radley, A. 118–19
rape 78
reformative implications 76
relational space *see* life-space
reminiscence museum 178–209; bedroom 202–8; 'hard times' 179–84; kitchen 192–201; sitting room 184–92
repressive erasure 69–70
responsibility for the past 76–7
restricted view of memory 25, 210
risk, mental health 160–1
rouge test 41

Said, E. 119
St Paul's Cathedral 134
sameness 6
Samuel, R. 70
Sandez, S.R. 1–2
scaffolded recollections 27–8
scaffolding 31
Schillmeier, M. 180
schizophrenia 165
Secor, A. 136–7
self-awareness 25–6
self-blame 77–8
self-defining memories 29
self-memory systems 26
semantic memory 11, 25–6
Semon, R. 68
Serres, M. 41–2
settlement *see* wellness
sexuality 173–4

sideboards (reminiscence museum) 191
Simonides 72
sitting rooms (reminiscence museum) 184–92
slave systems 23
smoking 161
social remembering approaches 25
social topology 157, 160–2
Sontag, S. 116
sorrowful affects 79
sound metaphors 7–8
space 17–18; *see also* life-space
spatial marking 58–9, 216, 218
specificity of remembering 221–2
spectral objects 118–27, 190–2
Spinoza, B. 15–16, 62, 78–9, 82, 151, 198, 223–5
Spitzer, L. 109
stability *see* wellness
steganography 73–4
sting operations 1
storehouse models 41
stream of thought 4–5

taking responsibility for the past 76–7
'tendency towards oblivion' 68–9
terror *see* London bombings
textile factories 48–53
The Art of Memory (Yates) 41
'the extended mind' 39–40
The Guardian 107–8
The Memory of the Modern (Matsuda) 41
Themistocles 72
The Moral Demands of Memory (Blustein) 75–8, 80–1
The One Show 140–1
The Sun newspaper 137
The Unknown Masterpiece (Balzac) 4
thick/thin relations 14
'thinking in diagrams' 212
thought categories 164–9
Tomkin, S. 61
topography, life-space 49
topology: child sexual abuse 97; life-space 17–18, 59–61; London bombings 136–7; mental health 157, 160–2, 168–9
'torque' 137
total institutions 157, 159
transcranial couplings of resources 40
transformative knowledge 79–80
transitional objects 123
translation 41–2

truth: adopted children 127–31; child sexual abuse 86–9
Tulloch, J. 134–5, 138, 140–3, 146–7, 152–3
Tulving, E. 25–6
typical antipsychotic treatments 169

Underground *see* London bombings
unmediated relationships to the past 218–20
unwarranted self-blame 77–8

Veterans Administration patients 12
vicarious memories 14, 109, 131
video 65–6, 111
'village square' (reminiscence museum) 182
visual metaphors 3–8
Vygotsky, L. 28

Wade, K. 128–9
wards *see* forensic psychiatric units

'war machine' (Kafka) 211
war on terror *see* London bombings
washing machines (reminiscence museum) 198
Watergate scandal 23–4
weight gain 170–3
Weinrich, H. 13, 69
wellness, mental health 161, 167–9, 171–2, 175–6
'Where have all the trousers gone?' (article) 107–8
Whitehead, A.N. 7, 63–4, 79–80, 94, 116, 212, 213
Winston's Wish 131
working self 26
'the workshop' (reminiscence museum) 181
World War memorials 56–7

Yates, F. 41
Young, A. 12